PELICAN BOOKS

THE NEW PSYCHOLOGY OF
DREAMING

Richard M. Jones, author of several books,
including *Ego Synthesis in Dreams* and *Fantasy and Feeling in Education*, is currently
Professor of Psychology at The Evergreen
State College, and working on a book dealing
with dream reflection as a learning tool.

THE
NEW PSYCHOLOGY
OF
DREAMING

RICHARD M. JONES

PENGUIN BOOKS

Penguin Books Ltd, Harmondsworth, Middlesex, England
Penguin Books, 625 Madison Avenue, New York, New York 10022, U.S.A.
Penguin Books Australia Ltd, Ringwood, Victoria, Australia
Penguin Books Canada Limited, 2801 John Street, Markham, Ontario, Canada L3R 1B4
Penguin Books (N.Z.) Ltd, 182–190 Wairau Road, Auckland 10, New Zealand

First published in the United States of America by Grune & Stratton, Inc., 1970
Viking Compass Edition published 1974
Reprinted 1976
Published in Pelican Books 1978
Reprinted 1978

LIBRARY OF CONGRESS CATALOGING IN PUBLICATION DATA
Jones, Richard Matthew, 1925—
The new psychology of dreaming.
Bibliography: p. 190.
Includes index.
1. Dreams. I. Title.
[BF1078.J65 1978]   154.6'3   77-12240
ISBN 0 14 02.2087 9

Printed in the United States of America by
The Murray Printing Company, Westford, Massachusetts
Set in Linotype Caledonia

This edition reprinted by arrangement with Grune & Stratton, Inc.

The following page constitutes an extension of this copyright page.

ACKNOWLEDGMENTS
Several lengthy passages of this volume have appeared in earlier versions in various books and periodicals:
Chapter One, "Dream Interpretation and the Psychology of Dreaming," was published under that title in the *Journal of the American Psychoanalytic Association*, 13:304-319, 1965.
Chapters Two and Seven previously appeared under the title "The Psychoanalytic Theory of Dreaming—1968" in the *Journal of Nervous and Mental Disease*, 147:587-603, 1968. Copyright © 1968 by the Williams & Wilkins Company, Baltimore. By permission of the Williams & Wilkins Company.
A section of Chapter Three was published as "The Problem of 'Depth' in the Psychology of Dreaming" in the *Journal of Nervous and Mental Disease*, 139:507-515, 1964. Copyright © 1964 by the Williams & Wilkins Company, Baltimore. By permission of the Williams & Wilkins Company.
Two sections of Chapter Nine are drawn from Jones, *Ego Synthesis in Dreams*, Cambridge, Mass., Schenkman Publishing Co., Inc., 1962, and from "An Epigenetic Approach to the Analysis of Dreams," in *Dream Psychology and the New Biology of Dreams*, M. Kramer, Ed., Springfield, Ill., Charles C. Thomas, Publisher, 1969.
In each instance these earlier works were modified or adapted for publication in their present form.

Acknowledgment is also made of permission to reprint excerpts from the following works:

The Individual Psychology of Alfred Adler, edited and annotated by Heinz L. and Rowena R. Ansbacher, New York, Basic Books, Inc., Publishers, 1956. By permission of Sanford J. Greenburger.

Andras Angyal, *Neurosis and Treatment*, edited by Eugenia Hanfmann and Richard M. Jones, New York, John Wiley & Sons, Inc., 1965.

Medard Boss, *The Analysis of Dreams*, New York, Philosophical Library, Inc., 1958.

W. Dement and E. Wolpert, "Relationships in the Manifest Contents of Dreams Occurring on the Same Night," *Journal of Nervous and Mental Disease*, 126:568-578, 1958. Copyright © 1958 by the Williams & Wilkins Company, Baltimore. By permission of the Williams & Wilkins Company.

Erik Erikson, "The Dream Specimen of Psychoanalysis," in *Psychoanalytic Psychiatry and Psychology*, R. Knight and C. Friedman, Eds., New York, International Universities Press, 1954. Copyright 1954 by International Universities Press, Inc., New York. By permission of International Universities Press.

Calvin Hall, *The Meaning of Dreams, New York*, Harper and Brothers, 1953.

Calvin Hall, "Out of a Dream Came the Faucet," *Psychoanalysis and the Psychoanalytic Review*, 49:113-116, 1962.

Carl Jung, *Modern Man in Search of a Soul*, New York, Harcourt, Brace, Inc., 1933.

George Klein, "Two Theories or One? Perspectives to Change in Psychoanalytic Theory," a paper presented at the Conference of Psychoanalysts of the Southwest, Galveston, Texas, 1966.

Samuel Lowy, *Foundations of Dream Interpretation*, London, Kegan Paul, Trench, Trubner and Co., Ltd., 1942.

Jean Piaget, *Play, Dreams and Imitation in Childhood*, translated by C. Gattegno and F. M. Hodgson, New York, Norton Library Edition, 1962. By permission of W. W. Norton & Company, Inc. All rights reserved by W. W. Norton & Company, Inc.

Ernest Schachtel, *Metamorphosis*, New York, Basic Books, Inc., Publishers, 1959.

Frederick Snyder, "Changes in Respiration, Heart Rate and Systolic Blood Pressure in Relation to Electroencephalographic Patterns of Human Sleep," *Journal of Applied Physiology*, 19:417-422, 1964.

Frederick Snyder, "Toward an Evolutionary Theory of Dreaming," *American Journal of Psychiatry*, 123:121-136, 1966. Copyright © 1966 by the American Psychiatric Association.

Frederick Snyder, "The Physiology of Dreaming," in *Dream Psychology and the New Biology of Dreams*, M. Kramer, Ed., Springfield, Ill., Charles C. Thomas, Publisher, 1969.

M. Ullman, S. Krippner, and S. Fieldstein, "Experimentally Induced Telepathic Dreams: Two Studies Using EEG-REM Monitoring Technique," *International Journal of Neuropsychiatry* (now *Behavioral Neuropsychiatry*), 2:420-437, 1966.

Montague Ullman, "Dreaming, Life Style and Physiology: A Comment on Adler's View of the Dream," *Journal of Individual Psychology*, 18:18-25, 1962.

Montague Ullman, "Altered States of Consciousness and the Problem of Vigilance," *Journal of Nervous and Mental Disease*, 133:529-535, 1961. Copyright © 1961 by the Williams & Wilkins Company, Baltimore. By permission of the Williams & Wilkins Company.

Robert White, *Ego and Reality in Psychoanalytic Theory*, Psychological Issues, Vol. 3, No. 3, New York, International Universities Press, 1963. Copyright © 1963 by International Universities Press, Inc. By permission of International Universities Press.

Herman Witkin and Helen Lewis, "The Relation of Experimentally Induced Presleep Experiences to Dreams: A Report on Method and Preliminary Findings," *Journal of the American Psychoanalytic Association*, 13:819-849, 1965.

For Susie

FOREWORD

This is a book about dreaming that will have a decisive impact upon anyone who takes dreams seriously, be he experimentalist, theorist, or therapist. In putting it this flatly my intent is not to be provocative, but to state as simply and directly as I can my estimate of the full worth of the author's effort. He has succeeded in writing a book about the psychology of dreaming that is comprehensively rooted in what has gone before, alertly oriented to what is going on now, and discriminatingly discerning about ideas that are apt to germinate more completely in the future. The timing is precisely right. Someone had to organize, within the covers of a single book, the contributions of a number of people whose ideas developed more or less in separation and whose work, in some instances at least, did not receive the attention it should, e.g., Lowy, Angyal. Someone had to reevaluate their contribution in the light of the enormous amount of new data now available to us from experimental sources as well as to attempt the task of integrating the novel insights each has provided. The author, despite the complexity of the subject and the limitations of a linear medium, has somehow managed to bring about a happening of this sort. His success lies in the combined use of three techniques: first, consummate skill in identifying and preserving the living core in the contributions of those who have gone before; second, a remarkably apt selection of quotations allowing each writer to speak for himself; and, finally, the injection at just the right places of original orchestration. To succeed in a task such as this requires the rare combination of the fidelity of a disciple with the courage of an innovator. Fidelity is too often packaged in compulsive intellectual allegiance. Only rarely does it come embedded in passion. When that happens, growth and change are possible in continuity with the past.

Here, in something close to the compelling quality of dialogue, Angyal, Erikson, Lowy, Piaget, Hall, Boss, and French rub shoulders with Freud, Jung, Adler, and Silberer. Add to this the stimulus to psychoanalytic thought in the contributions of Klein, White, and Schachtel, provide a concise and thoughtful review of the current experimental scene, buttressed by the integrative efforts of Dewan, Breger, Snyder, and Jones himself, and the reader will have a better idea of the range and comprehensiveness of the present inquiry.

A further word about the contributions of Jones himself. He is an instrumentalist as well as a maestro. Again his individual contributions reflect his capacity to combine in his person the role of disciple and of innovator. In his former capacity he has provided us with a much needed reminder and clarification of the differences between the issues involved in the interpretation of dreams and the issues involved in the understanding of a psychology of dreaming. His caveat concerning the ease with which these issues become confused is well taken, and the need for it is easily illustrated in the work of most writers on dreams and even, as the author shows, in the work of Freud himself.

As an innovator he has provided us with another dimension to our understanding of dream psychology through the epigenetic schema he has developed and the novel patterning that can be revealed, particularly in successive dreams of the night, when this method is applied. It appears to provide a helpful way to recognize and identify the historical patterning of dreams and their relationship to earlier developmental crises.

The inclusion in the text of an extended, scholarly, and brilliant review by Peter Castle of the contributions of Piaget to a psychology of dreaming should be specially noted.

A psychoanalytic mentor of mine at the time I was in training offered as advice for anyone going into psychoanalysis as a career the recommendation that Freud's book *The Interpretation of Dreams* be reread every three to four years. On this basis, I should have read it at least six times. I failed by half. I say failed because Jones's book reminds us of the rich heritage that resides in Freud's classic work, a heritage that has to be grasped and understood clearly before we can move ahead. But there is something else that calls all this to mind. There is something in Jones's own style that is reminiscent of Freud, something in the literary and yet scientifically satisfying skill with which he addresses himself to his subject matter. This book, too, will warrant frequent rereading. It captures the spirit that pervades the dream scene at the present time, the zest of the experimentalists and the concerns of the theorists and systematizers. He has responded to the new data with an appreciation of their consciousness-expanding potential while at the same time remaining true to his calling as a psychologist. He is more concerned with ensuring the flow of psychological knowledge in response to these new pressures than in controlling them through a system of dikes and barricades built up out of an entrapping loyalty to past systems. In helping to free psychoanalytic theory from, in the author's own words, its "Newtonian conscience" he is helping to bring it into a more felicitous relationship with a greater array of new data and a freer interplay of theoretical ideas.

Jones also offers a dream of his own and the associations that go with it. He uses this as a point of reference in comparing the interpolated approaches of other dream theorists. Going beyond the personal observations noted by the author and the extended interpretations suggested by the work of others, I think the dream has an important social reference and reflects aspects of an identity struggle that all of us involved with dreams are apt to experience in the face of so much that is new. This, however, the reader will have to judge for himself.

Let me conclude on the same note I began, namely, a statement concerning the importance of the book and its impact. This book should serve as a reminder, to those who have grown somewhat myopic, of the range and diversity of our own theoretical heritage. It should have a salutary, unsettling effect on all those who, by not going beyond Freud, have become compulsively smug on the question of what dreams are all about. It should serve as a stimulus to those concerned with moving toward a holistic grasp of dreaming in its phylogenetic, ontogenetic, physiological, and psychological dimensions.

It is with the certainty that this appreciative response will be shared by the reader that I invite his attention to the pages that follow.

MONTAGUE ULLMAN, M.D.
Director, Department of Psychiatry
Maimonides Medical Center
Brooklyn, New York

PREFACE

         The dramatic report by Dement and Kleitman (33) which first revealed the possibility of subjecting dreaming sleep to the methodological refinements of electronically aided observation came to my attention in 1960 when I was finishing *Ego Synthesis in Dreams* (120). I footnoted the Dement and Kleitman study in passing and thought little more about it, which indicates how deeply committed I then was to the clinical approach to dream research and how unimpressed I had always been with laboratory psychology in general. The reader who is familiar with *Ego Synthesis . . .* may recall that I was even then more interested in the functions of dreaming than in the contents of dreams and that I was prepared to extend or amplify Freud's method of dream interpretation if doing so seemed likely to offer a less obscured view of the process of dreaming. However, that I would ever come to question the fundamental assumptions of Freud's psychology of dreaming, much less that laboratory findings would prompt me to do so, was then a possibility undreamed of.

This changed during 1963 when, with the help of a National Institute of Mental Health Special Research Fellowship, I had the opportunity to work with Calvin Hall and Robert Van de Castle in the Institute for Dream Research, then located in Coconut Grove, Florida. My minimal chores as volunteer subject and occasional EEG monitor in this laboratory left ample time for me to indulge my theoretical bent, which in those leisurely surroundings gradually took the form of a fanciful game: What if I were Freud, being awakened repeatedly night after night and asked to report what had been going on in my mind? What if I were Freud and could pour over the graphic representations of my own brain waves the next day, could see how they looked before and after awakenings from which I had remembered dreams, how they looked before and after awakenings from which I had not remembered dreams? What if I were Freud and could sit before an electroencephalograph and observe the utterly predictable comings and goings of a remarkably consistent constellation of neurophysiological patterns which, it was increasingly coming to seem, were direct correlates of dreaming? What—if I were Freud—would I make of all this? And, more important, how would I change my theory of dreaming in response to what I made of it? If at first I played this game only within the privacy of my own thoughts and, in recognition of the presumptuousness involved, kept these largely to myself, I gradually played it with increasing assurance, in recognition of the apparent fact that I was the only one playing it.

On and off, I have continued to indulge myself in this way since, and the book before you contains the main outcomes to date. I mention this so as not to mislead the reader who may be mostly interested in the contemporary state of our knowledge of the psychophysiology of sleep. Chapters Three and Four provide something of a review of this knowledge, but more exhaustive reviews are to be found elsewhere. I do believe, however, that the questions which have both inspired and limited this volume—namely, how Freud might have perceived this knowledge, how he might have evaluated it, and how he might have modified the psychoanalytic theory of dreaming to accommodate it—are systematically pursued here for the first time.

Thus, to those who will say I have made too much of the REM sleep–dreaming association my reply is that I think Freud would have made no less of it. Not that he would have underestimated the dangers of the body-mind polemics involved, nor the limitations of objective research in so subjective a field of inquiry. But rather, I think Freud could not have resisted the pleasures of rethinking his favorite theory in such revealing new light, however indirectly shed. To those who will say that Freud would be unlikely to recognize his theory as modified in Chapters Seven, Eight, and Nine, I can, of course, have but one reply: *I* think he would.

A few words about the book's organization should dispel any impressions of whimsy that may have been made by the remarks above. The distinction between the psychoanalytic theory of dream interpretation and the psychoanalytic theory of dreaming, on which Chapter One dwells at length, may seem to some to be a needless postponement of meatier matters. A study of the history of dream psychology will show, however, that the blurring of this fundamental distinction has been the rule rather than the exception, thus making it necessary at the outset to clarify the basic vocabulary of our subject.

Similarly, Chapter Two, which traces Freud's original theory of dreaming to its manifold conceptual roots, may strike the knowledgeable reader as an exercise in academic virtuosity that might have been left for later on, if it had to be included at all. But if one sets out to modify a theory that has been as germinal as Freud's theory of dreaming has been, one must do something to see it as after all no larger than life. One way to cut a thing to life size is to trace it to its origins. In the instance at hand, this turned out to be a fortunate tactic in that the origins of Freud's theory, once traced, immediately suggested a plan for charting its future course. Thus Chapters Three, Four, Five, and Six are updated extensions of the same lines of thought and inquiry which constituted the initial theory.

The last three chapters include attempts to restate the theory in the light of these extensions. These attempts, of course, are not conclusive. My hope is only that they may make the psychoanalytic theory of dreaming a little more useful in sifting and organizing the mounting new facts and findings about dreams and dreaming.

Finally, I wish to express special gratitude to Louis Breger, Calvin Hall, and Montague Ullman, each in his own way a distinguished contributor to dream psychology, for their careful readings of the manuscript.

RICHARD M. JONES

CONTENTS

DREAM INTERPRETATION

Chapter One AND THE PSYCHOLOGY OF DREAMING

Twenty to twenty-five percent of our normal sleeping hours are now known to be spent in a highly eccentric condition. Terms coined to describe this condition include emergent stage one sleep, transitional sleep, rapid sleep, rhomben-cephalic sleep, pontine sleep, activated sleep, paradoxical sleep, and dreaming sleep. At this writing, the condition is known to consist of (1) rapid conjugate eye movements, (2) a distinctive low voltage desynchronized cortical EEG pattern, (3) increased variability in respiration rate, (4) increased variability in pulse rate, (5) increased blood pressure, (6) decreased muscle tonus, (7) high brain temperature and metabolic rate, (8) increased variability in arousal threshold, (9) full or partial penile erection in males, and (10) dreaming. The condition manifests itself with inexorable regularity in cyclical phases over the course of sleep every night in all people, and in all mammals—begging the question in the latter instance of dreaming. We shall have more to say of this condition in later chapters.

For now, consider that these definite *empirical* statements refer to the same unlikely object of scientific study as did psychology's most influential *theoretical* advance. It will merit the reflection of historians that two revolutionary events in the development of psychology as a science have turned on the subject of dreaming: (1) the introduction in Freud's *The Interpretation of Dreams* of dynamic psychology itself, and (2) the application of electro-encephalographic technology by Kleitman, Aserinsky, and Dement to the measurement of dreaming sleep (8, 33).

In the light of these two events, it is puzzling how few of the hundreds of studies which have taken advantage of EEG sleep monitoring methods in the fifteen years since their discovery have been designed in the interests of psychoanalytic dream theory. That the discovery and development of the EEG methods would have occurred if Freud had never advanced a dream theory is beside the point. He did advance such a theory; it is one of the foundations of modern social science; and the possibilities of refining it by means of the EEG methods are not obscure.

An explanation for our failure to take advantage of this break-through may lie in the excessive respect with which we tend to handle a theory that has served for seventy years without significant modification. Respect, however, should not make us overlook the fact that Freud's work included not one but two dream theories. One dealt with dream interpretation and the other with the process of dreaming. Until now it has been common to confuse the two, and in this chapter we shall seek to dispel some of this confusion.

Recall Freud's perception of the problem to which he addressed his major work. The second chapter, following the historical review, begins:

> As we have seen, the scientific theories of dreams [by which Freud referred to the pre-Freudian theories] leave no room for any problem of interpreting them, since in their view a dream is not a mental act at all, but a somatic process signalizing its occurrence by indications registered in the mental apparatus . . .The aim which I have set before myself is to show that dreams are capable of being interpreted; and any contributions I may be able to make towards the solution of the problems dealt with in the last chapter will only arise as by-products in the course of carrying out my proper task (65, p. 96).

What were the problems dealt with in the chapter referred to? They related to memory in dreams, the sources of dreams, the forgetting of dreams, the psychological characteristics of dreams, and the function of dreaming—in short, the potential psychology of dreaming. Freud was true to his purpose. The first six chapters of his book are devoted to setting forth a method of interpreting dreams. Only when he had convinced the most extreme skeptic that dreams were capable of being interpreted did he allow himself the seventh chapter in which he sought to erect a scaffolding for the eventual construction of a psychology of dreaming, feeling, as he says, justified "in giving free reign to our speculations so long as we retain the coolness of our judgment and do not mistake the scaffolding for the building" (65, p. 536).

One has only to read this book twice to sense Freud's personal preference: to understand the causes and conditions of dreaming, not just to show that dreams are meaningfully related to waking life. His commitment, however, and one that he met with such competence as to relieve all future psychologists from it, was to perfect a method of *interpreting* dreams that did not violate the trust which dream tellers tend to place in dream interpreters.

The insights into human mentality that followed Freud's researches tend to obscure the unsophisticated "science" from which he had to depart. We pause again, therefore, to see the problem of dreams as he saw it:

> Thus the lay world has from the earliest times concerned itself with "interpreting" dreams and in its attempts to do so, it has made use of two essentially different methods. The first of these procedures considers the content of the dream as a whole and seeks to replace it by another content which is intelligible and in certain respects analogous to the original one. This is *"symbolic"* dream-interpreting; and it inevitably breaks down when faced by dreams which are not merely unintelligible but also confused. . . . It is of course impossible to give instructions upon the *method* of arriving at a symbolic interpretation. . . . The second of the two popular methods of interpreting dreams . . . might be described as the *"decoding"* method, since it treats dreams as a kind of cryptography in which each sign can be translated into another sign having a known meaning, in accordance with a fixed key . . . (65, p. 96f).

It cannot be doubted for a moment that neither of the two popular procedures for interpreting dreams can be employed for a scientific treatment of the subject. The symbolic method is restricted in its application and incapable of being laid down on general lines. In the case of the decoding method, everything depends on the trustworthiness of the "key"—the dream-book, and of this we have no guarantee. Thus one might feel tempted to agree with the philosophers and the psychiatrists, and, like them, rule out the problem of dream-interpretation as a purely fanciful task. But I have been taught better. I have been driven to realize that here once more we have one of those not infrequent cases in which an ancient and jealously held popular belief seems to be nearer the truth than the judgement of the prevalent science today. I must affirm that dreams really have a meaning and that a scientific procedure for interpreting them is possible (65, p. 99f).

Thus, the title of Freud's central work: *The Interpretation of Dreams*. Thus, also, his oft-quoted and seldom appreciated introduction to Chapter Seven:

Hitherto we have been principally concerned with the secret meaning of dreams and the method of discovering it and with the means employed by the dream-work for concealing it. . . . It is only after we have disposed of everything that has to do with the work of interpretation that we can begin to realize the incompleteness of our psychology of dreams (65, p. 510f).

DREAM INVESTIGATION AND DREAM INTERPRETATION

If we designate "dream investigation," in contradistinction to "dream interpretation," as descriptive of the work of dream psychology, we must examine the differences between these terms. We may distinguish them on the basis of (1) their social significances, (2) their immediate purposes, (3) the criteria of success as regards the achievement of their purposes, and (4) their relations to each other.

1. Dream interpretation is a social event; dream investigation is a scientific event. Dream interpretation assumes the prior existence of an interpersonal relationship sufficient in its emotional linkage to support curiosity and trust on the part of the dream teller, and regard for the dream teller and a degree of expertise on the part of the dream interpreter. The dreams of strangers, on the other hand,

may be investigated in absolute solitude and the psychology of dreaming be advanced as a result.

2. The purpose of dream interpretation is to enhance the state of wakefulness. The purpose of dream investigation is to understand the state of dreaming sleep. Dream interpretation derives from the psychoanalytic theory of personality; dream investigation is an aspect of the psychology of thinking. These distinctions could not be more boldly implied than they were by Freud in a discussion of the problem of interpreting forgotten dreams: "... in quite a number of cases one can reconstruct from a single remaining fragment not, it is true, the dream—*which is in any case a matter of no importance*—but all the dream thoughts" (65, p. 517; my italics). Bear in mind that the "dream thoughts" have their origin in wakefulness, as has the apperceptive framework within which the interpretation which links the dream to the dream thoughts will be judged meaningful or not meaningful. Only within a social event which begins and ends in wakefulness could the dream in its own right be considered "a matter of no importance." Conversely, in recognizing Pötzl's experimental study of the modifications of day residue by the dream work, a research into the nature of dreaming, Freud was quick to say: "The questions raised by Pötzl's experiment go far beyond the sphere of dream-interpretation as dealt with in the present volume" (65, p. 182).

3. The criteria of validity in dream interpretation are that the interpretation should be consistent with the interpreter's knowledge of the dreamer and that this consistency should be reflected in the dreamer's meaningful response to the interpretation. The psychotherapist, therefore, typically cares less that his colleagues should agree with his interpretations than that his patients should feel challenged by them. Thus the recurrent pronouncements by clinicians of new "psychologies of dreaming," the credentials of which attest only to their being new methods of interpreting dreams.

The criteria of validity in dream investigation are the familiar scientific criteria of controlled replicability and dispassionate agreement, which psychologists could hardly aspire to achieve before the discovery of such objective methods of dream collection as have recently been made possible by electroencephalographic monitoring.

It is all the more important now, however, when we can place more reliance on the accuracy of dream reports, that we not forfeit the gain by confusing established principles of dream interpretation with hypothetical principles of dream formation. For example, the substitution of the latent content for the manifest dream is fundamental to psychoanalytic dream interpretation, but in the psychoanalytic study of dreaming this substitution is of dubious if not misleading value. "It has long been the habit to regard dreams as identical with their manifest content," said Freud, as he prepared to discuss the psychology of dream processes, "but we must now beware equally of the mistake of confusing dreams with latent dream-thoughts" (65, p. 580).

4. The relations between dream interpretation and dream investigation would be clearer now, I think, were it not for the charisma of Freud in all matters relating to dreams. For it was on this plane, the relations between the psychology of dream interpretation and the psychology of dreaming, that Freud did not always maintain his characteristic respect for their differences. And the oversight has grown with inheritance.

Dream interpretation is to dream psychology as engineering is to physics, as cross-cultural observations of child rearing practices are to developmental psychology, as, if you will, the summer behavior of squirrels is to upper air mass analysis. Several analogies are useful because each is imperfect in a different way. That something frequently works, or frequently has certain effects, or is frequently predictive of something else always implies lawfulness of some kind, although it rarely specifies what kind. Insofar as human intellect is instrumental in making the thing work, or in having the effects, or in making the prediction, some order of prescience must be assumed. This assumption obliges the scientist to seek a statement of the general laws thus implied. Each step in this process, each approximation to the formulation of lawfulness, can usually benefit from observations or manipulations of the event in question. Correspondingly, each such observation or manipulation can usually be accomplished more efficiently as the formulation of the law becomes more articulate. This process of mutual facilitation between the so-called applied and pure aspects of science can break down in three ways: (1) the interpretive devices, rules of thumb, and second-order working assumptions which govern applied work can become reified and perceived as substantive, first-order aspects of nature; (2) the same can be overgeneralized and indiscriminately given systematic hypothetical status with respect to the lawful relations of nature; and (3) conversely, systematic hypotheses with respect to the lawful relations of nature can be misapplied as interpretive devices, rules of thumb, or practical working assumptions. Doubtless, the advance of science can be charted by tracing the correction of such mistakes, which often must be made before they can be corrected. However, the time has come to begin dismantling some of the misconceptions that have characterized the commerce between the applied events of dream interpretation and the theoretical search for the psychological laws which govern dreaming.

I shall present one example of each of the misconceptions mentioned above, the first pertaining to the reification of the "latent content," the second pertaining to the overgeneralization of "dream distortion" or "censorship," and the third pertaining to the misapplication of the "wish-fulfillment" hypothesis.

Latent Content

In discussing the latent dream thoughts, Freud was fond of the analogy of the rebus:

The dream-content . . . is expressed as it were in a pictographic script, the characters of which have to be transposed individually into the language of the dream-thoughts. If we attempted to read these characters according to their pictorial value instead of according to their symbolic relation, we should clearly be led into error. Suppose I have a picture-puzzle, a rebus, in front of me? It depicts a house with a boat on its roof, a single letter of the alphabet, the figure of a running man whose head has been conjured away, and so on. Now I might be misled into raising objections and declaring that the picture as a whole and its component parts are nonsensical. A boat has no business to be on the roof of a house, and a headless man cannot run. Moreover, the man is bigger than the house; and if the whole picture is intended to represent a landscape, letters of the alphabet are out of place in it since such objects do not occur in nature. But obviously we can only form a proper judgement of the rebus if we put aside criticisms such as these of the whole composition and its parts and if, instead, we try to replace each separate element by a syllable or word that can be represented by that element in some way or other. The words which are put together in this way are no longer nonsensical but may form a poetical phrase of the greatest beauty and significance. A dream is a picture-puzzle of this sort, and our predecessors in the field of dream-interpretation have made the mistake of treating the rebus as a pictorial composition: and as such it has seemed to them non-sensical and worthless (65, p. 277f).

Now, as it was true that many of Freud's predecessors made the mistake of treating the manifest dream as a nonsensical pictorial composition, it is equally true that many of his successors make the mistake of accepting the analogy of the rebus literally and without regard for its limitations. A rebus is consciously designed to dis-semble; the discursive equivalents of its presentational symbols are calculatedly prefigured by the constructor of the rebus. No one can deny that it has proved useful for purposes of interpreting dreams to liken dream construction to rebus construction, but no one can seriously consider that the psychological processes which govern the construction of rebuses are, in reality, the same processes that govern the construction of dreams. In more systematic contexts Freud leaves no room for doubt on this issue:

A psycho-analyst can characterize as dreams only the products of the dream-work: in spite of the fact that the latent dream-thoughts are only arrived at from the interpretation of the dream, he cannot reckon them as part of the dream, but only as part of the preconscious reflec-tion (68, p. 274).

. . . now that analysts at least have become reconciled to replacing the manifest dream by the meaning revealed by its interpretation, many of them have become guilty of falling into another confusion which they cling to with equal obstinacy. They seek to find the essence of dreams in their latent content, and in so doing they overlook the distinction between the latent dream-thoughts and the dream-work. At bottom, dreams are nothing other than a particular *form* of thinking, made possible by the conditions of the state of sleep (65, p. 506).

Nevertheless, Freud did frequently refer to the "deliberate distor-tion" and "dissimulation" of latent dream thoughts in the process of manifest dream construction, to "the process of transforming the latent thoughts into the manifest content of a dream" (65, p. 310), and in other ways suggested that the latent content was substantively operative in the process of manifest dream formation. Perhaps this will turn out to be the correct view. Bear in mind, however, that all we can be sure of at the present stage of knowledge, and all Freud could be sure of, is that a latent content can usually be *inferred from* dreams by the psychoanalytic method of dream interpretation, i.e., that the latent content is an interpretive device, the utility of which probably reflects as yet undefined processes of dream formation.

Freud's own contribution to the conceptual inflation of the latent content seems to me to be based on a point of history. We know that he felt obliged to prove to a rationalist age that dreams were meaningful. He seems, therefore, to have felt obliged to show that they were *logically* so. I do not know how else to account for his superb dissertation on "the means of representation in dreams" (65, pp. 312-38) in which the manifest content emerges as the artfully erratic offshoot of an impeccably logical latent content.

Dream Censorship

We are introduced to the concept of "dream distortion" with uncharacteristic abruptness (65, p. 136). Freud has concluded his specimen interpretation of the Irma dream and has made his preliminary statement of the wish-fulfillment hypothesis. Then, without any of the disarming prose by which he typically led his readers to controversial theoretical positions, he simply proposes that we describe the aspects of dreams which render the wish-fulfillment hypothesis dubious as "the phenomenon of distortion in dreams." Actually, he had said thirty pages earlier:

> I have been engaged for many years . . . in unravelling certain psychopathological structures—hysterical phobias, obsessional ideas, and so on. . . . It was in the course of these psychoanalytic studies that I came upon dream-interpretation. My patients were pledged to communicate to me every idea or thought that occurred to them in connection with some particular subject; amongst other things, they told me their dreams and so taught me that a dream can be inserted into the psychical chain that has to be traced backwards in the memory from a pathological idea. *It was then only a short step to treating the dream itself as a symptom and to applying to dreams the method of interpre-*

tation that had been worked out for symptoms (65, p. 100f; **my** italics).

It was then but another "short step" to introducing the concept of "dream distortion" to account for the noncorrespondence between the dream's apparent meaning, or lack of meaning, and its interpreted meaning. Such a procedure had proved useful in interpreting symptoms; it continued to prove useful in interpreting dreams. However, this did not warrant the still *further* step of assigning to dream distortion a place in the *process* of dreaming. Freud knew this. Therefore he firmly insisted that distortion be viewed as imposed by the resistance characteristic of waking life; therefore, also, when focusing on the process of the dream-work rather than on the work of interpreting dreams, he spoke not of "distortion" but of "giving things a new form" (65, p. 507). And when he did sometimes take liberty and speak of dream censorship as if it were an integral part of the process of dreaming (designed as it were to defeat interpretations), he at least did not extend the license beyond immediate heuristic needs. ". . . We must always," he concludes, "be prepared to drop our conceptual scaffolding if we feel that we are in a position to replace it by something that approximates more closely to the unknown reality" (65, p. 610).

We would now seem to know sufficiently more about preconscious perception and preconscious cognition and about the psychophysiological conditions of dreaming sleep and of nondreaming sleep to resist all further attempts to confuse the interpretive notion of dream distortion with the psychological processes of dream construction.

Wish-Fullfillment

It is interesting how frequently a novice, on hearing Freud's emphasis on wish-fulfillment, proceeds to misapply the idea and yet often manages to meet the criteria of successful dream interpretation; i.e., he manages to be consistent with his knowledge of the dreamer, and he stimulates a meaningful response. He may, for example, as a friend of mine did, dream of a church collapsing in an earthquake and, without a moment's reflection as to the dream's latent content, conclude that Freud's theory must be right, because, "as I've always said, 'down with churches.'" It is tempting to agree that we have here a "Freudian wish" until we reflect that a wish to destroy churches, especially one that is so readily admitted, can in no way qualify as possessing "a psychical dimension of depth," which Freud insisted could not be absent, "without denying the standpoint of psycho-analysis" (68, p. 275). It is not, in other words, a *repressed infantile* wish. Therefore the collapsed-church dream was from Freud's point of view erroneously interpreted, because it succeeded only in extracting from the dream a sample of the dreamer's conscious reflections—a wishful reflection, to be sure, but not a repressed infantile wish.

> *My supposition is that a conscious wish can only become a dream-instigator if it succeeds in awakening an unconscious wish with the same tenor and in obtaining reinforcement from it . . . a wish which is represented in a dream must be an infantile one. . . .* In my view, therefore, wishful impulses left over from conscious waking life must be relegated to a secondary position in respect to the formation of dreams (65, p. 553f).

We come now to Freud's contribution to our confusion: his own interpretations of dreams frequently differ little from that of my friend. There is not, as a matter of fact, among the scores of specimen interpretations in the revised *Standard Edition* of *The Interpretation of Dreams,* a single one which meets his own standards.

What, for example, was the "wish" which Freud so painstakingly traced in the latent content of the Irma dream? It was, he tells us, the wish to be absolved from imagined reproaches against his professional competence: "Take these people away! Give me three others of my choice instead! Then I shall be free of these undeserved reproaches!" (65, p. 119). Is this a repressed infantile wish? No, it is not. But Freud warned us that he would keep much in reserve when interpreting his own dreams. The place to look, then, may be in his interpretations of his patients' dreams. What was the wish behind the dream of the lady who saw her young nephew lying dead in a coffin? Was it, as she feared, that she was such an awful person as to wish the boy dead? "I assured her," says Freud, "that this . . . interpretation was out of the question" (65, p. 152). There followed the usual associations and dream thoughts until the "true" wish was revealed. It was a wish once more to see a professor, a former object of the lady's affections, whom she had last seen at a child's funeral (65, p. 153). Is this a repressed infantile wish? No, it is not. But Freud was reluctant to use the dreams of his patients to illustrate his theory of dreams lest he be accused of generalizing to all people what was only true of neurotic people. Let us turn then to Freud's interpretation of a dream which was reported to him by a patient who had herself heard it in a lecture. It is the dream of the father who had for many days kept a vigil at the side of his child's sickbed and had, after the child's death, retired to the next room to lie down, leaving the door ajar so that he could see from his bedroom into the room in which his child's body was laid out with candles standing around it:

> An old man had been engaged to keep watch over it, and sat beside the body murmuring prayers. After a few hours' sleep, the father had a dream that his child was standing beside his bed, caught him by the arm and whispered to him reproachfully: "Father, don't you see I'm burning?" He woke up, noticed a bright glare of light from the next room, hurried into it, and found that the old watchman had dropped off to sleep and that the wrappings and one of the arms of his beloved child's dead body had been burned by a lighted candle that had fallen on them (65, p. 509).

Freud had no objection to the lecturer's understanding of this dream, which was that it served certain reality-testing purposes. He was not satisfied, however, that this was sufficient to explain the dream until he surmised its wish, which he thought could be the father's longing that his child be alive once more. But is *this* a repressed infantile wish? No, it is not.

I have made a thorough search of *The Interpretation of Dreams* and can report that there is not one illustration of wish-fulfillment which meets the criterion of reference to a repressed infantile wish. Every illustration posits a wish, but every wish is like the three just reported: it is either a wish of out-and-out conscious reflection, or it is a suppressed wish of post-infantile origin. One may, of course, consider the wishes revealed by these interpretations to be *derivatives* of repressed infantile wishes. There is no question that they are so and that it would be a simple task in each instance to establish the connections that mediate the derivations. But, considering the importance that Freud attributed to repressed infantile wishes as the motivating source of all dreams, why would he leave the task of ferreting these out entirely to his readers without a single illustration? One can imagine with what haste I re-examined other works of Freud to see if this peculiar omission held across his entire literature on the subject. No, only in *The Interpretation of Dreams* does this conspicuous absence obtain. In "An Evidential Dream," for example, Freud concludes the latent wish of the lady's dream (which is too lengthy to reproduce here) to be that of having sexual intercourse with her father and to have a child according to an anal theory of birth (68). Is this a repressed infantile wish? Yes, it is.

How shall we account for the incompleteness with which Freud advanced the point that he maintained was most essential to his theory of dreams? How shall we account for the fact that it is in his major and most popular work on dreams that this incompleteness is most in evidence, while in other works it is less in evidence? The answers must lie in the dual commitment to which Freud referred in speaking of his "theory of dreams": (1) his commitment to perfect a scientifically credible method of dream interpretation and (2) his commitment to begin a psychology of dreaming. *The Interpretation of Dreams* was devoted primarily to the first commitment. In Chapter Seven and in most of the later papers on dreams, the second commitment was uppermost. It was in these latter contexts that Freud held repressed infantile wish-fulfillment to be essential. Essential to what? Essential to the *formation* of dreams. For the *interpretation* of dreams, on the other hand, we have it from Freud's own example that any wish will do. But so, for this matter, will any mental act. Hence the polemics, which have plagued us since, over whether dreams are really hiding or really seeking.

What we have here is a converse example of the confusion which results from loosely employing the devices of dream interpretation in the formulations of dream psychology. For in this instance we have a systematic hypothesis overreaching itself as an interpretive device. This is not to say that the wish-fulfillment hypothesis may not be suggestive in the interpretation of dreams, nor is it to say that interpreted dreams are not useful data for testing the wish-fulfillment hypothesis. My point is only that as we should not expect to find the interpretive concept of the "latent dream thoughts" at the center of the psychology of dreaming, we should likewise not expect to find the hypothesis concerning repressed infantile wish-fulfillment at the center of all dream interpretations.

SUMMARY

What is, or ought to be, the relation between the psychology of dream interpretation and the psychology of dreaming? It is the relationship that should always obtain between the applied and theoretical aspects of a scientific enterprise. A diversity of interpretive schemes may meet the criterion of successful dream interpretation, as we will see in Chapter Five. The task for the future is not to show that these are consistent with one another, nor that they comprise a coherent whole; the task is to trace back to the psychological laws suggested by each, and eventually to seek consistency and coherence at that level in a systematic statement of the general psychology of dreaming. Some interpretive leads may then prove readily transposable as systematic constructs or observable realities; others may prove to have been useful approximations to more definitive constructs or more observable realities.

The relation of dream interpretation methods to dream investigation is, then, heuristic—purely so, and in this respect should not be judged on other grounds. Whatever their records of accomplishment as ways of making dreams meaningful to dreamers, which they may achieve in spite of all sorts of inconsistency, incompleteness, and even misunderstanding, if they work it is best assumed that these methods are suggestive of hypotheses. The hypotheses, once articulated and put to work in their capacity as predictors, must be held to an eventual record of achievement not only in refining methods of dream interpretation but in clarifying a spectrum of psychological issues relevant to sleep and dreaming.

THE PSYCHOANALYTIC THEORY OF DREAMING

Chapter Two

Freud's theory of dream formation may be stated most succinctly by quotation:

The situation is this. Either residues of the previous day have been left over from the activity of waking life and it has not been possible to withdraw the whole cathexis of energy from them; or the activity of waking life during the course of the day has led to the stirring up of an unconscious wish; or these two events have happened to coincide. . . . The unconscious wish links itself up with the day's residues and effects a transference onto them; this may happen either in the course of the day or not until the state of sleep has been established. A wish now arises which has been transferred onto the recent material; or a recent wish, having been suppressed, gains fresh life by being reinforced from the unconscious. This wish seeks to force its way along the normal path taken by thought processes, through the preconscious. But it comes up against the censorship, which is still functioning and to the influence of which it now submits. At this point it takes on the distortion for which the way has already been paved by the transference of the wish onto the recent material. So far it is on the way to becoming an obsessive idea or a delusion or something of the kind—that is, a *thought* which has been intensified by transference and distorted in its expression by censorship. Its further advance is halted, however, by the sleeping state of the preconscious. . . . The dream process consequently enters on a regressive path, which lies open to it precisely owing to the peculiar nature of the

15

state of sleep, and it is led along that path by the attraction exercised on it by groups of memories; some of these memories themselves exist only in the form of visual cathexes and not as translations into the terminology of the later systems. . . . In the course of its regressive path the dream process acquires the attributes of representability . . . it has now completed the second portion of its zig zag journey. The first portion was a progressive one, leading from the unconscious scenes or fantasies to the preconscious; the second portion led from the frontier of the censorship back to perceptions. But when the content of the dream process has become perceptual, by that fact it has, as it were, found a way of evading the obstacle put in its path by the censorship and by the state of sleep of the preconscious. . . . It succeeds in drawing attention to itself and in being noticed by consciousness (65, pp. 573-74).

Almost as afterthoughts Freud offered his "sleep-protection" and "safety-valve" notions, i.e., that the purpose of dreaming was protection of sleep, which it accomplished by arranging for partial release of disruptive psychological tensions.

A wealth of new knowledge about sleep and dreaming is in our possession as a result of the EEG sleep monitoring methods. More than enough to suggest that the time has come to honor our only systematic theory of dreaming with revisionary efforts. I propose in Chapter Seven to lay out for inspection one conceivable pattern as a guide to such an effort.

But first we should review origins. Freud had almost none of the empirical findings concerning sleep and dreaming that we have. What, then, was the pattern from which *he* worked? It can be observed to have derived from five sources: (1) observations of spontaneously recalled and reported dreams, in and out of the clinical setting; (2) extrapolations from established principles of dream interpretation to hypothetical processes of dream formation; (3) analogies supplied by the psychoanalytic theory of neurosis, particularly the theory of symptom formation; (4) commonsense assumptions regarding the modifications imposed on psychic functioning by "the state of sleep"; and (5) certain emphases which devolved upon all of Freud's specific theories from his general theoretical commitments, particularly as regards the determining influences of unconscious instinctual forces. To clarify the pattern of Freud's theory, each of these sources needs elaboration here.

OBSERVATIONS

The waking situations in which people tended to recall and report their dreams led Freud to the conviction that dreaming was a meaningful psychological process, occupying a distinctive place in the systems of normal mental functioning. He was sometimes impatient with the empirical details of dreams (i.e., manifest contents) when endeavoring to *interpret* them, but in seeking to understand the *process* of dreaming he was impatient with any but the most exhaustive attention to these same details. Other theorists had sought to explain dreaming by reference to one or another of the characteristic phenomenological properties of dreams: their regular inclusion of recent incidental perceptions and memories, their regular inclusion of hypermnesic perceptions and memories, their distinctively sensory qualities, and their distinctive sense of experiential presence. Freud's theory of dreaming remained the only one that sought to account for *all* of these observations. Thus, it is to its observational base that the theory owes its comprehensiveness, the primary role it assigns to psychological functions in the determination of dream content, and its underscoring of the normality of dreaming.

EXTRAPOLATION
FROM DREAM
INTERPRETATIONS

Odd though it may seem, comparatively little of the theory of dreaming was drawn from dream interpretations. So far as I can determine, only one of Freud's speculations concerning dream formation derived from this source—the assumption of functional interrelatedness between dreaming processes and waking thought processes:

> In view of the very great number of associations produced in analysis to each individual element of the content of a dream, some readers may be led to doubt whether, as a matter of principle, we are justified in regarding as part of the dream thoughts all the associations that occur to us during the subsequent analysis—whether we are justified, that is, in supposing that all these thoughts were already active during

the state of sleep and played a part in the formation of the dream. Is it not more probable that new trains of thought have arisen in the course of the analysis which had no share in forming the dream? I can only give limited assent to this argument. It is no doubt true that some trains of thought arise for the first time during the analysis. But one can convince oneself in all such cases that these new connections are only set up between thoughts which were already linked in some other way in the dream thoughts. The new connections are, as it were, loop-lines or short circuits, made possible by the existence of other and deeper-lying connecting paths. It must be allowed that the greater bulk of the thoughts which are revealed in analysis were already active during the process of forming the dream. . . (65, pp. 280-81).

In other words, not only could dreams be *made to* relate to waking experiences occurring before and after their formation, but they were assumed to be functionally related to such experiences *in statu nascendi*.

This assumption could only be academic at the time it was made, since there were no conceivable ways to substantiate it. Pötzl's Law of Exclusion (below-threshold day residues appeared in dreams while above-threshold day residues did not) and the laboratory findings which supported it were known to Freud, but several decades were to elapse before Fisher, Shevrin and Luborsky, and others were to refine Pötzl's methods and attempt to replicate his findings (179,44,45,46,204).

It bears re-emphasis that *only* this aspect of the theory of dreaming—the functional relation between dreaming and waking thought—owes its conceptual origins to the theory and practice of dream interpretation. The concepts of "latent dream thoughts" and "the censorship," for example, while integral to the theory of dream interpretation, did not emerge from the work of interpreting dreams (124,127,229). The utility and, hence, face-validity of these concepts were repeatedly *confirmed* by dream interpretations but they were *suggested* by another source of inference, the one to which we turn next.

ANALOGY

The contributions of Freud's theory of neurosis to the theory of dreaming cannot be overestimated. A preponderance of the hypothetical constructs which compose the theory were derived by analogical inference from the pre-existent theory of symptom formation. These include the censorship, the need of repressed material for points of transference to conscious material of weak associative power, the notion of compromise between opposing psychic forces, and the vicissitudes of interaction between the primary process and the secondary process, i.e., the dream-work. To this list might almost be added the wish-fulfillment hypothesis itself, except that this seems to have been predetermined by still another of Freud's conceptual wellsprings to be discussed further on.

The following quotations are a sample of the many that attest to Freud's reliance on this analogical source of inference:

> Thus we are driven to conclude that two fundamentally different kinds of psychical process are concerned in the formation of dreams. One of these produces perfectly rational thoughts, of no less validity than normal thinking; while the other treats these thoughts in a manner which is in the highest degree bewildering and irrational. We have already . . . segregated this second psychical process as being the dream-work proper. What light have we now to throw upon its origin?
>
> *It would not be possible for us to answer this question if we had not made some headway in the study of the psychology of the neuroses, and particularly of hysteria* [my italics].
>
> We have found from this that the same irrational psychical processes . . . dominate the production of hysterical symptoms. In hysteria, too, we come across a series of perfectly rational thoughts, equal in validity to our conscious thoughts; but to begin with, we know nothing of their existence in this form and we can only reconstruct them subsequently. If they force themselves upon our notice at any point, we discover by analyzing the symptom which has been produced that these normal thoughts have been submitted to abnormal treatment: *they have been transformed into the symptom by means of condensation and the formation of compromises, by way of superficial associations, and in disregard of contradictions, and also, it may be, along the path of regression* [Freud's italics]. *In view of the complete identity between the characteristic features of the dream-work and those of the psychical activity which issues in psychoneurotic symptoms, we feel justified in carrying over to dreams the conclusions we have been led to by hysteria* (65, pp. 597-98; my italics).

However many changes may be made in our reading of the psychical censorship and of the rational and abnormal revisions made of the dream content, it remains true that processes of this sort are at work in the formation of dreams and that they show *the closest analogy in their essentials to the processes observable in the formation of hysterical symptoms* (65, p. 607; my italics).

COMMONSENSE ASSUMPTIONS CONCERNING THE STATE OF SLEEP

Freud's notion of the "wish to sleep" has always been an anomaly in dream psychology, being lacking in the dynamic connotations with which he typically invested the concept of "wishes" in all other contexts. Today, of course, it runs directly counter to the empirical studies, to be reviewed in the next chapter, which show the human sleep cycle to be governed by neurophysiological processes that normally override the influence of psychological forces. It is interesting to note the exact point in his thinking at which Freud forged this weakest link in the theory. It was at the point where the symptom formation analogy broke down. As noted, almost every facet of the theory of dreaming had its inception in the theory of symptom formation. Then Freud notes an exception. Symptoms always have *two* main determinants arising from *two* systems in conflict, the Unconscious (Ucs) and the Preconscious (Pcs). Dreams had been shown to have but *one* main determinant arising from *one* system, the Ucs. Thus, in the apparent interests of maintaining the symmetry of his thoughts regarding the similarities between symptom formation and dream formation, he posited as the determinant of dream formation, which first opposed and then entered into compromise with the repressed wish, the "preconscious wish to sleep."

Nor was this the only point at which an inadequate understanding of sleep can be seen to have made for awkwardness. The crucial references to regression were similarly affected:

What modification is it that renders possible a regression which cannot occur in daytime? . . . No doubt it is a question of changes in the cathexes of energy attaching to the different systems, changes which increase or diminish the facility with which those systems can be passed through by the excitatory process. But in any apparatus of this kind the same results upon the passage of excitations might be produced in more than one way. *Our first thoughts will, of course, be of the state of sleep* [my italics] and the changes in cathexis which it brings about at the sensory end of the apparatus. During the day there is a continuous current from the perceptual system flowing in the direction of motor activity; but this current ceases at night and could no longer form an obstacle to a current of excitation flowing in the opposite sense. . . .

In explaining regression in dreams, however, we must bear in mind the regressions which also occur in pathological waking states; and here the explanation just given leaves us in the lurch. For in those cases, regression occurs in spite of a sensory current flowing without interruption in a forward direction. . . .

If we now bear in mind how great a part is played in the dream-thoughts by infantile experience or by fantasies based upon them, how frequently portions of them re-emerge in the dream content, and how often the dream wishes themselves are derived from them, we cannot dismiss the probability that · . . . the transformation of thoughts into visual images may be in part the result of the attraction which memories couched in visual form and eager for revival bring to bear upon thoughts cut off from consciousness and struggling to find expression. . . .

This indication of the way in which infantile scenes (or their reproductions as fantasies) function in a sense as models for the content of dreams, removes the necessity for one of the hypotheses put forward by Scherner and his followers in regard to internal sources of stimulation. Scherner supposes that, "when dreams exhibit particularly vivid or particularly copious visual elements, there is present a state of 'visual stimulation,'" that is, of internal excitation in the organ of vision. We need not dispute this hypothesis, but can content ourselves with assuming that this state of excitation applies merely to the *psychical* perceptual system of the visual organ; we may, however, further point out that the state of excitation has been set up by a *memory*, that is, a *revival* of a visual excitation which was originally an immediate one. . . .

Let us bring together what we have found out about the peculiar propensity of dreams to recast their ideational content into sensory images. We have not explained this feature of the dream-work, we have not traced it back to any known psychological laws; but we have rather picked it out as something that suggests unknown implications and we have characterized it with the word "regressive." We have put forward the view that in all probability this regression, wherever it may occur, is an effect of a resistance opposing the progress of thought into consciousness along the normal path, and of a simultaneous attraction exercised upon the thought by the presence of memories possessing great sensory force. In the case of dreams, regression may perhaps be further facilitated by the cessation of the progressive current which streams in during the daytime from the sense organs; in other forms of regression, the absence of this accessory factor must be made up for by a greater intensity of the motives for regression (65, pp. 542-48).

The reach of mind reflected in these speculations remains awesome. Freud might well have rested his regression explanation of the hallucinatory qualities of dreams on the "state of sleep," which obviously inhibits the potential for motor activity and obviously reduces the stream of external excitation characteristic of waking life. But his sensitivity to the similarities between normal dreaming and abnormal waking experiences, which we cited in a previous context as a potential source of misconception, deters him in this instance from taking an overly simple position: the same hallucinatory qualities could attach to waking experiences when they were under the dominant influences of infantile memories and related psychic phenomena. Thus, faced with the option of attributing the hallucinatory qualities of dreams primarily to the constraints of the state of sleep and secondarily to the attractions of repressed infantile wishes, or the converse, Freud chose the converse relationship. We can but wonder whether he would have reversed himself in this had he been in possession of contemporary knowledge that, although the conditions of sleep to which he referred obtain throughout the sleep cycle, dreaming mostly occurs during certain "activated" phases of the cycle.* Surely he would at least have reconsidered the option—as must we.

GENERAL
THEORETICAL
PREDILECTION

Why, we may ask, was Freud content to allow his otherwise tightly organized theory of dreaming the laxity

* Such activation, indeed, including excitation of the visual organ, per Scherner.

of the "wish to sleep" notion, and why did he repeatedly advance as a central hypothesis the unnecessary sleep-protection idea? Because both formulations were congruent with his reliance on the symptom formation analogy? Because they were both consistent with some dream interpretations? Because he had confidence in his knowledge of sleep? Apparently not. Rather, it would appear that these loose thoughts commended themselves to Freud primarily because they offered little resistance to his abiding ambitions: (1) to make psychology an exact science, ultimately referable to principles of energy distributions, according to the Newtonian model of his day, and (2) to bring psychology into line with the then revolutionary Darwinian geist to which all of biological science was conforming: man is an animal whose instincts are uniquely amorphous and atypically mediated, but an animal whose behavior is ultimately determined by energic forces better classified as instincts than as anything else. Thus, when all of his genius for observation, for extrapolation, for analogy, and for common sense had been brought to bear in support of his central hypothesis that the ultimate motivating force of dreaming was to be found in pressures for unconscious wish-fulfillment, he could still think to add this unabashed note of solipsism: ". . . it is self-evident that dreams must be wish-fulfillments, since nothing but a wish can set our mental apparatus at work" (65, p. 567).

It may prove to be one of the supreme ironies of scientific history that recent studies of the psychophysiology of sleep and dreaming have rejustified Freud's loyalty to Darwin in these matters (212) while showing his loyalty to Newton to have been a costly mistake (19,113,147). More on this in Chapter Six.

Each of these sources of evidence and inference, on which the psychoanalytic theory of dreaming is based, has been expanded and deepened since Freud's last revisions of the theory. In the next four chapters we shall review the main lines of these interim developments in preparation for suggesting our own revisions.

THE D-STATE, DEPTH OF SLEEP, AND SLEEP PROTECTION

Chapter Three

THE D-STATE

The fifteen-year record of electronic sleep monitoring investigations which followed Aserinsky and Kleitman's dramatic methodological breakthrough in 1953 has placed at our disposal vastly more knowledge of sleep than was available to Freud. Indeed, the psychophysiological state in which the pre-ponderance of dreaming is now thought to occur appears to be as different from "sleep" as "sleep" is from the waking state. Snyder, Fisher, Hartmann, Jones, and others have responded to these investigations by proposing that this other nonwaking state be conceived as a third basic form of human existence (208, 47, 104, 123).

Various investigators have been more than generous in seeking to provide this third state with an acceptable scientific name. Some of these were mentioned in Chapter One. At this writing there is no discernible consensus among the members of the Association for the Psychophysiological Study of Sleep, so, quite arbitrarily, we shall follow Hartmann in referring to it as the "D-state." Recall, very summarily, that it includes the concomitant presence of irregular pulse, blood pressure, and respiration; penile erection; rapid conjugate eye movements; sporadic activity of certain fine muscle groups; near absence of tonic anti-gravity muscle potential; a low voltage desynchronized cortical EEG pattern; high brain temperature and metabolic rate; and, in humans, a high positive correlation with ability to report dreams upon being awakened. As dramatically noted by Snyder:

> Since the relationship between REM [rapid eye movement] periods of human sleep and dream recall was first claimed in 1953, it has been reexamined in at least sixteen systematic studies, surely the most thorough test yet given to any psychophysiological relationship.
>
> The incidence of "dream reports" obtained from REM awakenings ranges from sixty to eighty-nine percent, the seventy-four percent first obtained by Aserinsky and Kleitman in 1953 being almost precisely the median (214).

The D-state rhythmically supervenes the sleep cycle about every ninety minutes through the night and lasts for increasingly longer periods of time ranging from about five minutes to about forty minutes. The D-state is ubiquitous; indeed only in extremely abnormal persons, or in normal persons under the influence of certain drugs, has it been found absent or deviant. The D-state is triggered by a noncortical system which is one of the lowest on the phylogenetic scale—the pontile-limbic system. It is a basic feature of mammalian life, all mammals so far studied showing clear evidence of it, and all nonmammals so far studied showing little or no evidence of it. Some form of mental activity is experimentally retrievable in humans at any stage of nonwakefulness, i.e., both in sleep and in the D-state. The quality of mentation involved, however, differs markedly in these two states, the D-state apparently being governed by the primary process although including some secondary process activity, and the sleep state apparently being governed by the secondary process although including some primary process activity.

The physiological correlates of the D-state and of non-REM (NREM) sleep have been discussed in detail by several writers. Oswald's *Sleeping and Waking* is probably the most competent review from the physiologist's standpoint—although it is a bit doctrinaire in its psychological interpretations (172). Hartmann's *The Biology of Dreaming* is the most exhaustive review available at this writing (106). For those who wish to view the new facts in the singular lights of metapsychology, Fisher's "Psychoanalytic Implications of Recent Research on Sleep and Dreaming" is commendable (47). I have especially enjoyed the authoritative and engaging perspectives on the physiology of sleep and dreaming which Frederick Snyder has projected in his three articles "The New Biology of Dreaming," "Toward an Evolutionary Theory of Dreaming," and "The Physiology of Dreaming" (208, 212, 214).

It will best suit our particular purposes to concentrate here on (1) the phylogeny of the D-state, (2) the ontogeny of the D-state, (3) speculations regarding the D-state's functions, and (4) the vexing questions posed by comparative investigations of REM and NREM sleep.

Although the D-state's biological functions are far from established, its exclusive association with mammalian life processes has been quite clearly established. It is a substantive component in the sleep cycles of opossums, mice, rats, rabbits, dogs, cats, sheep, goats, donkeys, monkeys, chimpanzees, elephants, and, of course, humans (106, p. 14). With one exception all attempts to detect its presence in reptiles have been unsuccessful (110, 132, 135, 209). Tauber reports the occasional presence of eye movements in the sleep of the chameleon, but these are not rapid conjugate eye movements, nor are they associated with any change in electro-encephalogram activity (228). Klein, *et al.*, observed brief periods resembling the D-state in birds, but so little of total sleep time was involved (0.5%) that it can at most be claimed that birds possess some precursive aspects of the D-state (148).

D-periods appear to occupy the largest portion of sleep among the carnivores. The omnivores are next, and the herbivores are last. The clearest pattern so far observed, however, shows the average length of D-periods to vary inversely with metabolic rate (106, p. 17).

In view of these phylogenetic studies it is easy to agree with Snyder that "the physiological state associated with human dreaming is a very old and basic biological characteristic of mammalian life" (213, p. 59).

That the D-state must serve some developmental function has been strongly suggested by numerous related ontogenetic studies, all of which show that it occupies much more time in the lives of the young than in the lives of adults. The newborn kitten, for example, would appear to spend almost its entire existence in the D-state (132). An interesting curvilinear pattern has been observed in the rhesus monkey, 31 percent of sleep being D-state at birth, 43 percent on the seventh day of life, 27 percent at the end of the first year, and 11 to 16 percent being characteristic of adulthood (165, 189). In humans the newborn infant spends about 50 percent of sleep time in the D-state. At age two the percentage is 40; at age five it is 25 to 30; during adolescence and adulthood it is 20; and at sixty years of age it is about 15. Human infants born prematurely spend approximately 75 percent of sleeping time in the D-state, and although intra-uterine electrographic instruments have not yet been perfected it seems likely that the human fetus may rival the newborn kitten in this matter (106, pp. 19-21).

What biological functions, developmental or otherwise, the D-state may serve is a matter for speculation. Dement has wondered if one function may not be that of clearing the nervous system of an endogenous metabolite deposited, as it were, by daily activities (25). Roffwarg, *et al.*, suggest that the developing cortex of the fetus and infant may require more sensory input than can be supplied by the periods of wakefulness characteristic of these early states, and that the D-state may provide an endogenous source of additional cortical stimulation (193). Weiss speculates that the D-state may serve to reorganize firing patterns in the central nervous system which have become disorganized during sleep (245). Ephron and Carrington have supposed that the D-state may be a homeostatic device providing periodic opportunities for recovery from the "sensory deprivation" of sleep (41). Snyder wonders if the D-state may not serve periodically to awaken animals whose survival would be jeopardized by lengthy periods out of contact with their surroundings (212). Berger is in the process of attempting to support the dual hypothesis that the D-state (1) provides a mechanism for establishing the neuromuscular pathways which serve binocularly coordinated eye movements in both phylogenesis and ontogenesis, and (2) periodically innervates the oculomotor system throughout mammalian life during extended sleep, in order to maintain facilitation of binocularly coordinated eye movement into subsequent wakefulness (14).

We shall take up the question of the possible psychological functions of the human D-state, including those relating to dreaming, in a later chapter. Whatever these may prove to be, they must certainly be quite late evolutionary elaborations of earlier biological developments, for clearly we are dealing with something primordial.

Both Snyder and I have previously suggested that the evolution of the mammalian D-state may be to human dreaming what the evolution of the mammalian ingestion and respiration systems have been to human speech. In a recent paper Snyder puts this thought even more picturesquely:

> If I may misappropriate Dr. Lewin's conception of the "dream screen," I can conceive that in some sense the primitive biological process of the REM state periodically provides the "energy" to illuminate the screen as well as the projector mechanism to crank the film, and possibly the film itself, but that, for reasons we cannot yet comprehend, all of this would go on regardless of whether the film contained the meaningful images we call dreams. For physiological answers to such questions as how the scripts of dreams are written, or the film produced, or why the entire process takes place, we can only wait hopefully and expectantly, but still very much in the dark (214).

We are sufficiently in the light, however, to be able to regard Freud's assumptions concerning the "state of sleep" as prescientific. At the very least we can now see that we must think of not one but two states of sleep, each of which is as different from the other as both are from the waking state, one of the differences apparently pertaining to nothing less than the conduction of dreaming.

We should be suspicious if the association of dreaming with the D-state seemed absolute, for, as Snyder has also noted, we can at best have but a third-hand hold on the data that suggest this association. There is first the distance from direct observation which is produced by the transition from the dreaming state to wakefulness; there is the further distance produced by the subject's translation of subjective experience into verbal reports; and, thirdly, there is the distance produced by the necessity of having to decide whether or not to regard the verbal report as a reflection of dreaming or of some other form of mentation. Under these circumstances it is remarkable that the weight of evidence is as noticeably on the side of associating dreaming with the D-state as it is. Nevertheless, one of the most provocative findings to have emerged from recent monitored sleep studies is that *neither* of the two kinds of sleep is psychologically quiescent.

The early replications of the original Aserinsky and Kleitman investigation, which confirmed the finding that reports of dreaming occurred on the average in 74 percent of awakenings from REM sleep, left the impression that those few dream reports which followed awakenings from NREM sleep were actually memories of previous REM sleep dreams. In other words, NREM sleep seemed to be, in nature, as Freud assumed dreamless sleep to be: a period of "abandonment of interest in thought processes" (65, p. 575). However, a doctoral dissertation completed in 1960 by David Foulkes not only showed this to be a misimpression but even raised the possibility that dreaming was not, after all, one of the distinguishing features of the D-state (55). Working with eight subjects for seven nights each, Foulkes made REM and NREM awakenings on each night but instead of asking if any dreams could be recalled he asked if any mental experiences could be recalled. A detailed interview was conducted after each report which sought to determine the qualities of the reported mental experiences—emotionality, clarity of imagery, etc. Foulkes found that his subjects were able to recall some kind of mental experience after 87 percent of the REM sleep awakenings and after 74 percent of NREM awakenings. The difference was statistically significant but far less dramatic than had previously been suggested. Moreover, the NREM recall rate was identical whether the awakenings followed uninterrupted REM periods or not, ruling out the possibility that the NREM reports were of previous REM dreams. Furthermore, almost the same percentages of NREM recall stemmed from stages three and four of NREM sleep as from stage two of NREM sleep, suggesting that the entire NREM period was capable of supporting mentation. (See Fig. 1, p. 32.)

How can the discrepancies between Foulkes' findings and those of previous investigations be accounted for? Foulkes attributed them to three sources: (1) Subject variability, for which it is difficult to control in a kind of research where large subject populations are prohibitively demanding of experimenter time and laboratory supplies. (2) The greater leniency of his requests; presumably subjects in previous studies, who were only asked about dreaming, reported only what they considered dreams. (3) Qualitative differences between NREM and REM mentation. NREM mentation is usually much less "dreamlike" than REM mentation, i.e., more likely to refer to some aspect of recent daily routine, less likely to contain symbolic elaborations, and more likely to "make sense" to the subject. So, whether the subject, or for that matter the investigator, considers a nocturnal report a dream depends on his criteria.

The doubts raised by Foulkes' early work thus had the very healthy effect of encouraging all dream researchers to explicate carefully the criteria by which they distinguished dreaming from thinking. Subsequent comparative studies of REM and NREM mentation, being careful to keep criteria explicit, have at this writing just about reached the point of restimulating the excitement which was set off by the studies of Aserinsky, Dement, and Kleitman which suggested, in the first place, that functional interrelations exist between dreaming and the D-state. Snyder has refocused this point as follows:

> There is complete agreement among [these] studies that reports from NREM awakenings are usually quantitatively and qualitatively different from those of REM awakenings, NREM reports tending to be brief fragmentary descriptions of thoughts, and REM reports tending to be longer more coherent descriptions of hallucinated dramas. If we are willing to accept the former as evidence of dreaming, then there is no specific relationship to REM, but if we insist upon the latter, then the relationship is as good as we might hope to obtain.
>
> That has been demonstrated best in three of the latest studies directed to this question (Goodenough, *et al.* 1965; Hobson, *et al.* 1965; and Monroe, *et al.* 1965). In these studies the last step in this procedure, the judgement as to whether a given report was or was not a dream report, was carried out by the investigators on a "blind" basis from transcripts, and although even such judgements are subject to varying preconceptions as to what constitutes a "dream report," the agreement among them and the original findings of Aserinsky and Kleitman is very impressive. . . .
>
> Since one of these studies (Monroe, *et al.* 1965) comes from the same laboratory that had previously challenged the REM dream correlation most severely, the conclusion of its authors is particularly significant. "These results seem to complete a full circle started with the work of Aserinsky, Kleitman, and Dement. It appears that REM periods are, after all, highly diagnostic of a kind of sleep mentation which has all of the characteristics associated with the term dreaming, of the kind of vivid, distorted, elaborated, visual-hallucinatory mentation which has been the major interest of the clinician" (214, in press).

However, what would have impressed Freud is not that REM mentation is more dreamlike than NREM mentation, but that NREM mentation exists at all. Because, taken all together, this means the "mind" is never at "rest." And the assumption that the mind needed "rest" was central to Freud's original view of dreams as guardians of sleep.

This is an appropriate juncture at which to take closer stock of the psychophysiology which was either assumed or implied by Freud's theory of dreaming, and to at least try to clarify the related erratic concept, "depth of sleep."

DEPTH OF SLEEP

A review of Freud's thinking will show that he did not trouble himself to be precise about the psychophysiology of sleep. There was not sufficient evidence at his disposal to warrant precision in this matter. Consequently, a metapsychological assumption had to suffice: the state of sleep was something that reduced the amount of energy at the disposal of the ego. Certain more precise conceptions about the psychological properties of sleep are implied in various others of Freud's formulations, but these are not consistent. For example, a conception of sleep as psychologically unidimensional and relatively quiescent may be inferred from the lengths to which Freud went to locate certain censorship activities and the secondary revision processes in the waking state (cf. Freud's reconstruction of Maury's guillotine dream: 65, pp. 495-97). On the other hand, a conception of sleep as psychologically active and multidimensional may be inferred from Freud's postulation of mounting tension in the system unconscious and of the successive organization of dream thoughts, first by the secondary process during which they are entirely rational and then by the primary process when they are transformed into the manifest dream.

> Thus we are driven to conclude that two fundamentally different kinds of psychical processes are concerned in the formation of dreams. One of these produces perfectly rational dream-thoughts, of no less validity than normal thinking; while the other treats these thoughts in a manner which is in the highest degree bewildering and irrational (65, p. 597).

Freud was not noted for leaving his basic assumptions so largely to inference. Therefore, at the risk of some oversimplification, we may conclude that while his intuitions went beyond it his theoretical commitment stopped at a conception of man as either awake or asleep, and of sleep as either dreaming or nondreaming sleep. The question of what the mind was up to during nondreaming sleep held little interest for Freud, his interest in sleep being subordinated to his interest in dreams. He merely speculated that when we were not dreaming, repressed infantile wishes caused cumulative tension until a dream formed, which absorbed some of the tension, dreams thus serving as the "guardians of sleep."

> A dream tells us that something was going on which tended to interrupt sleep, and it enables us to understand in what way it has been possible to fend off this interruption. The final outcome is that the sleeper has dreamt and is able to go on sleeping: the internal demand which was striving to occupy him has been disposed of (70, p. 223).

The graph with which Dement and Kleitman summarized the early EEG findings offers dramatic first-glance support for some kind of sleep-protection hypothesis (33). (See Figure 1.)

Figure 1

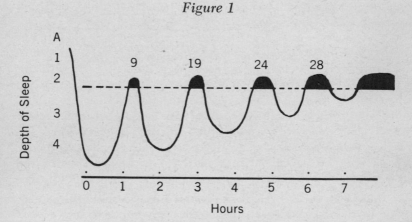

Along the vertical coordinate "A" signifies EEG "alpha waves," or wakefulness; the numbers correspond to EEG sleep stages 1, 2, 3, and 4. Shaded areas above the horizontal broken line represent Stage 1 (REM) sleep; the numbers directly above the shaded areas denote average duration in minutes.

On the average, a person's first seventy minutes of sleep includes a rapid "descent" into stage four, and a rapid "ascent" toward the threshold of waking. Just short of the threshold, and corresponding with the "emergence" into stage one, a dream begins. The termination of the dream signals the beginning of another "descent," another dream, and so on, the latter part of the night showing comparatively "shallow" descents into stage two, and the last dream of the night ushering the person into wakefulness.*

What more obvious conclusion to draw from this picture than that dreams are indeed the guardians of sleep, since they invariably occur as we are approaching wakefulness and they are invariably followed by another period of "deeper" sleep? This interpretation of the Dement-Kleitman graph is defended in some detail by Ostow (171).

A confirmation by way of modern electronic technology of a hypothesis generated by one man's imagination more than a half-century before would be most satisfying. It is therefore with some aggravation that the confirmation does not pass the test of second thoughts. The Dement-Kleitman graph presents an analogical conception of sleep, the analogy being in the name given its vertical coordinate: "Depth of Sleep." It is anyone's guess what the analogy is to. Let it immediately be noted that Dement and Kleitman were not engaged in testing the sleep-protection hypothesis; in their hands the graph was merely meant to summarize certain empirical findings. However, since the graph has been interpreted as confirmation of the sleep-protection hypothesis, certain words of caution are in order.

We had best place quotation marks around words like "descent," "ascent," "emergence," and "deep" in references to sleep. The evidence is not all in, but if future indications are consistent with the evidence that is now on hand, it may yet turn out that the only indisputable rationale for equating "up" with waking and "down" with sleeping is that these are the positions in space in which we customarily find our bodies during these periods. In other words, the spatial coordinates of the Dement-Kleitman graph may reflect no more than the persuasive influence of an analogical set.

* For the purpose at hand, we may overlook the fluctuations which the graph leaves out in its exclusive attention to averages.

Not that it should be dismissed on that account, but it certainly should be scrutinized within other frames of reference.

There are four other ways in which it is possible to conceive of sleep in terms of "depth": (1) in terms of the intensity of external stimuli required to wake a sleeper, as we say, "up"; (2) in terms of the rates of activity of the various physiological systems known to be functionally critical in the various stages of sleep; (3) in terms of the phylogenetic position of these respective physiological systems; and (4) in terms of the qualities of mentation found to be typical of the various stages of sleep. I shall pause here to sample and evaluate the kinds of evidence currently accumulating within each of these frames of reference:

Arousal Threshold

Dement and Kleitman have shown that the auditory thresholds during emergent stage one, i.e., stage one REM sleep, are significantly higher than during descending stage one, i.e., stage one with no eye movements (32). Assuming that we would expect "height" of auditory threshold to measure "depth" of sleep, we should be inclined to rate REM sleep as the deeper sleep. And yet we have routinely taken to referring to REM sleep as "light" sleep. This kind of inconsistency led Snyder and his co-workers to re-evaluate the question of sleep depth as measured by EEG patterns and by auditory arousal thresholds.

On any given night for a specific subject, the volume of sound necessary to produce arousal from sleep accompanied by EEG stage 3 and 4 . . . is considerably greater than that required to produce arousal from stages 1 and 2. However, it appears that the EEG pattern is a relative measure in relation to auditory thresholds since some individuals can be aroused from stage 4 more easily than others from stage 1, the dreaming stage, and to a lesser extent, there is some sort of variation in the same individual from night to night. Generally, the intensity of sound required to produce arousal from stage 2 is slightly greater than that required to awaken subjects from eye movement periods at about the same time of night. But this is a fine difference and it is sometimes reversed. It sometimes takes a greater volume to awaken the subject from an eye movement period than has been required to awaken him from spindling sleep 30 minutes before. The inescapable point is that there is a wide range of variability in the tone volumes required to awaken subjects from eye movement periods (123, p. 510).

The first frame of reference, then, yields considerations which are so difficult to pin down that it had best be set aside for now.

Physiological Activity Rates

Snyder, Hobson, Morrison, and Goldfrank have studied the correlations of heart rate, respiration, and blood pressure with the EEG patterns of sleep. They predicted that rate changes in these physiological measures would correspond to the cyclic changes in EEG patterns, the highest values of each corresponding to stage one (REM) sleep, the lowest to stages three and four, and the intermediate values to stage two. The prediction was confirmed in the case of blood pressure. However, respiratory and heart rate changes correlated significantly with EEG patterns in the direction opposite to that predicted (216). The second frame of reference instructs us, then, that it is first necessary to specify the physiological system the "depth" of which one wishes to assess, since there are certain inverse correlations among the systems upon which we otherwise run afoul. With certain of the physiological measures, even analogical bias seems to supply no conviction as to which is "deep" and which is "light." For example, the same study reports a very high correlation between REM sleep and variability of respiration rate. Leaving all other hints aside, this writer feels no inclination to call variable respiration either deeper or lighter than steady respiration. Even regarding the EEG patterns alone, while it has become customary, because it "feels" right, to equate deep with slow and light with fast, this feeling tends to disappear when we note that what slow really means is high voltage and what fast really means is low voltage. We may, of course, define our terms arbitrarily, but the evidence accumulating within this frame of reference is already sufficient to warn us that any such definitions will have to be exceedingly arbitrary and much too complicated to invite consensus.

Phylogenetic Position

As noted above, the same regularly recurring constellation of physiological changes known to be associated with dreaming in humans has been observed in other species. This is not, however, the most dramatic contribution of comparative psychophysiology to the problem before us. Using as his subjects decorticate cats and humans with gross cortical lesions, Jouvet has demonstrated a cortical origin for the high voltage, slow waves of the "deep" sleep stages, and a brain stem origin for the low voltage, fast waves of the "light" sleep state (134). We are thus cautioned against interpreting the physiology of the sleep cycle on the basis of cortical records alone.

Jouvet's findings suggest in general that, however intensified or variable the activity may be during REM sleep of neurological systems which are highest on the phylogenetic scale, REM sleep itself cannot occur without the triggering activity of a noncortical system which is one of the lowest on the phylogenetic scale. At the moment it seems safest to conclude within this frame of reference that, if we wish to relate depth of sleep in any way with phylogenetic "height," the evidence is ambiguous.

Psychological Correlates

The fourth frame of reference compounds confusion because we find ourselves immediately in the grip of a parallel analogical presumption involving "depth." For example, we are used to referring to primary process mentation as "deep" and secondary process mentation as less deep, even "shallow." Thus, if we continue to refer to stage one as light sleep we must explain to ourselves how it is that we find the "deepest" mentation accompanying the "lightest" sleep!

Thus the obfuscating properties of the "depth" analogy would appear to outweigh its iconic value. One of Lawrence Kubie's warnings seems especially well taken in this matter: "All such terms are descriptive metaphors borrowed from such other disciplines as geography, oceanography, physics, chemistry and mathematics. As descriptions, they have the limits and values of all models and diagrams whether verbal or graphic. If used as explanatory devices, they are verbal traps" (156, p. 46).

In the interests of avoiding the "depth of sleep" trap, I wish to propose a tentative alternate model for the representation of present and future EEG monitored sleep findings. A tri-phasic model seems most faithful to the data. (See Figure 2.)

The model seeks to comprehend "wakefulness," "dreaming sleep," and "thinking sleep." "Wakefulness" and "dreaming sleep" carry their usual phenomenological connotations, and are defined electroencephalographically by the alpha pattern and by the indices of stage one (REM) sleep, respectively. "Thinking sleep," since it has no natural phenomenological status, is defined electroencephalo-

Figure 2

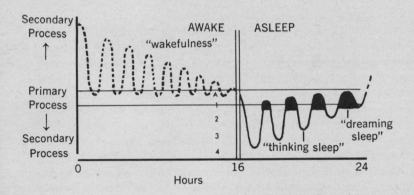

The two designations of the secondary process on the vertical coordinate are meant to suggest equivalence, in line with the evidence that sleeping mentation, as well as waking mentation, can include the secondary process. The double vertical line at hour 16 distinguishes phenomenological sleep from phenomenological waking life. The numbered gradations of this line refer to the EEG stages of monitored sleep.

The dotted wavy line, indicating EEG-defined wakefulness, is drawn to suggest its normally inhibited crest and trough variations, and its accessibility to primary process mentation. The solid wavy line, indicating EEG-defined nondreaming sleep, is termed "thinking sleep" on the strength of the non-REM findings referred to above.

The shaded portions correspond to the rhythmic recurrences of stage 1 (REM) sleep, termed by Snyder "dreaming sleep." They are drawn to suggest the inclusion in dreams of both primary and secondary process mentation. Their increasing duration over time is consistent with a preponderance of evidence. The comparatively greater dominance of the primary process in the later dreams is consistent with a presently slight weight of evidence.

graphically by the indices of stages two, three, and four; and psychologically by laboratory reports of non-REM mentation.

Snyder has made a convincing case for the term "dreaming sleep" (208, p. 381). "Thinking sleep" seems to describe nondreaming sleep most consistently with the non-REM findings. All three terms carry the conceptual advantage of making it difficult to mistake the model for anything other than what it is, namely a psychological model.

Wakefulness and thinking sleep may now be conceived in a two-dimensional perspective, much as the Dement-Kleitman graph depicts it, except for the twin continuum on the vertical coordinate, which shows both states tending toward secondary process mentation. Dreaming sleep is not to be conceived on this two-dimensional plane, but rather as a third dimension which supervenes the waxings and wanings along this plane at regular intervals, and tends toward primary process mentation. It is beginning to appear that questions of origination and timing of these regular pulsations of dreaming sleep are predominantly physiological questions, and that the physiological mechanisms behind these pulsations are also operative in periods of wakefulness, although normally inhibited then. This in no way obviates the necessity of studying those questions with respect to dreaming sleep which are psychological in emphasis: for example, the psychological correlates, if any, of the triggering mechanisms; the possibilities of psychological influence on these mechanisms; and the psychological structure and functions of dreams, which, however basically their conditions of occurrence may be governed by physiological releasers, are themselves psychological phenomena.

The tri-phasic model carries four immediate heuristic advantages:

1. While physical EEG criteria clearly yield a four-cycle breakdown in a night's sleep, the criterion of association with dreaming just as clearly yields only a two-cycle breakdown in a night's sleep. Dreaming occurs predominantly during stage one (REM) sleep. Nondreaming periods of sleep are characterized by repeated fluctuations between stages two, three, and four. We lose sight of these fluctuations in the graph, which only pictures averages, but they are as prominent an aspect of the individual EEG record as is the singular absence of such fluctuations during stage one (REM)

sleep. The model thus highlights what is most relevant to the future psychology of dreaming.

2. There are empirical observations that dreams may and do include all of the psychological qualities of experience which are typical of wakefulness and of thinking sleep. That these experiences are organized differently in dreams is beyond question. The tri-phasic model affords a way of depicting the dream both in its variable correspondences along the sleeping-waking continuum and as a qualitatively separable psychological entity.

3. The tri-phasic model is consistent with evidence that the physiological mechanisms which govern the rhythmical recurrence of the stage one (REM) sleep constellation are merely functionally inhibited during normal wakefulness. It is also consistent with corresponding psychological evidence that dream-like mentation may occur during abnormal periods of wakefulness; for example, under conditions of sensory deprivation or sleep deprivation or hallucination.

4. Finally, although the tri-phasic model is meant to orient psychological formulations, it is consistent with the overall gist of recent physiological findings. Thus, Snyder, Hobson, Morrison, and Goldfrank were led to conclude in the study mentioned earlier:

> Aside from disturbances surrounding transient arousals, the variability of our three measures (systolic blood pressure, respiratory rate, and pulse rate) during non-REM sleep, generally takes the form of a rhythmical variation around a reasonably stable base line, as though reflecting a continuous interplay of homeostatic compensations in a vegetative system. The changes seen during REM sleep are entirely different in that they take the form of unpredictable fugues of erratic and often marked change, presumably reflecting the same sort of activation in discrete physiological systems as do the bursts of eye movements (123, p. 513).

This statement is as reminiscent of Freud's conception of the process of dreaming as of the tri-phasic model:

> Two separate functions may be distinguished in mental activity during the construction of a dream: the production of the dream-thoughts, and their transformation into the content of the dream. The dream-thoughts are entirely rational and are constructed with an expenditure

of all the psychical energy of which we are capable. They have their place among thought processes that have not become conscious—processes from which, after some modification, our conscious thoughts too arise. However many interesting and puzzling questions the dream-thoughts may involve, such questions have, after all, no special relation to dreams and do not call for treatment among the problems of dreams. On the other hand, the second function of mental activity during dream construction, the transformation of the unconscious thoughts into the content of the dream, is peculiar to dream life and character-istic of it. This dream-work proper diverges further from our picture of waking thought than has been supposed even by the most deter-mined depreciators of psychical functioning during the formation of dreams. Dream-work is not simply more careless, more irrational, more forgetful, and more incomplete than waking thought; it is completely different from it qualitatively, and for that reason not immediately comparable to it (65, pp. 506-7).

The same cordiality of Freud's views with the tri-phasic model may be inferred from his careful tendency to speak of the waking aspects of dream formation in terms of "the censorship," and to speak of the sleeping aspects of dream formation in terms of "regard for the representative capacities of the sleeping psyche," with the exception that he never attempted in this context to distinguish the latter from the dreaming psyche.

SLEEP
PROTECTION

I think, however, that Freud would have been surprised at the non-REM findings which indicate representa-tive capacities in nondreaming sleep that are more like waking thought than like dreaming. Indeed, an intriguing question is whether he would have seen in the non-REM findings no less than the "latent dream thoughts" of psychoanalytic dream interpre-tation, which he was so careful to conceive of as a product of the waking psyche. Non-REM mentation is not normally conscious, but it is not, let us bear in mind, part of the system unconscious; i.e., it is not primary process mentation. The same may be said of the often misconceived "latent content."

If we assume the tri-phasic model to be valid, how is the sleep-protection hypothesis to be evaluated? It is first necessary to recall its specific evidential origin in Freud's thinking. This was provided by so-called "alarm clock" dreams. Some dreams seemed to respond to environmental or somatic stimuli by assimilating their perception into an on-going dream, thus prolonging sleep by a few minutes. In these instances, dreaming seemed to "guard" sleep. Freud had only a passing interest in the contributions to dream construction of environmental and somatic stimuli. Internal psychological stimuli preoccupied his attention. Indeed, he minced no words when it came to assigning priorities to these sources of stimulation in the construction of dreams. Somatic and environmental stimuli might sometimes have a hand in shaping the contents of dreams, but the indispensable motive source of dreaming was always to be found in internal psychological stimuli. The sleep-protection function, which the "dream-work" was imputed to serve in its treatment of somatic and environmental stimuli, was extended to apply also to its treatment of psychological stimuli. No evidence was adduced by Freud to support this extension, nor do the interests of logic make the extension mandatory. Moreover, it is clear in context why Freud did not feel obliged to seek support of the sleep-protection hypothesis on other grounds; it is not essential to his psychology of dreaming. It is merely consistent with what is essential to his psychology of dreaming, namely, the wish-fulfillment hypothesis.* Actually, Freud seemed to regard the dream's guardianship of sleep as a mere fact and not as a hypothesis at all. The sleep-protection idea was consistent with the wish-fulfillment hypothesis because the latter carried implications of tension reduction, and sleep was then vaguely conceived as a state of reduced tension. The crucial point is that the sleep-protection hypothesis is largely independent of psychological theories of dreaming. The dream is there to be understood psychologically if it serves some biological function other than the protection of sleep, or if it serves no biological function at all. The wish-fulfillment hypothesis which is essential to Freud's theory of dreaming will stand, fall, or be revised on the basis of psychological considerations, because the wish-fulfillment hypothesis is a purely psychological construct.

* Wish-fulfillment is used in its systematic sense, as in the psychoanalytic theory of thinking; not loosely, as in the concept of the "wish to sleep."

That Freud was not unmindful of the limitations of his proclivity for purely psychological constructs may be seen in his frequent references to the likely influence (for example, on symptom choice, psychoses, and character development) of unknown physiological factors. In respect to the matters with which Freud tended to concern himself, however, that was the trouble: physiological factors were usually unknown. In the instance before us, many physiological factors are no longer unknown. And it is hard to imagine Freud seeking to refute the clearly emerging fact that the almost metronomically recurring periods of dreaming sleep are basically governed by neurophysiological factors; that if dreaming serves purposes of its own, they are purposes which have issued from and based themselves upon pre-existent neurophysiological phenomena.

The issue of sleep protection thus becomes moot, which is just as well, since if we adopt the tri-phasic model we shall want to ask of ultimate hypotheses in dream theory that they account not only for the unique nature of dreams, but also for the unique nature of dreaming and thinking sleep.

Chapter Four

NEW OBSERVATIONS OF DREAMING

Modern electronic sleep monitoring procedures have vastly broadened the observational base for a theory of dreaming. More precise and diversified sampling procedures are now possible in both comparative and functional investigations. For example, dreams of persons who typically remember their dreams can be compared with dreams of persons who typically forget their dreams. And, freed of our dependence on spontaneously recalled dreams, we may now study whole dream sequences, thus opening up new vantage points for studying interrelations between dreams and between dream life and waking life. We may now also observe variations in dream content and structure in response to such experimentally induced variations in preceding states as hypnotic suggestion, sleep deprivation, special stimulations before and during dreaming sleep, and telepathic communication. Conversely, we may observe variations in the content and structure of waking states in relation to such experimentally controlled conditions as REM proximity, REM interruption, and REM deprivation.

In this chapter we shall sample some of the more suggestive findings from these new observational fields. More complete reviews are to be found elsewhere (47, 106, 172, 57, 255).

LABORATORY VERSUS "HOME" DREAMS

As soon as the promise of electronic sleep monitoring methods was appreciated the critical question arose: Are dreams reported in laboratory settings a representative sample, i.e., do experimentally retrieved dreams differ significantly from spontaneously recalled or "home" dreams? Initial studies yielded mixed results but subsequent findings have begun to settle into a sensible pattern. Domhoff and Kamiya reported that 30 percent of 219 dreams collected in the laboratory contained at least one overt reference to the laboratory setting (39). Whitman, *et al.*, who included references to the laboratory setting which were either explicitly mentioned or thinly disguised, reported a corresponding figure of 68.5 percent (253). Dement, *et al.*, in a study designed to control for expected inclusions of laboratory references in comparison with similar kinds of day residue, reported that the laboratory dreams of college students included about the same percentage of references to the laboratory as to their school work, thus suggesting that the laboratory references did not reflect a pre-potent or biasing factor. They further noted that other kinds of residue reflecting individually differing life preoccupations greatly outnumbered references to the laboratory (31). A subsequent investigation by Hall "confirmed in all major respects the findings of . . . Dement, *et al.* . . . that the incorporation of features of the laboratory situation into dreams can be reduced to a negligible minimum by observing certain conditions" (94, p. 205). In another study, however, Hall and Van de Castle reported that while laboratory and home dreams do not significantly differ as to content, they do differ significantly as to quality: home dreams tend to be more "dramatic" and laboratory dreams tend to be more "prosaic" (101). Snyder and his associates supported Hall's latter conclusion:

> In agreement with our introspectionist forebears, but in disagreement with popular and clinical impressions of dreaming, we find that REM dream reports are generally clear, coherent, believable accounts of realistic situations in which the dreamer and other persons are involved in quite mundane activities and preoccupations—and usually talking about them (217).

It should not surprise anyone that we tend to recall spontaneously our more interesting dreams, just as we tend to recall spontaneously our more interesting waking experiences. Therefore the sense of these investigations seems to be that the electronic sleep monitoring methods do in fact make possible the study of dreams that would not otherwise have been available for study, since they would not have been remembered, and that we should expect to find included in this expanded sample a higher percentage of "prosaic" dreams. Perhaps it should be noted that since the increase in dream recall ability under laboratory conditions hovers around the order of 90 percent, the individual investigator may rule out this tendency toward the prosaic, or rule it in, more or less at will.

DREAM RECALLERS
AND NONRECALLERS

Another question immediately raised by the electronic sleep monitoring methods was how frequently people who rarely recalled their dreams would be enabled to do so in the laboratory as compared to people who regularly recalled their dreams. The first attempt to answer this question found that a group of nonrecallers (said they dreamt less than once a month) recalled dreaming an impressive 53 percent of the times they were awakened from REM sleep. There were, however, significant differences between this group and a comparison group of dream recallers (said they dreamt about every night) who recalled dreaming 93 percent of the times they were awakened from REM sleep. Moreover, although both groups had the same average number of dreams per night (four), the dreams of the nonrecallers tended to be shorter in duration and less dramatic in quality (74).

Subsequent investigations have suggested that dream recall ability under both laboratory and home conditions is at least partially a function of personality structure, recallers being generally inner-oriented and nonrecallers being generally outer-oriented (5, 200, 160). It has recently been established, however, that time and speed of arousal are more consistent determinants of dream recall ability. Memory of dreaming appears to fade in proportion to the amount of time elapsed between the end of a REM period and arousal from sleep, approximately ten minutes being the maximum period permitting of dream recall (34). Whitman, *et al.*, concluded that this time factor was a more powerful determinant of dream forgetting than was dream content (253). Furthermore, sudden awakening seems to be more conducive to dream recall than gradual awakening (72, 203). Forgetting of dreams may therefore be as much a function of when and how a person awakes as it is a function of his personality structure.

Most pertinent to our interests is the fact that we can now study the dreams of persons who do not spontaneously remember their dreams. Accordingly it is regrettable that the contents of a group of recallers' dreams have not yet been systematically compared with the contents of a group of nonrecallers' dreams.

DREAM
SEQUENCES

One of the more notable advantages of electronic sleep monitoring methods is that they make possible the study of nightly dream sequences. Are the dreams of a single night related or are they unrelated? If related, how? Several investigations have been addressed to these questions.

Dement and Wolpert collected four or more dreams from eight subjects on each of thirty-eight nights. For example, the following dream sequence was collected from a normal male over the course of a single night of sleep:

1. "We were swimming and doing a lot of things. Everybody was in bathing suits at the swimming pool and I seemed to be admiring my body all the time. In one of the sequences there was this race, and then the racing stopped, and I was swimming down towards the end of the pool. I must have swam it awfully fast, although kind of leisurely. I climbed out and there was some guy sitting there who I immediately disliked. He seemed to epitomize all the guys who make asses of themselves parading around in bathing suits who I grudgingly admit do look good in bathing suits, but who are so conscious of it. And he was oiling himself. Anyway, it seemed as though I was afraid that my friend—I can't remember,

he is just a blank . . . or even she, is just a blank—was going to be attracted to this guy and not to myself. But for some reason I wasn't afraid as I ought to have been. I seemed to have some sort of metamorphosis. I became just like a strong-muscled Greek god. There was a lot of diving, and once my bathing suit almost came off. It seemed like I was in a white bathing suit. Then it seemed like we were all waiting for a TV program that Miss X [a well-known Hollywood actress] was to be on just before the bell went off."

2. "A and B [two prominent Hollywood entertainers] were lying on a bed in this room, and I was apparently with them. The door suddenly opened and B . . . no A . . . fired this gun, started firing his gun and the panels dropped out of the door and the whole door came crashing down. Then a half-visible man started walking in and said, 'I'm Mr. Blank, I want the plans.' He walked over to A and put his hands around his neck and started to squeeze. It was odd because he was intangible but it seemed as though A could feel him squeezing. We all started trying to squeeze him back and all of a sudden he became tangible or something, but anyway I started to hit him and I just knocked the hell out of him, the poor little fellow. And I remember standing there in a kind of a triumph just as the bell rang."

3. "I dreamed I was coming into this room and I didn't have a key. I walked up to the building and Charles R. was standing there. The thing was, I was trying to climb in the window. Anyway, Charles was standing there by the door and he gave me some sandwiches, two sandwiches. They were red—it looked like Canadian bacon and his were boiled ham. I couldn't understand why he gave me the worst sandwiches. Anyway, we went on into the room and it didn't look like the right place at all. It seemed to be some kind of party. I think that it was at that point when I started thinking about how fast I could get out of the place if I had to. And there was something about nitroglycerin, I don't quite remember. The last thing was somebody throwing a baseball."

4. "I was talking to my aunt about how you got in touch with the underground left over from World War II. She told me about a number of other undergrounds and we were just talking and wandering around the house and I played with my dog a little bit and so forth and she asked me about my work. Finally it seemed like it was time to get dinner and I knew that my mother had been cooking when we started talking. We went down to the dining

room and I asked my mother about the underground, and just as I was waiting for her to tell us what the World War II underground was, I said, 'Don't you think we can settle the question?' And the bell went off."

5. "Uh, this dream had something to do with a lecture. It was something about Economics but anyway, I was sitting watching Professor Z. and he was lecturing in a queer way. All the students were sitting down at the front of the lecture hall behind a long table, and Professor Z. was standing out in the middle of the room on one of the desks. All of a sudden, this big argument broke out while he was talking and they were both going on at the same time—his lecture and the argument. Claude R. and somebody else were arguing like that and all of a sudden I realized I was awake" (35, pp. 571-72).

Concluding that this dream sequence was related by way of its variable expression of the general themes of conflict and violence, the investigators elaborate as follows:

In dreams one and two of the series, an identical plot line is seen as the dreamer experiences a physical triumph over a male adversary. The triumph is associated with an abrupt metamorphosis in both cases. In the first dream, the dreamer becomes powerfully built "like a strong-muscled Greek god" and in the second, Mr. Blank suddenly becomes tangible and accessible to the dreamer's blows. Although the theme is constant, the setting is quite different; in one a bedroom, in the other a swimming pool. Only in the second dream does the conflict erupt into actual physical violence.

Dream three finds the dreamer on the receiving end of his friend's hostility as he is given the "worst" sandwich. He also dreams "something about nitroglycerin." This "something" and the ball thrown by "somebody" and the question of how fast he could get out if he had to would seem to signify that the dream was about to disintegrate into a more open expression of violence as the awakening occurred.

In dream four, violence is displaced in time to World War II and the underground, but the dreamer's query, "Don't you think we can settle the question," seems to imply a concern over some present conflict.

In dream five the violence is again verbal and is attributed to others whom the dreamer is watching from a distance.

Thus, in this sequence, the theme of violence and conflict builds up into an actual physical outbreak in dream two. It is then seemingly contained verbally in the last two dreams after being allowed abortive expression in dream three (35, p. 572).

In discussing these and similar findings Dement and Wolpert are quick to raise the possibility that the continuities observed may be a function of experimental artifact:

Not only is a dream abruptly and unnaturally terminated, but a series of events, namely the awakening, the description of the dream, and the handling of the recording apparatus, are added to the dreamer's store of "day residues," which may influence the subsequent dreams (35, p. 576).

In view of these limitations the authors are content to advance four hypotheses in accounting for the observed continuities:

1. If in undisturbed sleep each dream ends on some note of resolution, then the interruptions required by the monitoring procedure introduce an unnatural continuity by forcing each dream in a series to take up, as it were, where its predecessor left off.

2. If in undisturbed sleep each dream is related to the others in its series, then the observed continuities in experimentally collected dream sequences are diminished reflections of even greater continuities in natural sleep, since the repeated disturbances of sleep may be presumed to introduce an array of discontinuities.

3. The repeated awakenings and verbal reporting of dreams may be responsible for the observed continuities, each dream report constituting aspects of the subsequent dream's day residue.

4. The observed continuities may reflect the natural pattern of dreaming.

Concerning the collection of dream sequences for interpretive purposes Dement and Wolpert conclude:

Regardless of the mechanism, it is nonetheless true that many of these sequential dreams obtained through experimental intervention are definitely related to each other and occasionally a coherent dream thought seems to be maintained in all dreams of a sequence. Furthermore, when the manifest content of these related episodes is considered in its entirety, insights into the dreamer's personality are suggested that are not readily discerned by examining the manifest content of any single dream in the sequence (35, p. 578).

Clinical observations were combined with monitored sleep observations in a study conducted by Offenkrantz and Rechtschaffen in which 50 dreams were collected from a patient in psychotherapy over the course of 15 nights. Not only did this study support the findings of Dement and Wolpert in respect to the continuities of sequential dreams, but it discovered that similar elements in the manifest contents of dreams tended to recur in the same position in the sequence on different nights. Offenkrantz and Rechtschaffen concluded that their findings were generally supportive of French's ideas (to be discussed in Chapter 5) in that (1) patterns of "ego adaptive-defensive functioning" known to be characteristic of the patient's waking life were also found to characterize his dream life, and (2) the alternating ascendence of disturbing and reactive motives in the dream sequences seemed to be a function of previous dream gratification (169).

In a related study two subjects from whom intensive interview information and projective test protocols had been collected reported a total of 106 dreams over the course of 32 experimental nights. The following conclusions were drawn from exhaustive analyses of these materials:

1. A direct relationship among the manifest contents in the dreams of a night was rarely noted. However, the appearance of unique elements at similar points in a sequence, the lateral similarities of events from night to night and the confluence of similar dimensions suggest an organization of manifest contents into regular patterns.

2. Considering latent contents, we have noted a cyclic relationship which may be generally characteristic for sequential dreams. It seems that as need pressure accumulates in the early dreams of a sequence, it is discharged in a pitch of excitement either directly or by a highly dramatic visual representation, and is followed by a period of regression or quiescence. . . .

3. Dreams evoked by the method described . . . occur with striking regularity and consistency regardless of the nature or the intensity of particular conflict. The presence of apparent conflict thus appears to have no relationship to the frequency with which dreaming occurs . . . . this capacity for dreaming can be used by a variety of conflicts to discharge tension and represent attempts at conflict resolution (230, p. 606).

EXPERIMENTAL
PRESLEEP STIMULATION

In 1965 Herman Witkin and Helen Lewis described an elaborate method for studying the highly individualistic ways in which waking experiences become transformed and represented in subsequent dreams:

> The main feature of this procedure is to have the subject undergo an arousing experience just before he goes to sleep; this presleep event then serves as one reference point or "tracer element" for studying transformations. The presleep event we use consists, on some occasions, of an emotionally charged film; on other occasions (for comparison purposes) a neutral film; and on still other occasions, an encounter with another person through the medium of suggestion. The procedure has several other salient features. By means of a special technique the content of the subject's reverie between the presleep event and the time he falls asleep is obtained. The subject is awakened during all dream periods (identified by the concomitant occurrence of rapid eye movements and stage-1 EEG) and reports his dreams. Recordings are made of autonomic activity during the presleep event and during sleep. At the end of the sleep session an extended inquiry is conducted into each dream, including associations to the dreams, and into the subject's reactions to the entire experience.
>
> Each subject is intensively studied before participating in the experiment; additional knowledge is gained in the post-sleep inquiry of each experimental session of the series; and this knowledge is further supplemented by a biographical interview at the very end of the series of experimental sessions, in which dream associations are further pursued (254, pp. 846-47).

Witkin and Lewis, working in collaboration with Goodenough and Shapiro, have now concluded the data gathering phase of a multidimensioned research plan based on this method. Complete files exist on twenty-eight subjects, each of whom spent five nights in the sleep monitoring laboratory in addition to submitting to the screening interview and test procedures. It will be some years before these data are fully analyzed. The following preliminary findings and key queries are suggestive of the kinds of knowledge we may expect to gain from this laboratory.

One of the emotionally charged films (a film on childbirth) describes the Mahlstrom Vacuum Extractor and discusses its advantages as a method of delivery. It shows the exposed vagina and thighs of a woman, painted with iodine. The arm of the obstetrician is seen inserting the vacuum extractor into the vagina. The gloved hands and arms of the obstetrician, covered with blood, are then shown pulling periodically on the chain protruding from the vagina. The cutting motion of an episiotomy is also shown. The baby is then delivered with a gush of blood. The film ends by showing that only a harmless swelling of the skin of the baby's head results from the vacuum extraction method.

At his first awakening in a sleep session after he saw this film a subject reported having a dream about a group of college boys and girls singing in a park. The girls were dressed in white and carrying flowers. They had on long white gloves and were trying to "cover up their elbows and holding their arms so that they wouldn't be seen, the whiteness of the gloves wouldn't be seen in the dark." Before that, "somebody was catching bees for some laboratory purpose, and letting them go on the flowers, pollinating the flowers." At his second awakening the same subject reported a dream in which he was "flying around in an airplane," looking out through a hole, from which he could see the body of the plane. Through another hole, to the left, a coil of wire protruded, extending to the door of the airplane. There was a man who periodically pulled at this wire, making the door go up and down. It was "sort of a troop-carrier plane, people, parachutists, jumping out of the airplane." In another episode of the same dream he was conversing with some other man, a baseball player called "Lover," about the number of children each had. The baseball player was ahead of him in the "department of having children" (254, pp. 829-830).

A second emotionally charged film used in these studies shows a subincision rite as practiced by an aboriginal Australian group. It shows a number of older men preparing for the initiation of four young men. All the men are naked. Each initiate lies down across the backs of the other initiates, who are perched on all fours close to each other. An incision is made along the ventral surface of the penis and the scrotum with a sharp stone. The bleeding penis is then seen being held over a fire. The faces of the initiates clearly reflect their anguish. A hair dressing ritual is also shown. The film ends with a rhythmic ritual dance.

In one of the dreams of the sleep session which followed his viewing of this film the same subject had a dream about "two cowboy types" and "one was holding a gun on the other one. I could see the gun from the viewpoint of the man at whom it was pointed like I was looking into it, the barrel of the gun pointing directly at me, and I could see . . . the gunsight on top and two wing-like projections" (254, p. 831).

That a "tracer element" is successfully and regularly placed into the processes of the dream-work by these methods is more or less obvious: less obvious to those who require that the tracer element be literally represented in the subsequent dreams (for example Hartmann, 106, pp. 135-36); more obvious to those who take for granted the figurativeness of almost all dream representations. This writer looks to these studies, when fully analyzed and reported, to shed important new light on those all too familiar, and all too abstract, concepts: condensation, displacement, and symbolism.

Some of the more suggestive tentative findings reported to date are: (1) Dreams following emotionally charged presleep stimuli tend to highlight the more prominent elements of those stimuli, while dreams following neutral presleep stimuli tend to highlight the more peripheral elements of those stimuli. (2) The subjects' attitudes and conflicts in respect to the experimenter and the laboratory situation tend to be worked over in dreams much as are the more charged elements of the films. Far from being a biasing factor this may offer a unique vantage point for studying the dream-work, as, for example, the process of transference in psychotherapy offers a special vantage point from which to observe a patient's unconscious waking tendencies. (3) Although the specific contents of an individual's symbolic handling of conflict material in his dreams varies almost limitlessly, consistencies of pattern or style are sometimes discernible. For example, one person may consistently represent upsetting film elements by reversing them in his dreams; while another person may place the most noxious items in stories or dreams within dreams; while still another may favor the stratagem of being in the dream in spirit but not in person—and so on. (4) Dreams which tend to be forgotten are more likely to follow threatening presleep stimuli, as measured by simultaneous autonomic reactions, than to follow nonthreatening stimuli. (5)

Symbolic equations which are among the most transparent to the observer are frequently those which the dreamer himself denies. (6) A very promising hypothesis which has emerged from these observations is that dreams following neutral stimuli are more likely to reflect the person's present life experiences and that dreams following emotionally charged stimuli are more likely to tap memories of early childhood experiences.

A similar investigation involving presleep stimulation conducted by Lane and Breger sought to assess the effects of real life stress on dream contents by studying the dreams of five subjects on four separate days before they underwent major surgery, and comparing these with the dreams of the same subjects during a subsequent three day post-operative period. Changes in dream content between the two periods of dream collection were then compared with those of a control group who did not experience similar degrees of stress. The results indicated that anticipations of the stress of surgery did significantly influence the dreams of the experimental subjects and that the degree of incorporation of these anticipations into dream content was marked when the personal memory of surgery and the individual modes of psychological preparation for it were taken into account (158).

DRUGS

Another form of presleep stimulation which will surely yield further knowledge of the interrelations between waking and dreaming life is the administration of drugs. To date most studies involving drug administration have sought to determine the effects of various psychopharmacological agents on the amount, frequency, and duration of dreaming sleep. Dement and Fisher found that both Seconal and Amytal had a suppressive effect on REM sleep (29). Rechtschaffen and Maron found that Dexedrine or Dexedrine in combination with Nembutal markedly decreased REM sleep when administered for three or four consecutive nights, and that dramatic, apparently compensatory, increases of REM sleep were to be observed during subsequent "recovery nights" (185).

L.S.D. seems to have quite striking stimulant effects. In a study reported by Muzio, *et al.*, small doses of L.S.D. administered either before sleep or one hour after the onset of sleep increased the length of the second period of dreaming sleep from 30 to 400 percent above baseline averages and also resulted in an extremely atypical appearance of rapid eye movements in the adjacent period of stage two sleep (167).

Conspicuous in its attention to the effects of a psychoactive drug on dream *contents* is a recent report by Kramer, *et al.* (152). Having previously observed that short term administration of Imipramine in normal subjects resulted in an increase of hostile dream contents, the authors collected the dreams of ten severely depressed hospital patients who were under prolonged medication with Imipramine. There were two dream collection nights during the first week while the patients were on the placebo and then one dream collection night a week for three weeks while the patients were receiving Imipramine. By the end of the fourth week all ten patients had shown significant clinical improvement. Increased hostility was observed to be the main short term effect of Imipramine on the contents of these patients' dreams, as it had been on the contents of the normal subjects' dreams. The long term effect on the patients' dreams, however, was a decrease in hostility and an increase in heterosexuality. Kramer and his associates concluded:

> The essential psychopharmacological action of Imipramine in depression is a two-step effect in which hostility is mobilized, i.e., shifted from a bound to a free state, and then discharged by the time the depressed patient is measurably improved. Further, the dream data indicate that when hostile feelings recede in the depressed, tender feelings emerge . . . (152, p. 1391).

Probably wisely, these investigators do not raise the question of whether the observed changes in dream content reflected or were instrumental in leading to clinical improvements.

Ingestion of large quantities of alcohol is known to decrease REM time, and in dramatic relation to this fact it has been reported that withdrawal from alcohol in cases of advanced alcoholism leads consistently to large increases in REM sleep, with 100 percent increase being found immediately preceding development of delirium tremens (78). A study by Greenberg, *et al.*, of patients afflicted with Korsakoff's psychosis, which is preceded by prolonged alcoholism, is also suggestive. During the early months of the illness an increase in dreaming was observed. Thereafter a deviant sleep pattern emerged, although the amount of dreaming sleep reverted almost to normal. Greenberg and his colleagues speculate from this that the cortical lesion known to be associated with Korsakoff's psychosis prevents dreaming from completing its "task," which they theorize may be that of integrating internal emotional experiences and memories with daily external perceptual experiences, thus leading to the predominant symptom of Korsakoff's psychosis: impairment of recent memory functions (79).

PSYCHOTHERAPY

It might have been expected that by now there would be many reports of the effects of psychotherapeutic events on the contents of monitored dreams, but to date only one such study has been reported, this by Hunter and Breger (114). Four consecutive nights of "baseline" dreams were collected from each REM period of six subjects. Two of these subjects then became control subjects and the remaining four were brought together, with a therapist, to form a "sensitivity-therapy" group. Each experimental subject then served as the focus of the group's interaction for two consecutive nights. After each session the sleep of the subject focused upon was monitored throughout the night, and dream reports were collected from each dream period. The control subjects underwent two additional nights of dream collection five weeks after their baseline collection. The dream reports of all subjects—from both periods of dream collection—were then scored by independent raters for a variety of formal and content variables. The major findings were: (1) One-third of the dreams of the experimental groups directly incorporated other members of the groups. (2) All the dreams of the experimental subjects were directly related to the major thematic material dealt with in the preceding therapy session. (3) The post-group dreams of the experimental subjects showed significant increases, not matched by the control subjects, in unpleasant interaction between characters, inadequate or unsuccessful roles for the dreamer, and undesirable outcomes.

POST-HYPNOTICALLY
SUGGESTED DREAMING

Long before the development of sleep monitoring techniques, Schrötter and later Roffenstein and Nachmansohn had demonstrated that post-hypnotic suggestion might prove to be a powerful tool for influencing dream content and therefore for studying the processes of dreaming (201, 191, 168). Freud knew of these studies and was much impressed by them, as well he might have been, since they dramatically confirmed his views of the symbolization process in dreaming, especially those concerning sexual symbolism. For example:

> *Suggestion*: You will dream of sexual intercourse with your friend B., first in a normal, then in an abnormal fashion. You are to forget the suggestion and then dream it symbolically.
> *Dream* (in hypnosis): Sunday afternoon. I am expecting my friend B. We want to celebrate his name day. He brings a bottle of wine wrapped in a coat. Upon his request I take a glass from the cupboard and hold it up to him; he pours out some wine. I am frightened by that, cry out and drop the glass. It breaks and the wine spills over the floor. I am very angry with B. for ruining the rug. He consoles me: "I'll make up for that. Give me another glass for the wine." I bring another one. He wants to pour out the rest of the wine carefully into the glass. But after pouring a few drops, he snatches away the bottle (201, p. 242).

These early studies were subject to the criticism that the "dreams" reported were not true dreams but merely the obedient responses of subjects in nocturnal hypnotic states. EEG monitoring now makes it possible to check this possibility by awakening the subjects only at those times when it may be assumed they would normally be dreaming. Johann Stoyva did just this (218). From a population of 71, Stoyva selected 16 males who had shown complete post-hypnotic amnesia for a mild trance period and who had also shown ability to follow post-hypnotic suggestion. The subjects were readied for a night's sleep, put to bed, connected to the EEG, and put into hypnotic trance. Dream instructions were then given. ("You will dream in every dream tonight that you are 'climbing a tree.' You will dream of this in every dream tonight. You will dream only of this—that you are 'climbing a tree.'") After amnesia for the trance period was suggested the subjects were taken out of trance and allowed to lapse into natural sleep. The subjects were then awakened when EEG indices indicated approaching completion of dreaming periods and asked to report their dreams. Dream recall in accordance with instructions ranged for one group of seven subjects from 71 percent to 100 percent. For a second group of five subjects the range was from 43 percent to 57 percent. A third group of four subjects ranged from 0 percent to 33 percent. Dreams were considered to be in accordance with the suggested topic only if they contained identical or very similar images. For example:

Dream suggestion: "You will dream every dream tonight of climbing a tree."
Subject two: Awakened after 16.0 minutes in REM period 2. "There's this old *maple* in front of our house in Philadelphia. It used to scratch against the window and, ahhh, sometimes we had to cut off the *branches*. So I don't know, usually we just go out on the roof, but we were all *going up the tree* by the base to do it. All of us. The whole family and my grandmother—and she's been dead for five years now. We couldn't get up it and just scratching (sic) against the windows and making scraping noises."

Dream suggestion: "You will dream in every dream tonight that you fall from a horse."
Subject three: Awakened after 9.0 minutes in REM period 2.
"I was, it was in this field in the dark; it was at night. There was this horse, and I had a huge knife and I was chopping at it, and I was chopping at it, and I was chopping at it, attacking me (sic) and it wouldn't go away; cut it and chop at it, it's sumpin' awful! It wouldn't fall off, and, a, a, attacked the horse and it wouldn't go, just wouldn't go! I hated it! I don't know why, why I dream about horses, anyway. I hate horses! I don't dare get near a horse!" (218, pp. 289-90).

Taken in their entirety Stoyva's findings lend strong support to the earlier findings of Schrötter, Roffenstein, and Nachmansohn that some people can dream to order, as it were, in response to post-hypnotic suggestions. However, it is important to observe, with Stoyva, that despite the frequent explicitness of the inclusions of suggested topics, the natural dream-work always supplied a different and quite unpredictable embedding context. In other words, the suggestions did not enter the dreams as separate entities but were rather accommodated by the natural dream content.

A quite striking corollary finding of this study suggests that dreamers who are able to dream to order in this fashion may do so at some cost in the form of reduced amounts of dreaming. The seven subjects who regularly included the suggested topics in their dreams spent significantly less time in REM sleep as compared with their previously established baseline measures of REM time when no post-hypnotic suggestions had been operative. Following this lead Stoyva ran a pilot study with his five most suggestible subjects in which he increased the number of suggestions. He observed in four out of the five cases that although these subjects continued to include the suggested topics in their dreams their amounts of REM time were even further reduced. This is a particularly important set of observations because purely psychological factors have so seldom been found to have any appreciable effect on the duration of the highly stable and apparently physiologically programmed REM cycle.

An independently conceived study which turned out to be a nice variation on Stoyva's investigation has been reported by Charles Tart (226). Ten subjects were selected from a large group of students by standard tests of suggestibility and trained to reach a deep hypnotic state. In the experimental procedures the subjects were hypnotized and then told to dream during natural sleep that night about a narrative which was immediately played on a tape recorder. The narrative placed the subject in a threatening situation which evoked a realistic fear of bodily injury or death. It was emphasized that he would dream about the stimulus narrative in his natural sleep. Amnesia for the whole hypnotic session was then suggested. The subject was then dehypnotized, and slept in the laboratory for the night. Whenever his EEG and REM patterns indicated stage one dreaming, it was allowed to go on for a few minutes and then the subject was awakened for a dream report.

For five of the ten subjects, not a single element in their reported dreams corresponded directly to anything in the stimulus material. The other five subjects' dreams were affected, ranging from a minimal effect of two elements of the twenty-three in the stimulus narrative appearing in a reported dream to a high of thirteen of the twenty-three elements appearing in another reported dream. Two of the five subjects had only a single dream of the night affected, two others had two dreams affected, and the fifth subject had all five of his dreams strongly affected. Tart's findings support Stoyva's findings in that the reported dreams, even those showing the greatest effects of post-hypnotic suggestions, were not straightforward reproductions of the stimulus material. Rather there was considerable addition of extraneous detail and considerable embellishment. The "best" subject, in fact, repeatedly added a happy ending to his dreams after including the fearful topics that had been suggested. In conclusion, Tart implies a basis for explaining the reduced REM findings of Stoyva's investigation:

> It is as if the resulting dream were a product of a conflict between the suggested narrative and an autonomous, natural dream process which has, as it were, material of its own to present during the time of dreaming (223, p. 7).

Although this study did not speak to the possible negative correlation between amount of suggestion inclusion and amount of dreaming, Tart reports another study which addressed this question from the other side. Working with two subjects who had shown that their dreams were strongly affected by post-hypnotic suggestion, he sought to influence amounts of dreaming by four sets of direct post-hypnotic suggestions: (1) Wake up at the end of each dream. (2) Wake up at the beginning of each dream. (3) Dream all night long. (4) Don't dream at all.

Both "wake-up" suggestions proved to have a powerful effect. The two subjects had not awakened even once on their eight baseline nights but awakened a total of twenty-seven times, or an average of three awakenings per experimental night, on the "wake-up" nights. The "don't dream" suggestion had no significant effect with either subject, and the "dream all night" suggestions had no significant effect with one subject. For the other subject there was an increase in dream time of about half an hour per night, a 21 percent increase over baseline nights, which was statistically significant, but still far short of dreaming all night. Tart concludes that the timing and duration of dreaming sleep is probably basically under physiological control, and that psychological variables which can be generated in the laboratory may not be able to modify this physiological control more than about 20 percent (225).

TELEPATHIC
COMMUNICATION

In scientific circles there seems to be less resistance to entertaining the hypothesis that extrasensory perceptions may influence dreaming than the hypothesis that they may influence waking mentations. Perhaps this is because the conditions within which dreaming takes place make dreams so obviously remote from normal sensory stimulation, while yet dreams do undeniably exist, and are clearly not meaningless. The outer limits of the new observational vantages which the sleep monitoring procedures have made available to dream psychology may have been indicated in a series of recent reports on telepathic communication in dreams by Montague Ullman and his associates at Maimonides Hospital in New York.

The investigative procedure is as follows: the subject sleeps in a darkened room in which the experimenter, the EEG, and recording equipment are located. An "agent," located in a separate room approximately forty feet distant from the subject's room, chooses one of several envelopes containing "the target," a 5" x 8" reproduction of a famous painting. The choice is made using a procedure based on a random number table. The remaining envelopes are refiled by the agent before he inspects the target for the night. The agent then spends about thirty minutes associating to the target and writing down his associations. At the conclusion of the experimental session, the target is replaced in its envelope and set aside in a different file so as not to be reused. The experimenter is never told the target's identity for any given experimental session. The subject is awakened after five to ten minutes of REM sleep and asked to report whatever may have been going through his mind when being awakened.

Following is a summary of what at this writing is the most recent of these reports:

The possibility of experimentally inducing telepathic perception in the dreams of sleeping subjects was examined under conditions which controlled against ordinary sensory communication. EEG monitoring of periods of rapid eye movement and emerging stage 1 sleep was utilized for the collection of dream protocols from twelve subjects.

Two agents (one male, one female) selected target materials by random procedures from among a pool of twelve reproductions of famous paintings. They attempted to influence the subjects' dreams so as to introduce correspondence between the dreams and targets. Subjects at the close of their sessions ranked the potential targets against their recall of the night's dreams with the result that the actual targets were ranked in favorable positions more often than expected by chance (p = .05). Additional ranking done by three outside judges indicated better results from subjects working with the male agent (p = .05).

The male agent and the best of the twelve subjects were then paired for a seven night study of parallel design. The subject made his rankings (of targets against typed scripts of his dreams and associations) at the completion of the study rather than each night. He ranked the actual targets significantly more favorably than expected by chance (p = .05). The rankings of the three judges were significant at the .001 level. The results were evaluated by a specially adapted two way analysis of variance.

The statistical results of these studies, as well as the volume of striking anecdotal evidence of correspondences produced in them, suggest that telepathic effects in dreams are experimentally demonstrable. Further and broader investigations of these phenomena are now in process (239, p. 420).

The statistical significances quoted in this report will not much impress those who are unable to conceive the possibility that extrasensory perception may have even some trifling place in reality. Nor will descriptions of the elaborate experimental controls and exceptionally high scientific standards characteristic of Ullman's work much impress those who need to assume that extrasensory perception is an obvious fact. Those of us, however, who are simply impressed with the present limitations of our knowledge about how and why people dream must consider these findings. We shall focus here on some of the most striking anecdotes described in these reports. All of the examples were produced by the "best agent" and the "most gifted" subject:

1. The target was Dali's painting "The Sacrament of the Last Supper." It portrays Christ at the center of a table surrounded by his twelve disciples. A glass of wine and a loaf of bread are on

the table while a body of water and a fishing boat can be seen in the distance. Excerpts from the subject's first dream:

> There was one scene of an ocean . . . it had a strange beauty about it and a strange formation.

Excerpts from the subject's second dream:

> I haven't any reason to say this but somehow boats come to mind. Fishing boats. Small size fishing boats . . . there was a picture in the Sea Fare Restaurant that came to mind as I was describing it. It is a very large painting. Enormous. It shows, oh, I'd say about a dozen or so men pulling a fishing boat ashore right after having returned from a catch.

Excerpts from the subject's third dream:

> I was looking at a catalog . . . it was a Christmas catalog. Christmas season.

Excerpts from the subject's fourth dream:

> I had some sort of brief dream about an M.D. . . . I was talking to someone and . . . the discussion had to do with why . . . a doctor becomes a doctor because he is supposed to be an M.D., or something of that nature.

Excerpts from the subject's associations:

> . . . the fisherman dream makes me think of the Mediterranean area, perhaps even some sort of biblical time. Right now my associations are of the fish and the loaf or even the feeding of the multitude. . . . Once again I think of Christmas. . . . Having to do with the ocean—water, fisherman, something in this area. . .

2. The target was Degas's "The Dancing School." It depicts a dimly lit room with a dance class in progress. Girls in white ballet costumes stand in dance poses while others are adjusting their garments. Excerpts from the subject's first dream:

> A meeting. A group of people . . . it was some sort of meeting or get together.

Excerpts from the subject's third dream:

> I have the feeling of being in a house . . . it would be a large house, a mansion type house. As though I were in one of the rooms. High ceilings. Very elaborate.

Excerpts from the subject's fourth dream:

There's a girl . . . in it . . . a room in a house, an older house . . . a mansion, nineteenth century, perhaps.

Excerpts from the subject's sixth dream:

. . . I was in a class, a class made up of maybe half a dozen people . . . now, at different times, different people would get up for some sort of recitation or some sort of contribution . . . the woman—the instructor —was young. She was attractive . . . it felt like a school but I can't really say what the subject matter of the whole group was.

Excerpts from the subject's seventh dream:

I was finishing getting ready for bed, and we started having company . . . so I remember saying, "Oh, hell, I may as well go and get dressed." So I put on some pants and found a shirt. A shirt that had never been opened before . . . it seemed like all the buttons were on a tag . . . I was studying the instructions how to put them on . . . and as I was trying to read this, there was one little girl that was trying to dance with me. I remember ignoring her, trying to get these blame things on . . . a western shirt.

Excerpts from the subject's associations:

Well, I remember the one with the western shirt I was trying to put on at the party . . . it makes me think of yesterday. We were out at Cold Spring Harbor, I think, and in the store . . . it had a whole shelf of women's hose. . .

Assuming, for the purpose of discussion, that the agent's "sendings" are somehow being "received" by the subject and given a place in the formation of his dreams, what should once again most command our attention, I think, is that they are not simply being included in the dream contents in any direct representational ways. Rather, as apparently is true of every form of "external" influence on dreaming, they are transformed and assimilated into a dreaming process that does seem bent on some prevailing business of its own. For example, in another anecdote reported from the above study, which involved the same agent and another subject, the target was "The Sacred Fish" by di Chirico. In the painting, two dead fish rest on a wooden slab which has been placed in front of a candle. The subject dreamed of death, of going swimming, of a wooden table, and of lighting a candle. She also had several dreams about France and made repeated and pointed references to the word "poise." The authors immediately note that the French word for fish is "poisson." Now, this is precisely the kind of evidence which some scientists are unable to credit. What kind of "proof" is this that someone looking at a picture of a dead fish in an isolated room forty feet away from the subject has had any effect on that subject's dream? But, to the scientist who spends his work days interpreting and analyzing dreams this is the most convincing possible kind of evidence. For, it is precisely this kind of play on the data at its disposal that is at once the most distinguishing and most well established feature of the process of dreaming. Perfect for disguise if that is the purpose; perfect, also, for poetry, if that is related to the purpose.

EXPERIMENTAL STIMULATION DURING REM PERIODS

Ralph Berger sought to influence the contents of dreams by the direct method of repeatedly speaking personal names into the ears of sleepers during REM periods (13). Subsequent dream reports were then matched with these names by the subjects themselves and by independent judges. The subjects and judges did almost equally well in the matching, the subjects succeeding in 32 of 78 chances. The name was actually heard in the course of the dream in only a very few instances. Sometimes a person bearing the name appeared visually in the dream, either directly or in an identifiable transformation. Sometimes common associations linked the stimulus name with its dream representation. In most of the successful matchings, however, the linkage consisted of similar sounds connecting the stimulus names with dream constructions. Berger concluded:

. . . that perception of the external world, be it impaired, does occur in the REM periods associated with dreaming. However, the external origin of such perception is not normally recognized and external stimuli are perceived as belonging to the events of the dreams. Furthermore, it seems that perceptual awareness is coincident with cortical analysis of the stimulus, but is not dependent upon the significance of the stimulus to the sleeper . . . although the manner in which the stimulus is perceived sometimes appears to depend upon its meaning to the sleeper (13, p. 739).

REM
DEPRIVATION

With the tools at hand to determine when a person is dreaming, the opportunity exists to determine the effects on various sleeping and waking states of not dreaming. Several investigations have pursued this opportunity.

The normative effects of REM deprivation on subsequent sleeping states are already clear. On the average the more people are deprived of REM periods the more often must they be awakened in order to continue the deprivation. Also, again on the average, the more people have been deprived of REM time the greater are the amounts of it during subsequent nights of undisturbed or "recovery" sleep. Moreover, the "recoveries" are, on the average, in almost the exact amounts of the previous deprivation, as though some "deficit" was being made up (24, 27, 28, 139, 195).

The normative effects of REM deprivation on subsequent waking states have not yet been as well established. The first study designed to investigate this relationship indicated "anxiety, irritability and difficulty in concentration" to be possible effects (24). Later studies indicated that a further consequence of prolonged REM deprivation may be intense hunger associated with feelings of emptiness and depression, and hallucinatory tendencies (49). Two independent attempts to replicate these findings were unsuccessful (139, 213). A third attempt at replication confirmed the findings concerning hunger and food cravings, but reported mixed results regarding the other behavioral indices (194).

As to the effects of REM deprivation on the content of dream fragments left over from the deprivation procedure, one study reported an increase in aggressive contents (194), and two studies reported an increase in dream intensity (139, 194). It is, of course, possible that these findings were as much a consequence of the procedures necessary to prevent dreaming as they were a consequence of dream deprivation.

A recent report by Cartwright, *et al.*, promises to unravel the mixed implications of previous REM deprivation experiments by referring them to the influences of individual differences (21). After depriving ten subjects of their normal amounts of REM time for three consecutive nights, these investigators concluded that REM deprivation represents "a very different experience for even a highly homogeneous sample, in that some subjects need only be interrupted in their sleep a few times and some must be awakened very many" (21, pp. 302-3). Moreover, the more often subjects needed to be awakened to deprive them of REM time the more unstable were their electroencephalographic records during recovery periods, suggesting the possibility that the REM recovery reports for some subjects have, in the past, been spuriously high. These authors conclude that there may be at least three different patterns of response to REM deprivation, depending on individual factors: disruption, substitution, and compensation. The disruption pattern, manifested by repeated attempts to regain REM time and much subsequent EEG disturbance, seemed to be associated with weak ego controls and low tolerance for change in brain states. The substitution pattern was conceived to account for the finding that the more often a subject was able to report dreamlike content on being awakened from aborted periods of REM sleep the less was his REM increase during the recovery period. "These," say the authors, "may be the people who have more access to their fantasy under all conditions, for whom the dream stream can be tapped in a variety of states" (21, p. 303). The compensation pattern refers to the recovery phenomenon as classically described, and appears to be associated with good control, high perceptual field independence, and tolerance for delayed fantasy gratification.

An interesting variation on the REM deprivation experiment, conducted by Fiss, Klein, and Bokert, may prove to be still another way, made possible by EEG technology, to study the interrelations of waking and sleeping states (54). Instead of asking for dream reports after awakening their subjects these investigators asked for fantasies in response to TAT cards:

Continuous EEG and eye movement recordings were obtained from ten subjects who slept a full day in the laboratory. Subjects were awakened twice from rapid eye movement (REM) and twice from non-REM (NREM) sleep and each time asked to make up a TAT story.

Stories produced after interrupted REM sleep were longer, more complex, visual, bizarre, emotional, and vivid than stories produced after interrupted NREM sleep, and were more bizarre than stories told during control waking periods. "Dream" reports were strikingly similar in content to their corresponding fantasies.

The results strongly suggest that the distinguishing properties of a sleep stage are not "switched-off" following awakening but may persist into the waking state (54, pp. 550-51).

On the basis of these quite clear results the investigators found support for the theoretical position that REM and NREM sleep differ sharply with respect to cognitive qualities and that REM and NREM sleep are two distinct states, subject to separate regulative mechanisms. They were therefore drawn to subscribe to the view, which we adopted in the last chapter, that there are not two but three separate organismic states.

Chapter Five
NEW INTERPRETIVE APPROACHES

As we stated above, dream interpretation differs from dream investigation in that it seeks not to understand the process of dreaming but to employ dreams in deepening the self-awareness of dreamers. Although we must be careful not to confuse the assumptions, points of view, and techniques which make up the various approaches to dream interpretation with hypotheses and facts about the nature of dreaming, we may expect some of the former to be suggestive in respect to some of the latter. Thus, the regularity with which Freud was able to interpret dreams usefully as attempts to fulfill ego alien wishes led him to the hypothesis that *repressed infantile impulses* are the universal motivating forces of dream construction, even though, as was noted in Chapter One, we would be hard put to support this hypothesis on the basis of Freud's dream interpretations alone. Indeed, if dream interpretation had not been one of Freud's early interests, and had he founded psychoanalytic theory exclusively on his study of neurosis and the "psychopathology of everyday life," it is easy to imagine him deducing the psychoanalytic theory of dreaming as we know it from these other areas of research. Thus, the historical relationship between Freud's perfection of a method of interpreting dreams and his tentative formulation of a theory of dreaming stands as both stimulant and impediment to the further development of the theory: stimulant, in that useful dream interpretations did in fact lead directly on to systematic general theories, not only of dreaming but of a wide spectrum of human experiences; impediment, in that Freud's particular method for the employment of dreams in instructing the waking lives of dreamers happens to lead away from direct study of those manifestations of dreaming which are most clearly and most readily observable.

Although the Freudian method is well known, we shall refresh our memory of it here with an illustration, which will also serve to compare the first modern method of dream interpretation with subsequent ones. A manifest dream, one of my own, was written down some hours after awakening:

> I am driving fast on a two lane highway at dusk. I start to pass what I think is a truck. When abreast of it I see it is a long freight car on a truck—some new kind of vehicle, I think. I am committed to pass but realize with fright that I cannot see far enough ahead to be sure I'll get by before any cars might loom up from the opposite direction. Also, I see no leeway on the left; only a steep bank with almost no road shoulder. I slow down but then decide I am already too far out to get back in time if another car should appear. I decide to chance it and step on the gas. Just then I see a truck approaching. I also see that another truck is in front of the freight car truck of which I had not been aware. I dart into the space between them. By darting in I confuse everyone and endanger the oncoming truck. But after some swerving and upsetting of the drivers, fore and aft, it all turns out okay, leaving me feeling safe but sheepish.
>
> Then I pass the second truck and there is a clear straight stretch of road ahead. In the distance I see some low hanging branches which seem to envelop the road like a hoop. Suddenly feeling playful I step on the gas again, intending to fly through the hoop of branches. However, it turns out to be an old man on a haycart standing still in the middle of the road. I swerve very sharply and just barely miss him. As I pass I note that he is leisurely talking to someone. Further down the road I look back through the rear view mirror and see flames shooting up in the sky. Then I realize with an awful feeling in the stomach that the truck and freight car truck, not being as maneuverable as I, must have plowed into the haycart and the old man. I think to myself: "That poor old guy! Maybe I should go back to see if I can help. Maybe I should have stopped to warn him in the first place." But I continue on after thinking that there would be nothing I could do for him now in any event.

Recall that Freud's method of dream interpretation assumes the manifest dream to be a disguised (or distorted, or censored) rendition of certain "latent thoughts." It further assumes that it is these latent thoughts which will most expand or enhance the dreamer's waking views of himself, and that the best way to pierce the disguise (or correct the distortions, or circumvent the censor)—thus to reveal the latent thoughts that are lurking, as it were, in the wings of the manifest dream—is to request the dreamer to associate "freely" to the various manifest dream elements, until some coherent rationale emerges which may be made pertinent and acceptable to the dreamer's otherwise impertinent or unacceptable views of himself.

My first association to the dream was to the word "abreast." It is not a word I would typically use to describe being alongside a moving vehicle. I reflect that it is not even a very stable part of my vocabulary and that if I found myself using it in waking life it would certainly be a reference to being alongside something stationary. But, of course, *a breast* is something else again. How clever! And how transparent! Too much so, indeed. So, beware; the very transparency of this word play may be the dream's best disguise.

The long freight car on a truck is one of those dream images that translate poorly into words. In the dream itself it was much more than that, and much different. In the dream it was something suprisingly novel, not awesome, but very, very interesting, such that one could feel a pleasant sense of possessiveness at having merely seen it (like the electric trains under the Christmas trees of friends, which I knew my family could never afford but which I enjoyed nonetheless, or like the year I found a new wagon under my Christmas tree and could hardly contain the joy of being its owner). It was not at all the kind of thing one expects to come upon routinely driving across the country (which it now occurs to me I was doing in the dream). And now I remember that despite my fright at that moment in the dream I felt a twinge of annoyance that I could not give more attention to this new conception of a truck.

My thoughts turned next to the obvious day residue. The day before I had finished conducting a teacher training seminar which for a week had thoroughly consumed my thoughts. Now I could turn to the more personally pressing matter of moving to California where some months previously I had accepted a new position, after resigning from my post of ten years in Massachusetts. It had been ten good years. Would I regret the move? How strongly would I miss my friends—and they me? And the patients and students— was I wrong in not considering their needs before my own? But could I have been to them what I was when I felt fully committed? Ah, there's that old guilt! The bottomless stomach, the tight throat, the aching frustration of not being able to feel—and thus to control— another's pain. Remember how it first came out in analysis: the screen memory of being haunted with guilt at age ten, after seeing an old woman miss a bus, knowing I had no part in it, knowing my reaction was out of all proportion to the event, but feeling an overwhelming pity and sorrow and sense of responsibility all the same?

Returning to the dream, I noted the particular situation I was in on the highway to be an apt symbolic portrayal of my situation in life: at a point of no return, decisions and commitments made, but not yet fully acted upon, with all the insecurities of not being certain of what might lie ahead. A more sweeping parallel then occurred to me: I am a skilled and assertive driver but not one to take unnecessary risks. Yet, on occasion, I have found myself in exactly the situation in which the dream placed me: having begun to pass the car in front of me only to discover I had overestimated the margin of safety, thus being forced to rely more heavily on speed and skill than is wise. Looking back over the course of my life I saw a similar pattern; for the most part it had run a smooth, steady course, more characterized by deliberation and caution than by impulsiveness. Yet, the record was there of a series of radical changes, seemingly out of character, made on impulse (and usually involving abrupt disengagement from familiar persons or situations). Consequent mixed feelings toward myself in the two perspectives were also parallel: as a driver, pride in having had the skill to out-maneuver some very close shaves, and twinges of shame over having allowed them to be so close; as a person, pride in having concluded so many interesting life chapters, and twinges of shame that there was not more apparent consistency running through them. There were also unsettling thoughts about the confusing and possibly harmful effects my various moves had had on others; but, being out of sight, these were quickly put out of mind.

The experience of driving through the "hoop of branches" was distinctive. At first sight, at a distance, they seemed mysterious and sinister; immediately, however, there was the sense of recognizing them as familiar, even inviting. The associations were to memories of a large bush in back of the house in which I spent my early childhood, and long unrecalled memories of "tongue-touching" and similar "games" indulged in within its privacy with a female cousin who lived in the same house. Unaccountably my thoughts shifted to a vivid "memory" of being in a movie house as a child, watching a movie of a burning house and then discovering that it was the one in which I was sitting. Another screen memory, of course, probably based on a childhood dream, since I had surely never experienced such an event. But the memory carried the quality, nonetheless, of referring to something in real life.

The flames in the rear view mirror, and the haycart, and the old man presumably killed by the truck converged, by way of a web of associations too long and involved to report here, around my grandfather who, I fear, died without knowing from me how I loved and respected him. He had been the steady center of the otherwise broken family of my childhood, and I had taken the occasion of our last meeting, when I was seventeen, to declare my independence from him and his influence in awkward teenager ways, which could have left doubts about his value in my life. How often, since his death, had I wished I might have been at his deathbed to make amends! But that had been impossible, so I would never be absolutely sure he died knowing I had accepted his life as a valued part of my own. Then, a loose stream of associations (deathbed—center—darting into a space between—"a breast"—feeling safe but sheepish—unsettling both drivers) terminated in vivid memories of my early childhood home: my grandfather's room, my mother's room, my crib placed against (I could say abreast of) her bed, my cousin, the backyard bush. . . .

Some of this dream's rationale, that is to say its latent content, may now be inferred. Doubtless it included the · conscious wish that my decision to start a new life in a new world would turn out all right, that whatever adventures and dangers might lie ahead would be interesting ones and at least safely managed. From the associations of guilt and concern for those left behind I take one of the dream's ego alien wishes to have been that I would be sorely missed in Massachusetts, possibly that I might leave in my wake a wreck. I can attest that a review of certain fleeting thoughts confirmed both of these inferences and that my self-awareness was deepened as a result.

A repressed infantile wish was probably concerned with phallic desires to get into a space the nature of which may be obliquely suggested by the images of my mother's bed and of the "bush." I cannot say that subsequent reflections on this inference appreciably deepened my sense of self, but they do convince me that repressed infantile experiences do figure somehow in the construction of dreams.

The associations to this dream and the interpretations drawn from them are not exhaustive, but they will serve to keep Freud's approach in focus for the purpose of comparing it with more lately developed approaches to dream interpretation.

Since Freud's last revision of *The Interpretation of Dreams,* a number of dream theorists have developed supplementary interpretive methods that may prove important in refining the theory of dreaming. These are, in roughly the chronological order of their published works: Jung, Adler, Silberer, Lowy, Hall, French, Ullman, Erikson, and Boss. Although working independently, all but one of these theorists (French) gave primary attention to manifest dreams, an observation of some importance in itself. In the remainder of this chapter I shall briefly review the principal points of view, assumptions, and techniques which comprise these diverse approaches, illustrating them where possible in relation to the dream described above. The reader who is interested in the fine points of dream interpretation should consult the original texts, as I shall not attempt to be exhaustive in representing the various points of procedural emphasis or technical nuance. Rather, I shall try to marshal those interpretive notions which seem to me to be most immediately suggestive in relation to the psychology of dreaming.

CARL JUNG

Contrary to Freud's view of the manifest dream as a disguised version of certain latent thoughts which more truly represent the dreamer's subjective state, Jung took the view that the manifest contents of the dream were natural facts, which, if properly understood, gave the truest picture of the dreamer's subjective state:

> Perhaps we may call the dream a facade, but we must remember that the fronts of most houses by no means trick or deceive us, but, on the contrary, follow the plan of the building and often betray its inner arrangement. . . . We say that the dream has a false front only because we fail to see into it. We would do better to say that we are dealing with something like a text that is unintelligible not because it has a facade, but simply because we cannot read it. We do not have to get behind such a text in the first place, but must learn to read it (137, pp. 12-13).

This said, Jung followed Freud closely in his regard for the limitations of conscious reflection, but kept his sights on the authenticity of the manifest dream:

> The dream gives a true picture of the subjective state while the conscious mind denies that this state exists or recognizes it only grudgingly. . . . When we listen to the dictates of the conscious mind we are always in doubt. . . . The dream comes in as the expression of an involuntary psychic process not controlled by the conscious outlook. It represents the subjective state as it really is (137, pp. 4-5).

Jung's assumptions concerning the dream-work, from which he derived his particular interpretive procedures, followed from his more central assumptions concerning conscious and unconscious processes and their interaction. These are best understood in respect to his principle of psychic self-regulation, in which unconscious processes tend to function in a compensatory relation to conscious processes:

> I expressly used the word compensatory and not the word opposed because conscious and unconscious are not necessarily in opposition to one another, but complement one another to form a totality which is the self. According to this definition, the self is a quantity that is superordinate to the conscious ego. It embraces not only the conscious but also the unconscious psyche and is therefore, so to speak, a personality which we *also* are. . . . The unconscious processes that compensate the conscious ego contain all those elements that are necessary for the self-regulation of the psyche as a whole. On the personal level

these are the not consciously recognized personal motives which appear in dreams, or the meanings of daily situations which we have overlooked, or conclusions we had failed to draw, or affects we have not permitted, or criticisms we have spared ourselves (138, pp. 186-87.)

The concept of compensation is to be understood not only in this general reference to relative quantity of self-awareness but also in process terms:

The psyche is a self-regulating system that maintains itself in equilibrium as the body does. Every process that goes too far immediately and inevitably calls for a compensatory activity. Without such adjustments a normal metabolism would not exist nor would the normal psyche. We can take the idea of compensation so understood as a law of psychic happening. Too little on one side results in too much on the other. The relation between conscious and unconscious is compensatory (137, p. 17).

In defining this self-regulation process as it pertains to therapeutic dream interpretation, Jung makes a definite point of emphasizing that the compensatory activity is a two way and not a one way affair:

Dreams give information about the secrets of the inner life and reveal to the dreamer hidden factors of his personality. As long as these are undiscovered they disturb his waking life and betray themselves only in the form of symptoms . . . [therefore] there must be a thorough-going conscious assimilation of unconscious contents. By assimilation I mean *mutual* interpenetration of conscious and unconscious contents and not as is too commonly thought a one-sided evaluative interpretation and deformation of unconscious contents (137, p. 16; my italics).

Nevertheless, in all of his examples of dream interpretation Jung took the view that the compensatory process involved in producing dreams is one in which the unconscious seeks to correct unbalanced or inadequate conscious experience. Indeed, in the following quotation Jung rather precisely anticipates Silberer's notions of dream symbols as automatic "pre-rationative" responses to "apperceptive deficiency" and "apperceptive insufficiency"—of which we shall say more below:

It is far wiser in practice not to regard dream symbols as signs or symptoms of a fixed character. We should rather take them as true symbols—that is to say as expressions of something not yet consciously recognized or conceptually formulated (137, p. 21).

From these points of view and theoretical assumptions Jung derived three specific interpretive procedures which distinguish his method of interpretation: (1) The dream should be amplified by way of "exegesis" rather than by way of association. (2) The question "what for?" should be put to the dreamer more often than the question "why?" in order to elucidate the excessive or inadequate conscious experience for which the dream stands as a compensation. (3) The dream should be regarded as a real, rather than a merely symbolic, experience—the better to take advantage of its compensatory effects.

If we associate freely to a dream our complexes will turn up right enough, but we shall hardly ever discover the meaning of the dream. To do this we must keep as close as possible to the dream images themselves. When a person has dreamed of a deal table, little is accomplished by his associating it with his writing desk which is not made of deal. The dream refers expressly to a deal table. . . . In such cases, I say to my patients: "Suppose I had no idea what the words deal table mean. Describe this object and give me the history in such a way that I cannot fail to understand what sort of thing it is." We succeed in this way in establishing a good part of the context of that particular dream image. When we have done this for all the images in the dream, we are ready for the venture of interpretation (137, pp. 12-14).

A purely causalistic approach is too narrow to do justice to the true significance either of the dream or of the neurosis. A person is biased who turns to dreams for the sole purpose of discovering the hidden cause of the neurosis, for he leaves aside the larger part of the dream's actual contribution. The dreams I have cited unmistakably present the aetiological factors in a neurosis; but it is clear that they also offer a prognosis or anticipation of the future and a suggestion as to the course of treatment as well (137, p. 6).

Although compensation may take the form of imaginary wish fulfill-ment, it generally presents itself as an actuality which becomes the more strikingly actual the more we try to repress it. We know that we do not conquer thirst by repressing it. The dream content is to be taken in all seriousness as something that has actually happened to us; it should be treated as a contributory factor in forming our conscious outlook. If we do not do this we shall keep that one-sided conscious attitude which evoked the unconscious compensation in the first place (137, pp. 17-18).

In these perspectives, what stands out in the highway dream is its repeated presentation of situations in which quick decisions are made in a highly mobile context, followed by self-assertive actions taken with only secondary regard for the comfort and well being of others. I am thus prompted to ask if this dream may not have been a compensatory response to a conscious pattern of living too much in contemplation and thought and not enough in action, of tempering my decisions too much by regard for their consequences on others, and, perhaps, of underestimating the abilities of others to acquit themselves adequately in response to my actions. I can say that these were relevant and useful considerations, all.

Furthermore, I am encouraged to dwell on the phenomenological reality (i.e., the dream experience) of having found myself at a point of no return in a situation fraught with risk in which I behaved as well as circumstances would permit; of having been free, even under these strained conditions, to appreciate a novel sight; and, finally, that I committed myself to the dimly perceived beckonings of the road ahead with a sense of adventure. I can say that these were instructive and reassuring memories, all.

ALFRED ADLER

We must suspect that Adler did not remember many of his dreams, for he repeatedly spoke of dreams, and of dreaming, in prejudiced ways:

> The subjectively felt difficulty of the problem always acts as a test of social interest, and *can be such a burden that even the best of us will begin to dream*. We should expect, therefore, that the more the individual goal agrees with reality, the less a person dreams; and we find that it is so. *Very courageous people dream rarely for they deal adequately with their situation in the daytime* (2, p. 359; my italics).

Adler's writings on dream interpretation are inconsistent and often contradictory. However, since these writings may have anticipated the more orderly and thoughtful work of later theorists (notably

French, Lowy, and Ullman), we are obliged to note them in passing.

There are three ideas to be found in Adler's writings on dreams: (1) Dreams express the unity of personality, i.e., the dreamer's "life style." (2) Dreams are forward looking and problem solving experiences. (3) Dreams produce emotions which can carry over into waking life with possible adaptive consequences.

Adler expressed the first idea as follows:

> The supreme law of both life forms, sleep and wakefulness alike, is this: the sense of worth of the self shall not be allowed to be diminished. . . . It may be well to remark that the psychologist is not disturbed if somebody says to him, "I will not tell you any dreams for I cannot remember them but I will make up some dreams." The psychologist knows that the person's imagination cannot create anything but that which his style of life commands. His made up dreams are just as good as those he genuinely remembers for imagination and fancy will also be an expression of his style of life (2, pp. 358-59).

Are the ways in which dreams express the unity of personality significantly different from the ways other kinds of experiences express it? This is a question Adler did not pursue, and we are unable to infer the answer from his few illustrations of dream interpretation. Thus, we can only wonder whether by this idea he meant to affirm or to oppose Jung's view of dreams as compensation in the service of "psychic self-regulation."

Adler expressed the second idea as follows:

> The self draws strength from the dream fantasy to solve an imminent problem for the solution of which its social interest is inadequate. . . . Thus, every dream-state has an exogenous factor. This, of course, means something more than and something different from Freud's "day residue." The significance consists in that a person is put to the test and is seeking a solution. This seeking of a solution contains the "forward to the goal" and the "whither" of Individual Psychology in contrast to Freud's regression and fulfillment of infantile wishes. It points to the upward tendency in evolution, and shows how each individual imagines this path for himself. It shows his opinion of his own nature and of the nature and meaning of life (2, p. 359).

Again, he does not go on to say *how* he conceives dreams to seek solutions to problems, nor how they exercise their forward looking propensities, and his implicit suggestions on these points are contradictory. For example, having dismissed Freud's work out of hand, Adler's one suggestion regarding the process by which dreams seek to solve problems refers to a form of self-deception which to this writer is indistinguishable from Freud's "dream censor."

> In dreams we fool ourselves into an inadequate solution of a problem, that is, inadequate from the standpoint of the common sense, but adequate from the standpoint of our style of life. We do this by dismissing important facts and leaving only a small part of the problem which can, if everything is put to figurative metaphorical form, be solved easily. . . . For example, a young man wants to get married but hesitates and expresses contradictory views regarding the important step he is considering. A friend may say "don't be a jackass!" The friend thus reduces the whole complicated problem to being a jackass or not and thus enables the young man to find an easy solution to it (2, p. 360).

As we will see, French does much better by the idea of the dream as a problem solving experience.

The third idea was expressed as follows:

> The purpose of the dream is achieved by the use of emotion and mood rather than reason and judgement. When our style of life comes into conflict with reality and common sense, we find it necessary, in order to preserve the style of life, to arouse feelings and emotions by means of the ideas and pictures of a dream, which we do not understand.
>
> In a dream the individual's goal of achievement remains the same as in waking life, but a dream impels him toward that goal with increased emotional power. . . . In dreams we produce the pictures which will arouse the feelings and emotions which we need for our purposes, that is, for solving the problems confronting us at the time of the dream, in accordance with a particular style of life which is ours (2, pp. 360-61).

Typically, Adler immediately proceeds to imply a refutation of his own position by illustrating it with a negative case:

> Thus, people frequently get up in the morning argumentative and critical, as a result of an emotion created by the night's dream. It is like a state of intoxication and not unlike what one finds in melancholia, where the patient intoxicates himself with ideas of defeat, of death, and of all being lost (2, p. 361).

I shall not attempt to apply Adler's views to the highway dream except to note that the reflections of the patterns of my life course, which were included in the initial associations, may exemplify the idea that dreams express a dreamer's "life style."

HERBERT SILBERER

Herbert Silberer was one of the very few of Freud's younger contemporaries whose work on dreams Freud found worthy of favorable comment, possibly because like Pötzl but unlike Adler, Maeder, and Stekel, Silberer had developed a disciplined method of observation which promised to supplement Freud's method of free association, thus perhaps adding to the scientific credibility of psychoanalytic theory as a whole. Silberer's was not a clinical method, nor was it designed to be applied to nocturnal dreams; rather it was designed to observe the related symbolic phenomena of hypnogogic hallucinations. In his early studies of one of the ubiquitous features of this form of symbolism—its transformation of the abstract into the concrete—Silberer observed two psychological conditions to be especially conducive to such transformations: apperceptive deficiency and apperceptive insufficiency.

Apperceptive deficiency refers to situations in which a person is unable to maintain rational mastery of intellectual achievements which are normally routine for him, and falls back, as it were, on their pre-rationative approximations. He may be fatigued, drowsy, in a fevered condition, in emotional conflict, or under the influence of drugs, or may in some other way have lost the fine edge of his optimal mental state. *Apperceptive insufficiency* refers to situations in which a person, in full command of his optimal mental state, has momentarily assumed challenges which just barely elude his best intellectual efforts. He may then receive an assist from these same pre-rationative approximations. We sometimes call this "inspiration."

Silberer arranged to catch these passing pre-rationative assists on the fly, so to speak, by training himself to observe his reveries under a delicate blend of the two conditions. At the first signs of drowsiness he would set himself to contemplating some intellectual problem of which he was not yet quite master. When the elusive concept gave way to its perceptual sequel he would alert himself to wakefulness and ponder the two versions of what he called the "autosymbolic phenomenon."

I think of human understanding probing into the foggy and difficult problem of the "Mothers" (Faust, Part II).

Symbol: I stand alone at a stone jetty extending out far into a dark sea. The waters of the ocean and the dark and mysteriously heavy air unite at the horizon.

Interpretation: The jetty in the dark sea corresponds to the probing into the difficult problem. The uniting of air and water, the elimination of the distinction between above and below, would symbolize that, with the Mothers, as Mephistopheles describes it, all times and places shade into each other so that there are no boundaries between "here" and "there," "above" and "below." It is in this sense that Mephistopheles says to Faust: "Now you may sink!—I could as well say: rise" (205, p. 202).

I am trying to think of the purpose of the metaphysical studies I am about to undertake. The purpose is—I reflect—to work my way through ever higher forms of consciousness, that is, levels of existence, in my quest after the basis of experience.

Symbol: I run a long knife under a cake as though to take a slice of it.

Interpretation: My movement with the knife represents "working my way through." To clarify this apparently silly symbol I must give a detailed explanation. The symbol-basis, that is, the relationship which makes the picture here chosen usable for autosymbolic representation, is the following: At the dining table it is at times my chore to cut and distribute the cake. I do this with a long and flexible knife, necessitating considerable care. It is particularly difficult to lift the slices; the knife must be carefully pushed *under* the slice (this is the slow "working my way through" to arrive at the "basis"). There is yet more symbolism in the picture. The symbol is a layer cake, so that the knife cutting it penetrates several layers (levels of consciousness and existence) (205, p. 203).

From the many observations which he collected by this method Silberer concluded that the "regressive" symbols which comprise most hypnogogic hallucinations and most dreams can be classified in three categories: material symbols, functional symbols, and somatic symbols. It was this contribution which Freud described as "one of the few supplements to the dream theory, the value of which is indisputable" (206, p. 361). *Material* symbols are those which refer to *what* the person was thinking, i.e., to the objects of thought which are transformed into symbols. Thus the many sided conceptual meaning of Mephistopheles' statement to Faust, "Now you may sink!—I could as well say: rise," is transformed into the concrete symbol of standing on a jetty where "the waters of the ocean and the dark and mysteriously heavy air unite at the horizon." *Functional* symbols are those which refer to *how* the person was thinking, i.e., with ease, hardship, laziness, joy, restraint, defiance, perseverance, attraction, repulsion, conflict, etc. Thus, the peculiar mental state of tension and poise with which Silberer approached the working through of ever higher forms of consciousness in his quest for "the basis of existence" is transformed into the concrete symbol: "I run a long knife under a cake as though to take a slice out of it." *Somatic* symbols are those in which somatic occurrences and states of all kinds are reflected symbolically—external as well as inner feelings, sense impressions of pressure, feelings of temperature, etc.

> . . . before falling asleep my head feels heavy and pains; the pain is stifling. I see before me a box of matches arranged upside down, the heads of the matches at the bottom of the box. The heads of the matches are symbolic of my head. I feel myself inflamed; this is the source of the image of the matches, which are as inflammable as my head feels and which can erupt as the illness which might erupt in me. As the matches stand heads downward, so do I feel as if I am standing on my head . . . (206, pp. 368-69).

The material and somatic categories added nothing really new to Freud's classifications of dream symbols, but, as Freud acknowledged, the functional category was a novel and valuable contribution to the psychology of dream symbolism.

As for dream interpretation, Silberer took a somewhat wider view of the meaningfulness of dreams than did Freud:

> . . . There is indeed the wish life of a man always mixed into his emotions; and it is certainly so that emotions are the base of all dreams. But it is doubtful whether the constant focus on this viewpoint would always enable the observer to emphasize the most characteristic, the most important part of the dream, i.e., its leitmotif.
>
> I would prefer a more general formula, even though I am in accord with the theory of hidden wishes and their disguised appearance. My formula in essence is: the stimulus of the dreams is always an emotional factor of high valence which arouses our interests with lustful or unlustful coloring. It incites in us gay expectation, complacent self-mirroring, anxious apprehension, worried reflections, bitter accusation, or any other inner reaction animated by affect (206, p. 376).

As for interpretive methods, Silberer seemed to steer a middle course between placing emphasis on manifest and latent dream contents and between relying on associative materials and on direct interpretation. On the one hand, his interpretations suggest that he considered contemplation of the waking problems and states of mind which are revealed by the material and functional symbols of dreams to be more rewarding to the dreamer than contemplation of the symbols themselves. On the other hand, he appears to have deemed it sufficient to have a thorough knowledge of the dreamer and his life situation, and of course an understanding of the symbolizing process, to assist in both the revelational and contemplative aspects of the interpretive procedure.

Disregarding the somatic symbols that may have figured in the highway dream, a retrospective search for its functional symbolism settled intuitively on that moment of annoyance and resigned frustration in the dream when I found myself unable to ponder the intricacies of the novel vehicle I was passing, or even to identify it, because of the requirements of steering a safe course. This state of mind, I then recalled, precisely paralleled one that I had repeatedly experienced in the teacher training workshop I had just concluded. It had been an extremely intense experience, fourteen hours a day for seven consecutive days. As might be expected, under these circumstances, the participants had come to know each other intimately. However, as leader of the workshop, whose responsibility it was to keep it on its prescribed course, I repeatedly felt constrained to steer clear of certain personal involvements, to which, in less urgent circumstances, I might rather have given myself over. Moreover, the teachers had impressed me as exceptionally interesting people, but, since they represented various school systems from all parts of the country, it was extremely unlikely that I would meet them again. Thus, the urgent feeling tone in the dream: here is this really interesting spectacle that I can only know in passing and shall probably never see again.

These reflections on my recent experiences in the workshop proceeded to bring to light several "material" symbols not previously noted. For some years, as a consultant to the curriculum designing organization which supported the workshop, I had unsuccessfully professed an approach to the teaching of elementary social studies which called for eliciting, rather than avoiding, strong emotional reactions in both teachers and pupils.* Previous efforts to win converts to this approach had failed because I had not succeeded in convincing the various workshop leaders of its value. Therefore, I had offered, this one last time, to conduct the workshop myself. In this I ran the risk of seeing five years of work exposed as misguided and misleading, for, truth to tell, I was more sure of the theoretical than of the practical merits of my position. However, having committed myself, as it were, to assume the driver's seat, I had acted, as in the dream, with single minded purpose. This had taken the form of showing the teachers at the first meeting, and with no introduction, the most threatening film of those from which they would later be free to choose in teaching a new course on the evolution of Man. It showed an Eskimo boy catching and tying a seagull and then stoning it to death before the proud eyes of his mother. I had decided to start the workshop in this manner over the objections of two respected colleagues. As the workshop ran its course it became clear that I had been right in not heeding their advice, as they were later to acknowledge. In fact, at its conclusion the workshop had been commended by all concerned as the most successful yet undertaken. So much for the symbolism of successfully stepping on the gas despite the consternation of the other drivers. But there was more: the teachers had learned all that could have been expected of this new and potentially dangerous approach in one week's time. However, would it blow up in their faces when they tried to apply it unassisted in their own classrooms? This thought, as a matter of fact, had flitted across my mind as I went off to sleep the night before the dream, while also looking forward to the new challenges of my own which might conceivably blow up in *my* face. Thus, the material symbol of the flames of surmised origin in the rear view mirror.

SAMUEL LOWY

As the title of Samuel Lowy's major work, *Psychological and Biological Foundations of Dream Interpretation*, indicates, he shared Freud's professional ambivalence. Engaged daily in the practice of psychiatry, thus in the interpretation of

---

* This position is detailed in my *Fantasy and Feeling in Education* (128).

dreams, he was nonetheless primarily interested in the natural functions and processes of dreaming.

Lowy conceived the process of dreaming to be an emotion producing and emotion regulating process. Although produced by the conditions of sleep and reflected in the conscious symbolisms of remembered dreams, this process, as Lowy conceived it, has its primary origins and serves its primary purposes at the psychosomatic level of "psycho-affective homeostasis":

> . . . just as the "physical metabolism" carries out the task of guaranteeing the constancy of physiological events, so have the multiform events, occurring within the subconscious and unconscious spheres, the dreaming process included, to effectuate the psycho-affective homeostasis (162, p. 65).

Lowy's contribution to dream interpretation was less a matter of method than of a certain attitude of largesse which he took toward dreams, which followed from his assumption concerning the primary function of dreaming. He made this attitude most explicit in discussing the fact that only a small percentage of dreams are remembered.

> The recollection of the dream has always to surmount some resistance, some counter-pressure of varying intensity. . . . This, surely, is a strange phenomenon! Why do we possess at all a faculty for remembering our dreams in the waking state, if complete remembering is impeded in this way? It seems almost as if dreams were not destined for the knowledge of our waking consciousness. . . . This fact seems to constitute a certain argument against the view held by some that the dream is a finger-post for the waking life, a guide for the correct solution of the various problems of one's existence. However fitting and clever many of the examples may be, which are quoted in support of this view, the fact that dreams are usually forgotten speaks strongly against it. Dreams which appear to be of such an "advising and warning" kind might be actually something different, something more. They contain not a mere plan for later life, not a counsel, nor a purely theoretical principle; but they represent a self-contained, *concrete process* within the compass of the psyche. When, for instance, we refuse to see some real difficulty, some threatening complication, and exorcise it from our conscious thoughts, and then this reality appears in our dreams, this is probably not mere exhortation, or warning, but

a sign that the subconscious psyche is usefully dealing with the difficulty in question, that it is mobilizing and integrating the thought-processes relating thereto, that it is preparing itself for and against the eventuality, forming, as it were, "antibodies," and *thus making up for what our conscious thinking neglected to do because it was unable to cope with it.* If, then, the real difficulty actually occurs, the psyche, the nervous system, the personality are not unprepared, not quite without mental "antitoxins". . . . Eventual memory constitutes a secondary gain (162, pp. 3-5).

In other words the primary function of dreaming is a kind of psychic self-regulation, much as Jung described it. However, for Lowy this process fully accomplishes its purposes *outside* of waking consciousness. If a dream happens to be remembered in waking life, and if then it happens to be interpreted such that the parameters of waking consciousness are increased in quantity or broadened in quality, so much the better for waking consciousness—but this is, as we sometimes say, "the gravy."

Although . . . the dream is not primarily destined for conscious memory, it is clear, on the other hand, that it is definitely destined for being "consciously" experienced during sleep. What the subconscious puts at the disposal of the dream-ego, is meant to become "conscious" during dreaming. These two different modes of becoming "conscious" ought not to be confounded (162, p. 5).

Moreover:

The world of dreams appears as dissociated only in comparison with the world of conscious thought, in relation to the world of logical reality. But why assume and take for granted that the world of dreams wants to be compared with, and related to, the world of reality and realistic thinking? *The contrary is much more probable. The world of dreams is a world apart* (162, p. 56).

Thus, since a remembered dream was fair game for just about anything, Lowy proceeded, in his interpretive practices, to make the most of his license. It is not made clear in writings of the dream theorists whose work we have yet to discuss to what extent Lowy's work contributed directly to their assumption of increased interpretive liberties. However, Lowy's working principles may be seen to have anticipated almost all of the major approaches to dream interpretation that have followed the first English publication of his work in 1942. These principles may be summarized as follows:

1. Since the primary function of dreaming pertains to the production and regulation of emotion, the interpreter does well to draw the dreamer's attention to the "affective reverberations" of dream memories, thus including the conscious spheres of personality organization in the revitalizing processes in which, it is assumed, the unconscious spheres of personality organization were involved during the experience of dreaming.

2. Since the symbolic qualities of dreaming consciousness have a purpose of their own that is separate from any purpose that might conceivably be served by waking consciousness, and since these symbolic qualities are presumably sufficient to the achievement of their distinctive purpose, we are hardly called upon to view the manifest dream as a distorted representation of waking concepts. Better, says Lowy (here seconding Jung), to learn to appreciate the idiom of dream consciousness on its own terms, if we wish to enjoy the secondary gain which is all that dream interpretation can yield.

3. Since dreaming is oriented toward unity and constancy in the psyche, interpretation should concentrate on neither the past nor the present. Rather, it should concentrate on the synthesizing connections of past *and* present which are engineered by the condensations of dream symbolism.

By means of the dream-formation, details of the past are continually re-introduced into consciousness, are thus prevented from sinking into such depths that they cannot be recovered. Those of our experiences which are not at the moment accessible to consciousness are thus kept in touch with consciousness, so that in case of necessity association with them may become easier.

This connecting function of the dream-formation is reinforced considerably by formation of symbols. When this function takes a hand and condenses masses of experiences, perhaps a whole period of the dreamer's life, into one single image, then all the material which is contained in this synthesis is reconnected with consciousness. Dream-formation thus causes not only a connection of single details, but also of whole "conglomerations" of past experience. But this is not all. Through the constancy and continuity existing in the process of dreaming, there is created a connection with this dream-continuity. Which fact greatly contributes to the preservation of the cohesion and unity of mental life as a whole (162, pp. 201-2).

4. Since a dream is the highly over-determined product of the convergence in dreaming consciousness of multitudinous material, functional, and somatic symbols* we are hardly justified in viewing the manifest dream as merely a useful set of departure points for collecting waking associations. The free association method is sometimes indicated for the achievement of certain limited and strictly therapeutic goals, but the fullest and potentially most enriching interpretations are based not on parts of dreams, much less on associations to parts of dreams, but on the dream totality. And, since the qualities of dream consciousness are refractory to the qualities of waking consciousness, the meaningfulness of the totality of dreams is better appreciated by intuition and induction than by logic and deduction.

". . . the . . . interpreter should feel himself into the dream-event ("empathy"), should let the image in its totality pass through his own psyche . . . then his own inner fund of experience will supply him with the necessary supplements; with whatever is needed to transform the verbalized dream-image into a "living content." Just in the same manner as *the apparently monochromatic ray of sunlight is decomposed into its individual and differently coloured components, by being passed through a prism.* Every image which belongs to the dream, every object which plays a part in the delineation of a scene, signifies *something*, means "intra psychic life." But, again, this is only theory. In actual practice we have to rest content with discovering single motives, and for psychotherapeutic purposes actually only certain elements and relations are important. *The primary significance of the manifest dream* is, of course, a natural presupposition. If the dream mechanism finds it necessary to create the manifest dream then it is not justifiable to take it as entirely nonessential" (162, p. 196).

We should not be surprised that our previous interpretations of the highway dream have already illustrated applications of the first three of these principles, as these undoubtedly reflect the influences on Lowy's thinking of Freud, Jung, Adler, and Silberer. Thus, I have already allowed the dream's aftereffects of exhilaration, fear, confidence, apprehension, regret, guilt, resignation, and hope to

* Lowy subscribed to Silberer's conclusions.

bathe my recognition of its memory; I have already sought to re-experience its drama as lived, and not merely as remembered; and I have already had occasion to appreciate the niceties with which it synthesized patterns that are representative of my past and present. It only remains to apply Lowy's fourth principle as regards the dream's totality.

The phrase "point of no return" presents itself as the verbal entry to this approach. This, I sense, is what this dream is all about—its dwellings on the old and on the new, its refraction of the sense of commitment, as much in the confident sensation of the sole of my foot on the gas pedal as in the fears for my safety, as much in memories of my skill as a driver as in my reliance on the equanimities of others, as much in the moment of sheepishness as in the moment of playfulness, as much in the reassurance of being able to act as in the doubts over the consequences of acting. This, it now occurs to me, is not interpretation as much as it is entertainment. Just possibly, then, it is the *entertainment* of dreams, rather than their interpretation, that Lowy had in mind when he spoke of the "secondary gain" to be derived from remembering dreams.

CALVIN HALL

Calvin Hall, the arch-empiricist of dream psychology, has collected, classified, scored, and interpreted tens of thousands of dreams over the last quarter of a century. A postcard to Dr. Hall will bring from his Institute of Dream Research a sample of male dreams, female dreams, white dreams, black dreams, Indian dreams, psychologists' dreams, gamblers' dreams, the dreams of the first scalers of Mount Everest—or, pretty much, what have you. An academic psychologist with only passing interests in the clinical arts, Hall is less interested in dreaming, or for that matter dreams, than he is in what dreams can tell us about people—individual people (103), groups of people (86), and all people (85). His contributions to dream interpretation have been more on the side of discipline (objectification, codification, and interpreter reliability) than on the side of artfulness (100). Nevertheless, Hall has made two quite distinctive contributions to the field of dream interpretation, one methodological and one theoretical.

Eschewing single dreams in favor of dream series (as did Jung before him and French after him), he has proposed a method of interpretation which he describes as the *spotlight* method.

Often the meaning of one dream is self-evident and illuminates a major conflict like a spotlight shooting its beam into the darkness. Armed with the hypothesis drawn from a spotlight dream, the other dreams of the series are scrutinized for projections of the same basic conflict. If a number of dreams of an individual fit in with the same interpretation this interpretation is felt to be corroborated and is assigned to the dream series (95, p.120).

Here is an example:

Case A—Subject: female, 20 years, college junior. Basic conflict: desire to establish an autonomous and independent life either through a career or marriage, preferably the latter, versus fear of leaving the security provided by the family.

Spotlight Dream A 1
I dreamed that I volunteered to go overseas as a teacher. I went to Italy to teach the children there. My dream consisted of leaving my family and being very graciously welcomed in Italy by an army officer and his wife. I was married shortly after my arrival there. Most of my dream was the difficulty I had leaving home.

Interpretation
The basic conflict is clearly projected into this dream. She does leave home, even the country, yet despite the presence of parental substitutes in Italy and a speedy marriage, much of the dream is concerned with the difficulty she has in leaving her home.

Dream A 2
I dreamed last night I was in a train station with my sister. We were supposed to make a certain train but for some reason neither of us could find the right track. It was most confusing and all I can remember is the two of us racing about trying to find that train in a large depot that had many tracks and entrances.

Interpretation
She wants to get away from home but the threat of insecurity prevents her from finding the proper train, even though she has the companionship and support of her sister.

Dream A 3
I dreamed I was back in high school again.

Dream A 4

My dream last night was quite confusing. I was attending college classes but was in high school. I was in the high school building attending classes with my high school friends, but the classes themselves were those I now attend. It was rather a review of a typical day as I used to have them in high school. We were planning to attend a football game after school and things were quite exciting.

Interpretation

These are regressive dreams. If she were back in high school it would not be necessary for her to make the choice between family security and individual freedom. *A4* shows that intellectually she prefers college to high school but it would be less threatening to her if the classes were held in the high school building. Regression offers a neat solution to her problem.

Dream A 5

I dreamed I got infantile paralysis and found I would have a permanent affliction. I had to quit school and life seemed pretty miserable.

Dream A 6

I dreamed I had an accident and broke my leg. The rest of the dream I was in the hospital getting just loads of attention and sympathy. Friends came to see me and one of my overseas friends was given a furlough to come home for awhile. The pain I might have had from a broken leg never entered the dream. It was all very pleasant and I was the center of attention.

Interpretation

The solution found in these two dreams portrays the desperation she feels. She is willing to endure infantile paralysis in order to resolve the conflict. The leg fracture, while not as serious, is equivalent to infantile paralysis, since it immobilizes her. In either case, she cannot leave the family. Moreover she becomes the recipient of attention and sympathy, and a boyfriend is even given a furlough to visit her. But these gratifications are merely the by-products of the primary wish-fulfillment to remain with the family.

Dream A 12

Last night I dreamed my sister and I were in a play. All I had to do was sing a song but they didn't give it to me until the last minute and I couldn't seem to learn the song. My sister had the lead and for some reason I was always appearing on the stage when I wasn't supposed to. I did sing my song finally and it turned out to be a success, much to my surprise.

Interpretation

This is a fine example of sibling rivalry. Her sister has the "lead" and the dreamer intrudes when she is not wanted. The dreamer feels rejected because the parents prefer the sister. Therefore the interpretation which she places upon their insistence that she become independent is that they want to get rid of her in favor of her rival. The dream ends on a reassuring note. She does sing her song successfully. The singing of the song probably symbolizes a satisfactory transition to maturity (95, pp. 68-76).

As an interpreter of dreams, Hall might be termed a Freudian expressionist. On the one hand, he follows Freud's wish-fulfillment directives to the letter. On the other hand, he will have none of Freud's notion of the dream as a disguise:

We believe there are symbols in dreams and that these symbols serve a necessary function, but it is not the function of disguise. We believe that the symbols of dreams are there to express something, not to hide it (91, p. 95).

Moreover, for Hall, dreams not only serve to express human interests; often they seek to express them at their best, to improve, clarify, or beautify them.

Why then are there symbols in dreams? There are symbols in dreams for the same reason that there are figures of speech in poetry and slang in everyday life. Man wants to express his thoughts as clearly as possible in objective terms. He wants to convey meaning with precision and economy. He wants to clothe his conceptions in the most appropriate garments. And, perhaps, although of this we are not too certain, he wants to garnish his ideas with beauty and taste. For these reasons, the language of sleep uses symbols (91, p. 108).

Since it is not possible to illustrate Hall's interpretive approach by application to our single specimen dream, I should like to take this opportunity to quote at length from one of his shortest articles, "Out of a Dream Came the Faucet." In my opinion, it conveys the essence of his contribution to dream psychology.

This is the dream that invented the faucet. It was dreamed by a young man on the 216th anniversary of the birth of George Washington.

"I dreamed I got out of bed and went into the bathroom and attempted to turn on the water faucet. I turned and turned but no water came out. I then decided to call the plumber. Soon afterward the door opened and an individual dressed in coveralls approached me. Upon closer examination I discovered the plumber was a female. I scoffed at the idea of a lady plumber. But unruffled she went to the basin, turned the faucet, and water immediately flowed. This was when the emission occurred."

In this wet dream, faucet equals penis. Faucet is the symbol object, penis is the referent object. Ask a person why this analogy between faucet and penis exists in the mind of the dreamer, and he will probably respond with the commonsense answer of association psychology—"because they resemble one another." True enough, a faucet from which water flows is analogous to a penis from which semen flows. Isn't *cock* a common slang word for penis? In order to remove any doubt that such a resemblance exists, the dreamer obligingly ejaculated when water started to flow from the faucet. He knew what the faucet in his dream stood for.

Why did the dreamer choose to represent his sex organ by a faucet instead of by any one of the other hundreds of symbols in dreams and language for penis? We dealt with this question in a previous article. The gist of what we said then was that a dream symbol represents a conception of a referent. In the present example, the choice of faucet expressed the dreamer's conception of his penis on the night of February 22, 1948. Since a person has many conceptions of the same thing, on another occasion he would probably employ another kind of symbol—tree, gun, or syringe, for example. Each of these symbols depicts a different idea of the penis. In fact, a week after the faucet dream, the young man represented his sex impulse by a different metaphor.

"In this dream I found myself lying in bed in the early hours of the morning. It was a cold, dull morning and I seemed to feel a chill run through my body. Suddenly the sun rose and the room seemed to fill with warmth. It was during this period the emission occurred."

Why are there symbols in dreams? Why doesn't a person just dream about the referent? Sometimes he does. Our ever-obliging young man had just such a dream on May 10, 1948. We quote only the last sentence of his dream report.

"I tried to seduce her only to find that my organ seemed to be too large for her vagina, thus making intercourse impossible."

No symbolism is this dream. Penis is penis (a big one), vagina is vagina (a small one). Then why the symbolic faucet in his Washington's Birthday dream? Surely not to disguise the penis, or if that was the reason it proved to be a pretty flimsy disguise.

We think one reason a symbol appears in a dream in place of a referent object is that the dreamer is dissatisfied with the referent object and creates a better one. Our young dreamer thought to himself, "wouldn't it be nice if my penis could be turned on and off as easily as a faucet." No sooner thought than visualized.

In support of this thesis, contrast the satisfactory outcome of the faucet dream or the rising sun dream with the frustrating outcome of the May 10th dream in which there was no symbolization.

Important as these questions are—why are there symbols in dreams, and why does a dreamer select a particular symbol for a referent object—there is an even more basic question. Why do such things as faucets exist which can be used to symbolize the penis? No, we are not being prankish. Obviously, the faucet did not invent itself. It was invented by someone or by a number of people independently. Why was it invented? Commonsense answers, "Because it serves a useful purpose." In our opinion, all purposive explanations are rationalizations. The motive power for behavior is a wish, not a purpose. The faucet was invented for the same reason that the young man dreamed his penis was a faucet. The inventor of the faucet was acting out *his* fantasy of a penis which could be turned on and off at will. That his fantasy proved to have utility is a consequence, and not an antecedent or cause, in the same manner that the survival value of a mutation is a consequence of the mutation and not its cause. Genes do not mutate in order to annihilate or to evolve a species. Nor was the faucet invented in order to supply man with a convenient and controllable source of water, although once in existence it proved to have such a use.

The faucet was invented by a man who wanted a better penis. Money was invented by someone who wanted to accumulate a bigger pile of feces. Rockets to the moon were invented by a group of dissatisfied oedipal animals. Houses were invented by wombseekers, and whiskey by breastlings. . . .

What we are proposing is a *tabula rasa*—not of the mind which asserts that objects evoke fantasies—but a *tabula rasa* of the environment which asserts that fantasies create objects.

At birth, a baby whose mind is filled with fantasies enters an *empty* world. Out of his fantasies, he fills the world with faucets, fountains, hoses, and sprinklers. He invents the world. He is still inventing the world . . . (85, pp. 113-15).

THOMAS FRENCH

Probably the most carefully devised clinical method of dream interpretation since Freud's is the *focal conflict* method of Thomas French (63). Working recently in collaboration with his colleague Erika Fromm, French's central assumption is that dreaming serves the purpose of seeking solutions to interpersonal problems. He does not take issue with Freud's thesis that unconscious wishes activate dreams; however, he considers the dream itself to be a network of problems organized around a recent focal conflict in interpersonal relations. The dream-work seeks to solve these problems by substituting analogous ones, which are strategically more amenable to the nonverbal, practical, socially isolated, empathic thinking that is characteristic of the state of sleep. Within the network of related problems which make up the manifest dream there is usually one problem which is a reaction to a recent emotional dilemma of the dreamer, upon which congruent earlier problems converge and around which similar contemporary problems gravitate. This *focal problem* is conceived to be within possible range of ego functions involving active growth and learning.

The dream's successive attempts to find a solution to the focal problem constitute a hierarchy of substitutions of one problem for another. The hierarchy is assumed to derive from a similar pattern of successive attempts in the dreamer's past to find solutions to critical developmental conflicts. This prior hierarchy of problems, and attempts at solutions, French calls the dream's *historical background*. The constellation of defensive and integrative mechanisms which relate the dream's historical background to its focal problem and to the dreamer's present life situation as reflected in his associations is the dream's *cognitive structure*. Usually the cognitive structure will show the manifest dream to be interpolated between the focal problem, with its related fears and hopes in the present, and the historical background, with its related traumatic and reassuring memories. Often the chronological succession of episodes which make up a manifest dream reveals an initial attempt to deny the focal conflict by means of a reassuring hallucination, followed by further symbolic representations of the focal conflict and subsequent attempts to imagine reality based solutions.

The goal of interpretation is to comprehend the cognitive structure of the dream as a whole and to confront the dreamer with it in such a way as to facilitate successfully defensive or integrative solutions in real life, depending on the therapeutic goal of the moment. Interpretation of dream symbols may combine any of three modes of analysis: (1) direct symbol translation, which assumes that certain objects have almost universal symbolic meanings; (2) functional analysis, in which the analyst takes into account the ordinary function of the object which was used as a symbol and inquires into how this function may relate to the focal problem with which the dream is struggling; and (3) literal interpretation, in which the analyst tries to account in literal detail for the manifest text of the dream, including its symbolism, in reconstructing the historical background.

As to interpretive procedure, French employs Freud's free association method but relies much more heavily than did Freud on intuition and "empathic imagination" in making inferences concerning the latent content or, for French, the "cognitive structure." In this, French's approach is much like Lowy's. However, French's concept of the dream's cognitive structure enables him to make a much more disciplined use of intuition in the interpretive process, since there are clear criteria by which to judge the validity of this or that intuitive lead. Every interpretation must contribute to the intelligible fitting together of the dream's multiple references to distinctive themes in the past. Every interpretation must also fit the resulting configuration relevantly into the dreamer's present emotional situation.

French prefers to work with dream series; however, his directives are sufficiently ordered and specific to allow us to illustrate his approach in reference to the highway dream. In scanning the associations to the dream, we are led intuitively to the conclusion that the focal conflict is only implicitly represented. There is mention of mixed feelings concerning those I am leaving behind but what comes very explicitly to my mind now is a luncheon conversation I had had several weeks prior to the dream with a dear and highly respected older friend and colleague. This conversation still lingered in my thoughts at the time of the dream. My friend had made no secret of her personal chagrin at the prospect of my departure, but she was mostly at pains to be reassured that my decision was in my own best interests. Leaning on her intimate and long standing knowledge of my personal strengths and weaknesses, she proceeded to ask a number of pointed questions regarding my motives, which, although leaving the courage of my convictions intact, exposed a number of inconsistencies which I was unable to explain. For myself, I was content that there should be such inconsistencies, as I had never doubted my decision stemmed from other than logical considerations. But I was unnerved to think she might interpret the inconsistencies to mean I was withholding pertinent information.

The questions on which my thoughts had lingered after this conversation were as follows: (1) Since my friend's probings had been not only personally informed but clinically astute, was my decision a mature one? (2) Had I, in fact, been withholding pertinent aspects of my motives? The point of convergence of these two questions I shall consider the dream's focal conflict. The moral issues implicit in the previously recorded associations concerning my childhood explorations under the backyard bush will qualify as historical background to the first question, as will the ruminations on the infrequent but regular role that impulsiveness had played in my life. Similarly, previously recorded concerns over withholding and separation in respect to my grandfather will qualify as historical background to the second question.

We may infer from direct translation of the long freight car-truck symbol, of the symbols of darting into a space between, of plunging through a hoop-like encirclement, and of shooting flames that traumatic and reassuring memories concerning phallic adventures have converged on the focal conflict. Further, we may infer by functional analysis of the entire highway motif that a variety of problems and solutions involving mobility and transition gravitate around this point of convergence between the focal conflict and its psychosexual antecedents. Thus, the outlines of the dream's cognitive structure begin to emerge, in which a network of past and present problems are indeed apparently being confronted by way of a network of analogous problems and solutions.

As for the defensive and integrative qualities of this cognitive structure, consider the shift which links the dream's two major episodes. The central action in both episodes is one of phallic intrusiveness. However, the first episode takes place in respect to a familiar situation and the mood is one of concentration and concern, whereas the second episode takes place in respect to a mysterious object (the hoop-like circle of branches in the distance) a "literal analysis" of which suggests a playful, even cavalier attitude. We may infer from this that the degree of reality-oriented ego strength which was brought to bear on the focal conflict by memories of skill in passing trucks was not sufficient to resolve the pressures of the focal conflict, thus requiring regression to the symbolism of jumping through a hoop. As to the respective defensive and integrative qualities of this regression, I think we would have to declare this a moot question at the time this dream was dreamt.

MONTAGUE ULLMAN

The first dream theorist to take account of the Aserinsky-Kleitman discovery, which suggested the relation of dreaming to the REM phase of the sleep cycle, was Montague Ullman. Ullman concluded from the earliest laboratory findings described in Chapter Three that the REM period is a state of partial arousal brought about recurrently through the night as a result of physiological factors impinging upon and influencing the threshold of the reticular activating system. It followed, according to Ullman, that

> To understand the formal characteristics of the dream—the concrete sensory quality, the hallucinatory aspect—it becomes important to remember: at the time the dream is occurring the brain is in a state of partial arousal in response to the initial corticopetal impulses mediated through the reticular activating system; and its efferent system is oriented not to somatic efferents mediating activity in the external world, but to corticofugal efferents to the reticular system influencing the threshold in that system. The cortex in this sense becomes another source of afferent stimuli feeding into the reticular system, along with all the other afferent stimuli impinging upon this system. It is in conjunction with this mode of functioning, namely, where the cortex provides a source of afferent stimuli, afferent to the reticular activating system, that the formal characteristics of the dream assume an afferent or sensory quality (237, p. 19).

By an incisive deduction from this position Ullman advanced the hypothesis that the function of dreaming is not to preserve sleep but to maintain an optimal state of vigilance.*

The significance of dreaming is related to the general adaptive significance of the cyclic variations in depth of sleep during the sleeping

---

* Ullman may thus be seen to have anticipated Snyder's evolutionary theory of dreaming before the bulk of phylogenetic evidence, on which Snyder bases his theory, was available.

phase of the sleep-wakefulness cycle. The dream is essentially bi-directional: It may be oriented toward bringing about full arousal, or play a role in the return to sleep (237, p. 20).

Ullman's views on dream interpretation follow consistently from these views on the significance of dreaming:

> The content of dreams can best be viewed as a dialectical unity in which new perceptions leading to new levels of self-revelation are struggling to gain expression in an area where outmoded techniques of self-deception are beginning to weaken and crumble.
>
> The remarkable feature of the dream content lies in the dreamer's ability to express in symbolic or metaphorical terms the connection between a present problem and aspects of the past experience related to the problem and culled from all levels of the longitudinal history of the individual. The dream states more about the problem and the healthy and defensive reactions evoked by it than is immediately accessible to waking consciousness.
>
> To understand this aspect of dream consciousness two things have to be borne in mind. During these states of partial arousal the individual may experience affects which are disturbing enough to warrant full arousal. If this be so, then a certain sequence of events must follow involving the recticular system and the cortex. The interplay of impulses between the former and the latter produces a qualitative transformation in the level of consciousness, and waking consciousness is reinstituted. This change involves a far greater transformation in the level of awareness than ever occurs in the waking state in response to a distressing or threatening stimulus.
>
> The second point is a derivative from this. To achieve this drastic change in consciousness the individual has to state, usually in visual terms, much more about a problem area, its genetic roots, and the implications for his entire defensive structure than he is ever called upon to do in the waking state. Hence deeper truths are revealed concerning one's personality than are immediately accessible in the waking state (237, pp. 19-20).

Ullman concludes from his assumptions about the nature of dreams and dreaming, and it should not be overlooked that these were the first such assumptions to be derived from both clinical and experimental evidence, that dream interpretation is best guided by the view that the unique quality of dream content is its capacity for revelation rather than concealment:

> The affective overtones of the dream are direct, though often subtle, clues to the objective truths involved in the problematic situation. If

anything, self-deception is more difficult to effect in a dream than in waking life. This is so because the individual has to explain in depth— that is, in a more complete and historically or genetically integrated fashion—the nature of the threat or upset that besets him (237, p. 24).

I am quite sure that Ullman would accept the interpretations of the highway dream which we proposed in illustration of French's focal conflict approach as illustrative as well as his own "revelational" approach, although he would no doubt insist on some alterations in terminology. There is, however, an additional interpretation of this dream which has not previously been brought to light, which I believe to be valid, and which occurred to me as I sought to invoke Ullman's perspective. This pertains to the objective fact that I was alone in the dream. The other people involved were either transients, enclosed like myself in their own vehicles, or were persons who were merely to be noted in passing. Indeed, now that I reflect upon it, the pervasive affective overtone of the dream was one of vague loneliness. I may infer from this observation that one of the self-revelations which was struggling to gain expression in this dream pertained to a tendency toward isolation, toward an avoidance of intimate and lasting personal relationships. In other words, what the dream, from its wider and deeper points of view, may have been noticing is that despite my increasing confidence and agility in handling situations in which there is the possibility of harm to myself and others, I am not even confronting situations in which there is the possibility of lasting closeness between myself and others.

ERIK ERIKSON

All of the dream theories described to this point were formulated either in reaction to or independently of Freud's theory. Erik Erikson's contributions are therefore all the more notable for having been conceived from within the orthodox Freudian fame. In their extensions of Freudian principles and methods, however, Erikson's contributions to dream theory are both stimulating and strikingly original. For example, Erikson was the first traditional psychoanalyst to rescue the manifest dream from the scientific and clinical attic to which several generations of institutional seminars on dream interpretation had unthinkingly consigned it.

> The psychoanalyst, in looking at the surface of a mental phenomenon, often has to overcome a certain shyness. So many in his field mistake attention to surface for superficiality, and a concern with form for lack of depth. But the fact that we have followed Freud into depths which our eyes had to become accustomed to does not permit us, today, to blink when we look at things in broad daylight. Like good surveyors we must be at home on the geological surface as well as in the descending shafts. . . . Unofficially, we often interpret dreams entirely or in parts on the basis of their manifest appearance. Occasionally, we hurry at every confrontation with a dream to crack its manifest appearance as if it were a useless shell and to hasten to discard this shell in favor of what seems to be the more worthwhile core. When such a method corresponded to a new orientation, it was essential for research as well as for therapy; but as a compulsive habituation, it has since hindered a full meeting of Ego Psychology and the problems of dream life (42, pp. 139-40).

In a conceptual vein running parallel to that first struck by Adler, although far more richly mined, Erikson proceeded to draw attention to the manifest dream's distinctive reflectiveness of the dreamer's life-style:

> In addition to a dream's striving for *representability,* then, we would postulate a *style of representation* which is by no means a mere shell to a kernel, the latent dream; in fact, it is a reflection of the individual ego's peculiar time-space, the frame of reference for all its defenses, compromises, and achievements (42, p. 143).

Not content to permit the concept of the "ego's peculiar time-space" to recommend itself merely by its felicitous phraseology Erikson provided an outline for its systematic analysis, both latitudinal and longitudinal, which has yet to be employed in dream research as much as it deserves.

Chart 1. Outline of Dream Analysis

I. Manifest Configurations
    Verbal
        general linguistic quality
        spoken words and word play

Sensory
  general sensory quality, range and intensity
  specific sensory focus

Spatial
  general quality of extension
  dominant vectors

Temporal
  general quality of succession
  time-perspective

Somatic
  general quality of body feeling
  body zones
  organ modes

Interpersonal
  general social grouping
  changing social vectors
  "object relations"
  points of identification

Affective
  quality of affective atmosphere
  inventory and range of affects
  points of change of affect

Summary
  correlation of configurational trends

II. Links Between Manifest and Latent Dream Material

Associations

Symbols

III. Analysis of Latent Dream Material

Acute sleep-disturbing stimulus

Delayed stimulus (day residue)

Acute life conflicts

Dominant transference conflict

Repetitive conflicts

Associated basic childhood conflict

Common denominators
  "wishes," drives, needs
  methods of defense, denial, and distortion

IV.   Reconstruction

Life cycle
present phase
corresponding infantile phase
defect, accident, or affliction
psychosexual fixation
psychosexual arrest

Social process: collective identity
ideal prototypes
evil prototypes
opportunities and barriers

Ego identity and lifeplan
mechanisms of defense
mechanisms of integration

(42, pp. 144-45)

Two of the dimensions specified in this outline, *psychosexual fixation* and *psychosexual arrest,* merit particular attention in that they imply much of what French referred to as the dream's "cognitive structure." Erikson elaborates these concepts:

> In our general clinical usage we employ the term fixation alternately for that infantile stage in which an individual received the relatively greatest amount of gratification and to which, therefore, his secret wishes persistently return and for that infantile stage of development beyond which he is unable to proceed because it marked an end or determined slow-up of his psychosexual maturation. I would prefer to call the latter the point of *arrest,* for it seems to me that an individual's psychosexual character and proneness for disturbances depends not so much on the point of fixation as on the *range* between the point of the fixation and the point of arrest, and on the *quality* of their interplay. It stands to reason that a fixation on the oral stage, for example, endangers an individual most if he is also arrested close to this stage, while a relative oral fixation can become an asset if the individual advances a considerable length along the path of psychosexual maturation, making the most of each step and cultivating (on the very basis of a very favorable balance of basic trust over basic mistrust as derived from an intensive oral stage) a certain capacity to experience and to exploit subsequent crises to the full. Another individual with a similar range but a different quality of progression may, for the longest time, show no specific fixation on orality; he may indicate a reasonable

balance of a moderate amount of all the varieties of psychosexual energy—yet, the quality of the whole ensemble may be so brittle that a major shock can make it tumble to the ground, whereupon an "oral" fixation may be blamed for it. Thus, one could review our nosology from the point of view of the particular field circumscribed by the points of fixation and arrest and of the properties of that field. At any rate, in a dream, and especially in a series of dreams, the patient's "going back and forth" between the two points can be determined rather clearly. Our outline, therefore, differentiates between a point of psychosexual fixation and one of psychosexual arrest (42, pp. 167-68).

In the paper from which these quotations were taken Erikson illustrates the manifold utilities of his approach by using it to amplify none other than Freud's interpretation of his own "Irma" dream, the date of which, the reader may recall, was the one mentioned in Freud's letter to Fliess, in which he indulged the fantasy that his summer home might one day be adorned with a tablet bearing the inscription "in this house on July 24, 1895, the Mystery of the Dream unveiled itself to Dr. Sigm. Freud." Erikson's rationale for choosing this particular dream as his "specimen" reveals his preference for an epigenetic rather than a merely genetic point of view.

Such autobiographic emphasis . . . supports our contention that this dream may reveal more than the basic fact of a disguised wish-fulfillment derived from infantile sources; that this dream may, in fact, carry the historical burden of being dreamed in order to be analyzed, and analyzed in order to fulfill a very special fate (42, p. 133).

There is space here neither to review the enhanced stature and warmth with which Freud comes to life again in Erikson's careful and loving re-examination of the Irma dream, nor to represent Erikson's quite singular technical virtuosities as a clinical interpreter of dreams. For these pleasures, the reader must go to the body of the text. For our purpose here we quote only its conclusion:

The Irma dream documents a crisis, during which a medical investigator's identity loses and regains its "conflict-free status". . . .
    It illustrates how the latent infantile wish that provided the energy for the renewed conflict, and thus for the dream, is embedded in a manifest dream structure which on every level reflects significant trends

of the dreamer's total situation. Dreams, then, not only fulfill naked wishes of sexual license, of unlimited dominance and of unrestricted destructiveness; where they work, they also lift the dreamer's isolation, appease his conscience, and preserve his identity, each in specific and instructive ways (42, p. 170).

After publication of this paper Erikson's interests drew him away from interpretations of autobiographical dreams toward interpretations of autobiographies, and it now appears that dream psychology must be content with this one major contribution. However, in an earlier monograph, in which I sought to adapt Erikson's interpretive method for service in research pertaining to the process of dreaming, I described an extension of Erikson's approach. Of this, more in Chapter Nine.

MEDARD BOSS

Medard Boss introduces his major work with this oft-quoted statement by Chwang-Tse:

> Once upon a time, I, Chwang-Tse, dreamed I was a butterfly, fluttering hither and thither, to all intents and purposes a butterfly. I was aware only of following my fancy as a butterfly and unconscious of my human individuality. Suddenly, I awoke, and there I lay, myself again. Now I do not know whether I was then a man dreaming I was a butterfly or whether I am now a butterfly dreaming I am a man (18, p. 11).

He then takes the position that to ask this question seriously is to run the risk of diluting one's capacity fully to appreciate one's dreams. For Boss, we exist no less in dreams than we do in waking life. Thus, he is concerned with *experiencing* dreams to the exclusion of either studying them or interpreting them. His argument seems to be not with any particular scientific approach to dreams but with the scientific approach itself.

All approaches to the scientific study of dreams, whatever their theoretical differences, would have to agree that any scientific knowledge of dreams is dependent on two successive phases of observation in the waking state, both of which submit to varying degrees of accuracy and reliability: (1) the retrospective observation of the dream by the dreamer, and (2) the observation of the dream report by the investigator. Boss holds that we "outrage" a dream if we try to do more than participate in it, and that we reduce such participation to the extent of any effort to observe the dream on either of these levels. Rather, he advises that we should not try to view a dream as representational or symbolic at all.

If, then, we should hold Boss to the requirements of logical thinking, it is difficult to see how we could avoid attributing to his position the suggestion that to truly understand a dream one should stay asleep. In practice, however, Boss does observe dreams from the standpoint of the waking state and he does interpret them.

For instance, a twenty-five year old student related the following dream: I am in a former home with my governess who acted as my mother. I can see a stream flowing round and round in our garden. By merely exerting all my will power, and without any physical actions on my part, I managed to lead the stream out of its old bed and so to bend its course that it can flow away from the garden. I had to exert my will to the utmost and constantly. As soon as I stopped willing, the stream tries to return to its old bed.

This was a dream of a young man who had been suffering from increasing neurasthenia over many years. Although he looked the picture of health and possessed great will power, yet even the smallest physical or mental exertion produced such fatigue that insomnia, colitis and exhaustion appeared with great intensity. In spite of his more than average intelligence he was therefore forced to postpone taking his long overdue University examination.

This brought the extremely ambitious patient close to despair and suicide. However, shortly after the dream had revealed his real state to him, he managed to pass his examinations with distinction and without any special effort. The dream had been able to teach him, and he was struck by it as if by lightning, that he had been utterly and completely arrested in his childhood stage of life and that he was always going around in circles. He saw that all his energy had been consumed by his incessant attempts to oppose the pull of these infantile life attitudes and to direct the current of his energy towards the outer world. So he had no strength left for acting and thinking in the world at large. . . .

This dream could easily have misled us into an interpretation on the objective level, in which the circular stream enclosing the dreamer would have become the "symbol" of the mother's womb. Just as easily, it could have lent itself to an interpretation on the subjective level which would have contended that the inner psychological stagnation of the dreamer had here been projected into the "symbol" of the unalterable path of the stream coursing around the parental garden guarded by the governess. . . .

In reality, the dream phenomenon itself neither justifies the assumption of any symbolization of an external object nor that of a projection of subjective inner conditions nor yet of an expression or a reflection of an existential direction. It rather discloses to us no more than the fact that the patient's whole dream existence was one of stern resolve to lead the river out of its usual circular path. His entire existence was nothing more than this special relationship towards the dream thing. In the light of his infantile disposition, this world could show itself as a world stamped by no other dream thing than the parental home and the governess. From this resolute endeavor to make the river flow along a straight path, he could understand his own debilitating striving towards progress in life. Since, however, his efforts were only of a volitional, ambitious and overcompensating nature, they were bound to be wrecked on the rocks of his fundamental childishness (18, pp. 129-30).

What Boss seems to be attempting to do here is raise a clinical truism to the stature of a theory of dreams. Every therapist knows that before any kind of dream interpretation can be therapeutically effective the dreamer must first experience the dream in such a way as to lead to his accepting responsibility for it. Without this essential existential prerequisite any interpretation will be understood as either arbitrary, irrelevant, or unimportant. Boss's contribution to the arts and disciplines of dream interpretation, therefore, may be seen to consist primarily of his lengthy dwellings on the existential elements of Jung's and Lowy's contributions. The singularity of his concentration on these elements, however, does draw particular attention to two observations to which we shall return when we re-address the theory of dreaming: (1) the hyperconsciousness of the dream experience, and (2) the communication values of remembered dreams.

From Boss's point of view I must of course be presumed incapable of appreciating the highway dream's true essence, because I have by this time imposed upon it so many subjective and objective interpretations. I deny this, but let it be.

SUMMARY

This concludes our review of the approaches to dream interpretation that have been developed since Freud. The reader may question why it is that such well regarded writings as those of Maeder, Stekel, Horney, Sullivan, Fromm, Binswanger, and Bonime were not included. To this question let it first be said that the reader who is primarily interested in dreams and dream interpretation should by all means consult the works of these authors, for they do include many noteworthy and distinctive interpretational nuances which have not been covered here. Let it then be re-emphasized that our primary focus throughout this book is on dreaming, not on dreams. And, from the point of view of the psychology of dreaming, it may, I think, be safely said that no significant heuristic leads have been overlooked. Which is to say, in brief, that in this writer's judgment French has incorporated Maeder; Lowy has included Stekel; Ullman has improved on Horney and Sullivan; Hall has incorporated Fromm; Boss has covered Binswanger; and Bonime has brought to a high clinical polish the roughly presented suppositions of Lowy.

NEW
Chapter Six THEORETICAL
FRAMES

We noted in Chapter Two that in formulating his theory of dreaming Freud's particular observations, interpretations, and intuitions were constantly under the general influence of his abiding commitments to an instinctivist position. All forms of human behavior were assumed to stem, ultimately, from the motivating forces of human instincts. Moreover, these forces were assumed to be ultimately reducible to physical energies, and distributions of physical energies, awaiting only the development of proper instrumentation to reveal themselves as substantive and measurable. It was these two assumptions which distressed Freud's followers and led to the various cleavages within the psychoanalytic movement.

Finding both of these assumptions to be obstructive in the study of historical and social influences on human behavior, the neo-Freudian revisionists (Jung, Adler, Fromm, Horney, Sullivan) dismissed them both out of hand, although they proceeded to build their various socio-cultural theories of motivation on Freud's developmental, topographic, and structural assumptions. Recognizing the same obstructive consequences of Freud's dynamic and economic assumptions, as they have come to be called, a loyalist group of "ego psychologists," led by Hartmann and Rapaport, sought to elaborate and refine Freud's instinct and psychic energy concepts so as to render them compatible with the study of historical and social determinants. This they did primarily by way of such concepts as "neutralized energy," "desexualized libido," and the "conflict-free ego sphere." Each of these offspring schools of thought remains viable today in that sizable numbers of clinicians and theoreticians continue to order their observations and thoughts within their respective frames of reference. I think it is safe to say, however, that there are no signs of either school seeking a rapprochement with the other, from which we may conclude that each has managed to take a position which is in some ways unalterably removed from reality.

A third school of psychoanalytic thought, as yet unnamed, has begun to show a way around this impasse. This school of thought, traceable to the independent works of Kardiner and Polanyi, finds its initial impetus in the observation that neither the revisionist nor the loyalist position has commended itself to the scientific community by virtue of supporting an evolving pattern of empirical research. This third position, most recently and articulately stated by Holt, Klein, and Rubenstein, is that Freud's dynamic assumptions, which give "drives" a central role in the determination of human behavior, are tenable because they generate hypotheses that are conceivably subject to empirical treatment, but that his economic assumptions concerning the energic substance of the drives are untenable because they cannot generate hypotheses that are subject to empirical treatment.

We shall subscribe to this position and for that reason will describe it in some detail. Let it immediately be noted that the source materials at hand for this purpose, namely the works of Kardiner, Karush, and Ovesey, of Rubenstein, of Holt, and of Klein, are not of one harmonious mind in respect to all of the origins of the dilemma or in respect to all of the implications of their solution to it. However, they do all agree on the solution as broadly stated above. Klein's statement is, in this writer's opinion, the clearest.

GEORGE KLEIN

Klein begins by asking us to consider that psychoanalysis is unique among psychological theories in consisting of two kinds of theory: a clinical theory, based on evidence and inference; and a metapsychological theory, based on hypothetical premises and deductions therefrom. The clinical theory had its beginnings in Freud's attempts to find meanings in behaviors previously believed to be meaningless such as dreams, slips of the tongue, jokes, and symptoms, and has left a rich heritage of principles and points of view for ordering observations of all kinds of human behavior. The metapsychology had its beginnings in Freud's ambition to translate his clinical findings into terms of a quasi-thermodynamic system of energy distributions and has left a spurious debt to Newton which, if we insist on continuing to pay it, threatens to cut us off from the true wealth of psychoanalysis. Moreover, so much did Freud's scientific training in the Bruecke-Meynert laboratory lead him to value the metapsychology over the clinical theory that it has become tacit in the training of psychoanalysts to view the metapsychology as *the* theory, and the clinical theory as only an approximation thereto. This is a serious error of judgment, in Klein's view, and made all the more difficult to correct by its tacitness. On the contrary, says Klein, it is the metapsychology which cannot pass muster as a scientific theory, since it seeks merely to explain another theory:

> The existence of the two theories—the two cultures of psychoanalysis—is, I believe, a historical aberration traceable to Freud's philosophy of science—(1) that concepts of purposefulness and meaning are unacceptable as terms of *scientific* explanation; (2) that an acceptable *explanation* must be purged of teleological implications; (3) that ultimately, the regularities described with purposivistic concepts will be *explainable* through the use of purely physiological models which disclose the causes of which the purposive principle is simply a descriptive expression (147, p. 4).

It is true that Freud discarded and never returned to his "Project for a Scientific Psychology," in which his adherence to this philosophy of science was most obvious. But his reason for discarding the "Project" was not that he wavered in his conviction that an adequate psychology must be neurophysiologically grounded. Rather, he believed only that the "right" neurophysiological model would not come to light during his lifetime:

> I have no inclination at all to keep the domain of the psychological floating, as it were, in the air without any organic foundation. But I

have no knowledge, neither theoretical nor therapeutic, beyond that conviction so that I have to conduct myself as if I had only the psychological before me (147, pp. 5-6).

However, having done his best by the psychological before him, as, for example, in the momentous first six chapters of *The Interpretation of Dreams,* Freud felt impelled to do what he could by way of marking out a path for the guidance of his followers, who might live to see the day when the "right" neurophysiological model would be available. These markings took the form of his discussions, in Chapter Seven, of energies, forces, cathexes, systems, layers, mechanisms, and physical analogies, by which he tried to provide a potential explanatory frame of reference within which to consider the meanings of dreams "more scientifically."

> The explanatory language was a new one. It was designed to tell how the mind functioned in impersonal terms and *without employing the language of purpose.* The latter being the phenomena that were to be explained. This was the birth of the so-called economic point of view. Thus, the economic point of view was Freud's substitute for the neurophysiological model of the Project. Its terms were different, but its intent was the same—to provide a non-teleological, causal account of the phenomena of purposefulness and intention as these reveal themselves in the psychoanalytic situation. The assumptions belong to the general outlook of materialism which was that phenomena are to be understood, and ultimately explained, in terms of their physical-chemical nature (147, pp. 6-7).

Notwithstanding that Freud's effort in this regard was a marvelous act of creation, Klein argues that it was his most misleading achievement. *Not,* and this is the heart of the argument, because it was inadequate, but because it was irrelevant. It was irrelevant because the clinical theory is sufficient in itself, fully capable of directing the course of psychoanalysis as a science, and not in need of another theory to explain itself:

> The essential *clinical* propositions concerning motivation have nothing to do with reducing a hypothetical tension; they are inferences of *directional* gradients in behavior, and of the *object-relations* involved in these directions; they describe relationships needed and sought after, consciously and unconsciously, how they are lived out and how they are fulfilled through perceptual encounters, conception, symbol, and action. The key factors in the psychoanalytic clinical view of

motivation are relational requirements, encounters, crises, dilemmas, resolutions, and achievements—not a hypothetical "tension" reduction. . . . In short, the metapsychology is neither distinctively human, nor distinctively psychoanalytic. It is, moreover, a reduction to a conceptual domain which requires a different kind of observational datum than is available in the analytic situation. What neurophysiologist studies his "datum" by talking to it, as is the case in the psychoanalytic situation? It leaves at the wayside the fundamental intent of the psychoanalytic enterprise—that of *unlocking meanings*. Terms like cathexis, hyper-cathexis, bound-cathexis are drained of psychological meaning, and belong in a different universe than psychoanalytic psychology (147, pp. 10-11).

What does psychoanalytic theory look like when disabused of its Newtonian conscience? This view is revealed by highlighting the two characteristics which distinguish the clinical theory of psychoanalysis from other theories of human behavior. First:

Psychoanalysis . . . attempts to specify coherences in behavior in terms of *intention*. Not purposes solely on the level of conscious intent, but purposes arising out of the dynamics of aborted wish, conflict, defense, anxiety, guilt and unconscious fantasy. When a psychoanalyst sees a pattern of behavior taking on the meaning of a "defense," for example, he is stating the significance of a pattern of behavior—a statement about its purpose or intentionality. The regularities to which an analyst becomes sensitized are unique in that they have distinctively to do with intentionality—aims frustrated, conflicted, aborted, regressive, defended against . . . they [also] have to do with trends in the development and changes of purpose and intention over the course of a person's life—conceptions of *crisis, conflict, defense*, and *modes of resolution*, which determine the evolution of purposes in behavior. These concepts include among others: ego development, psychosexual development, repression, consciousness-unconsciousness, transference, identification, conflict, defense, drive, fantasy. All are crucial in different ways in pointing to units or coherences of behavior that would otherwise not be noticed without such concepts . . . (147, pp. 16-19).

Second:

. . . Psychoanalysis is a psychology of the *meanings and syntheses arising out of crises in an individual's lifetime*. Freud's central contribution was not merely the discovery of sexuality or aggressive determinants of behavior, though these were also fundamental. It was that of understanding behavior as *syntheses* which evolve from *conflict*—as modes of *resolution of conflict*. . . . The key, then, to the profundity of Freud's insights is the effort to look at life as a problem solving venture, involving a constant adjudication of incompatible polarities, actual or fantasied, in which structures are the products of a synthesis of opposing tendencies, with symptoms viewed as solutions carried to pathological extremes (147, pp. 19-21).

In these lights psychoanalysis emerges as a theory uniquely equipped to explain the *why* of behavior and not the *how*—its purposes, and not its causes. As for whether this qualifies psychoanalysis as a science, Klein rests his case on these assertions, drawn from Polanyi's contributions to the philosophy of science:

1. An intention and a function are as directly observable, no less specifiable, than a neurological discharge and, in that sense, just as "real."
2. A statement of function or intention is as adequate a basis for explanation as a neurophysiological one.
3. Meaning, purpose, intentionality—unconscious and conscious— define principles of regularity that are translatable to, but not reducible to, physiological and neurophysiological specifications (147, p. 22).

Since so much of our concern in this book is with the increased possibilities of cooperative effort between psychologists and physiologists, made possible in the study of dreams and dreaming by advances in electronic technology, we shall do well to consider the special emphasis which Klein places on the third of these assertions:

It is not simply that we do not have the data in the psychoanalytic situation for a physiological conception of psychoanalytic facts; I would suggest further that no such data would ever substitute for the constructs of personal meaning which constitute psychoanalytic psychology, the latter being of an entirely different level of *perceived order*, involving different units of analysis. These cannot be known from or deduced from principles of physics and chemistry or of mechanical, attentional or physiological models, and therefore, it is of secondary, not primary, importance for psychoanalysts to concern themselves with translations to physiological models of explanation (147, pp. 22-23).

ROBERT WHITE

An alternative strategy for resolving the dilemma posed by the economic point of view in psychoanalytic theory is that of Robert White, as described in his "Ego and Reality in Psychoanalytic Theory" (247). White's concern is with the demonstrated weakness of psychoanalysis in dealing with questions of normal learning. He traces this weakness not to the concepts of instinct or psychic energy but to Freud's insistence that instinctual energy is the *sole* mover of human behavior. "How," White asks, "does a creature of instinct come to recognize that the world is there all the time whether he likes it or not, and that it follows laws of its own whether he likes them or not?" (247, p. 54). It was in response to this order of question that Hartmann and Rapaport sought to refine the economic point of view by proposing that when motives did not behave in the peremptory and periodic ways of the instincts they were powered by "neutralized" energy. Thus, friendly behaviors, which carried no hint of sexual elements, could be conceived as motivated by desexualized libido; and assertive behaviors, which carried no hint of aggressive elements, could be conceived as motivated by energies which have become neutralized by a process of "deaggressivization." With Kardiner, White sees these and similar attempts as little more than semantic devices, which, in substituting one descriptive terminology for another, can only encourage circular reasoning and could not in any event add anything to our understanding of friendliness or assertiveness. However, White's strategy is not to discard energic considerations from psychoanalytic theory but to add to them in order to take account of adaptive behaviors such as exploration, manipulation, locomotion, language, and the development of plans and intentions, which are awkwardly perceived as seeking the reduction of sexual or aggressive tensions:

> On the face of it, the adaptive processes . . . do not press toward erotic or destructive instinctual aims. Some theorists have thought that this discrepancy was only a matter of appearance. If one stretched the definitions of the two instincts sufficiently, and if one made generous allowance for unconscious and symbolic forms of gratification, perhaps all behavior could be brought under the twin scepters of Eros and Thanatos. Such a view was found wanting by Freud himself, who amended it by postulating a process whereby libido could be desexua-

lized and thus made freely available for the neutral aims of the ego. This hypothesis, expanded by Hartmann and his associates to include the neutralization of both kinds of instinctual-drive energy, provides the ego with its own allowance, so to speak, but reminds us that this came from the pockets of the parent instincts (247, pp. 183-84).

White agrees with Hartmann that the energies which support adaptive behavior must be neutral with respect to instinctual aims, but he does not agree that neutral energy is a transformation of instinctual energy. Rather, he proposes that most adaptive behaviors are motivated by a separate and independent form of "ego energy" which he calls "effectance." Effectance differs from instinctual energy in that it has its origins in the central nervous system itself, rather than in appetitive body tissues; seeks its own maintenance (and sometimes increase), rather than its own discharge; and seeks alterations not in internal organic states but in the environment:

> The playful, exploratory and manipulative activities of children provide the basis for a theory of independent ego energies. Examining them closely, we can see that more is involved than a random overflow of activity. It is noticeable in young children—indeed even in young animals—that attention is given longest to objects upon which it is possible to have large effects. Studies of preferences show that the most interesting objects are the ones with which the most can be done. Even when an external stimulus obviously starts the transaction, the response tends to have the character of a series of varied actions producing whatever effects are possible. . . . It is proposed here to refer to the energy behind such behavior as *effectance,* and to the affect that attends it as the *feeling of efficacy.* Effectance thus refers to the active tendency to put forth effort to influence the environment, while feeling of efficacy refers to the satisfaction that comes with producing effects.
>
> Independent ego energies and their satisfactions are conceived to be just as basic as the instincts. They are not, however, related to particular somatic sources or to consummatory patterns of discharge. Conceivably they can be equated with the inherent energy of the nervous system. But their significance for development lies in their direct relation to the formation of psychic structure. Effectance is a prompting to explore the properties of the environment; it leads to an accumulating knowledge of what can and cannot be done with the environment; its biological significance lies in this very property of developing *competence.* Instinctual energies, of course, likewise pro-

duce action, effects, and knowledge of the environment, thus making a contribution to competence. But their contribution is necessarily narrower than that of neutral energies which stand ever ready to promote exploration for its own sake. It will be noted that this conception of independent ego energies tends to reduce the sharp metaphorical distinction between energy and structure. If we conceive of structure as competence, we are giving it the dynamic character of patterns of readiness for future action (247, pp. 185-86).

White is careful to ascribe additive rather than replacement functions to h:s concept of effectance motivation. In a showdown, it is the drives that do the replacing. By definition, however, such showdowns must be periodic:

When instinctual drives are aroused, the activity of the nervous system—the "ego apparatus"—is directed toward instinctual aims. Only when drives are quiet does the system operate in the pure service of feelings of efficacy, and with the breadth and non-specificity that is most conducive to the growth of varied competencies (247, p. 85).

This is not the place to scrutinize the respective merits of the Kardiner-Holt-Klein and White solutions to the energy problem in psychoanalysis. Each, for our purposes, has the merit of questioning the value of explanations which only satisfy the criterion of showing how they can specify the process of tension reduction. Klein's solution has the special merit of giving focus to human intentionality. White's solution has the special merit of giving focus to a gradient of human intentionality which may be crucial to understanding the function of dreaming, as Hall has already anticipated: Man's inclination to affect and to change his environment. Whether we dispense with the hypothetical concept of psychic energy altogether, or whether we choose, with White, to assume two kinds of psychic energy, with different origins and aims and functioning according to different principles, is a matter of no immediate concern to the psychology of dreaming. What is germane to our interests is the implication of both these solutions that we may seek to explain the phenomena of dreaming by discovering its psychological functions without necessarily defining its neurophysiological causes.

TOWARD
Chapter Seven # A NEW THEORY OF DREAMING

The new stores of information and more refined perspectives which have been reviewed and discussed in Chapters Three through Six suggest it would be timely to take a long second look at the psychoanalytic theory of dreaming, as presented in Chapter Two and, where indicated, to propose modifications of this theory. Toward these objectives I should like, first, to propose a basic and very general re-centering assumptive proposition about the nature of dreaming, which, it seems to me, follows from the post-Freudian lines of advancing knowledge that have been traced above. Then, I shall ask the reader to consider certain modifications of the extant theory's major conceptual components—wish-fulfill-ment, dream-work, day residue, and the roles of preconscious and conscious symbolization—which seem to me to be suggested by this proposition and by the theoretical and empirical considerations that prompted it.

The proposition is: Dreaming is the augmentative *response* of the *human* psyche to the distinctive neurophysiological conditions of the mammalian D-state.

The primary advantages of this view are four in number: (1) It leaves conceptual space for assigning psychological functions to the D-state, over and above its neurophysiological functions, by presum-ing that whatever psychological functions dreaming may serve have been exploitive of more fundamental organismic conditions characteristic of the species, much as, as previously noted, the functions of human speech have exploited the arrangements for respiration and ingestion characteristic of the higher primates. (2) It skirts the question of whether other mammals dream, which, although interesting, need not preoccupy us. (3) It yields to the weight of evidence which suggests that neurophysiological factors are primary in the governance of the sleep cycle while permitting speculation that, as regards dreaming, relations of mutual facilitation may obtain between neurophysiological and psychological processes. (4) It shifts the burden of the theory's proof from questions of psychological causation, which are rendered passé if the D-state is in any event not primarily governed by psychological processes, to questions of psychological *organization*.

WISH-FULFILLMENT

Suppose we were to accept Klein's argument, as reviewed in the previous chapter, that Freud's preoccupation with Newtonian notions of energy distributions had all along misled him, i.e., that the economic point of view in general psychoanalytic theory was all along superfluous. It would follow in the theory of dreaming that the wish-fulfillment hypothesis, as originally formulated, would need to be reconsidered. What, for example, would our position be in respect to the support Freud drew for the wish-fulfillment hypothesis by way of extrapolation from interpreted dreams? Actually, as we noted earlier, this support was not as extensive as it can appear to have been when we allow ourselves to confuse Freud's investigations of dreaming with his interpretations of dreams. But there was support from this quarter for associating repressed infantile wish-fulfillment with the process of dreaming, and it was impressive. How are we to accommodate our present view to this evidence? I suggest that this is best done by assigning to wish-fulfillment in dream formation the status of *consequence* rather than *cause*.

The ubiquity of the D-state makes it more credible that it introduces conditions conducive to the excitation of unconscious wishes than that the excitation of unconscious wishes introduces conditions that trigger the D-state. In other words, it is more credible that the ego takes advantage of the D-state to further its several purposes than that the id takes advantage of the "sleeping ego's preconscious wish to sleep" for the single purpose of achieving partial discharge of repressed psychic energy. It may be that the D-state affords the ego special opportunities for promoting the interests of the id, but the present view assumes the ego to avail itself of these opportunities in ways that are "mindful" of its other responsibilities—to the super-ego, to reality, and to itself.

One of Freud's favorite metaphors helps to clarify this revision. Recall that he visualized a kind of *quid pro quo* arrangement in which the ego was the entrepreneur of the dreaming enterprise and the id was the necessary capitalist:

> Daytime thought may very well play the part of the entrepreneur for a dream; but the entrepreneur, who, as people say, has the idea and the initiative to carry it out, can do nothing without capital; he needs a capitalist who can afford the outlay, and the capitalist who provides the psychical outlay for the dream is invariably and indisputably . . . a wish from the unconscious (65, p. 561).

We are now assuming that the true capitalist in this enterprise is an as yet unknown psycho-biological function as old as mammals, that the ego and all of its functions remains the entrepreneur, but that unconscious wishes must accept their place as creditors along with the superego, reality, and the ego's normal concern for its own abilities to serve all three.

Still another way of putting this revision of the wish-fulfillment construct is to paraphrase Freud's view of the role of somatic stimuli in dream formation. In that view extrapsychic stimuli were conceived as being subjected to the dream-work, as were the day's residues, and woven into the on-going dream, thus determining certain aspects of the staging and content of the dream. But these extrapsychic stimuli were viewed as incapable in themselves of initiating the dream process; this role was reserved to intrapsychic stimuli, i.e., repressed infantile wishes. Similar limitations are placed on unconscious wish-fulfillment as soon as we view it as a consequence rather than as a cause of dreaming. We are drawn, that is, to liken the role of unconscious wishes in dream formation to the role already ascribed to somatic stimuli: during the D-state these unconscious wishes may be incorporated into a dream, thus influencing its staging and content but like somatic stimuli they are incapable of *initiating* the process of dreaming.

Let it be emphasized that by altering our conception of the role of unconscious factors in dream *instigation* we are not thereby obliged to′ alter our conception of the role of unconscious factors in dream *construction*. Everything else in the original theory concerning regression and the interplay of the systems Unconscious and Preconscious can remain the same. We can even continue to refresh our thoughts with these metaphors:

> Thus the censorship between the unconscious and the preconscious, the assumption of whose existence is positively forced upon us by dreams, deserves to be recognized and respected as the watchman of our mental health. Must we not regard it, however, as an act of carelessness on the part of the watchman, that it relaxes its activities during the night, allows the suppressed impulses in the unconscious to find expression, and makes it possible for hallucinatory regression to occur once more? I think not. Even though this critical watchman goes to rest—and we have proof that its slumbers are not deep—it also shuts the door upon the power of movement. No matter what impulses from the normally inhibited unconscious may prance upon the stage, we need feel no concern; they remain harmless since they are unable to set in motion the motor apparatus by which alone they might modify the external world. The state of sleep guarantees the security of the citadel that must be guarded (65, pp. 567-68).

We have taken the position that "shutting the door on the power of movement" is not entrusted to the psyche at all, but is rather an integral condition of the D-state. But the rest of Freud's speculations concerning the interaction between unconscious and preconscious processes can remain intact. Indeed these speculations are strengthened by attributing the inhibition of motor activity to a more reliable agency.

THE
DREAM-WORK

In all future reconsiderations of the theory of dreaming, let us resolve to substitute the term "transformation" whenever we encounter the terms "disguise," "distortion," or "censorship." Speaking from within the theory of dreaming, i.e., leaving the interests of dream interpretation aside, this is hardly a revision, since it was the meaning Freud preferred when his concern with questions of dream *formation* was unambiguous:

> Two separate functions may be distinguished in mental activity during the construction of the dream: production of the dream-thoughts, and their *transformation* into the content of the dream (65, p. 506; my italics).

However, as documented elsewhere, Freud's formulations of the dream-work were sometimes lax in that they confused the theory of dreaming with the theory of dreams, with the result that he sometimes referred to "distortion" or "censorship" when "transformation" would have carried his meaning better (124).

To illustrate: A young woman reported a dream in which, in a state of high excitement and suspense, she was attempting to put a wild horse into a corral. While thus engaged she kept thinking how nice it would be if the horse was not a hired one but was her very own. She was also impressed in the dream with the horse's penis. Surely, we would not stir much controversy among a group of clinicians were we to suggest that the repressed infantile wish expressed in the process of this dream's formation was a wish for a penis of the dreamer's own. A really intuitive dream interpreter, say a Wilhelm Stekel, might surmise in addition that the day residue was a recent memory of having had sexual intercourse, and perhaps also that her lover was somehow less than "eligible."

There was no way to test the hypothesis as regards the repressed infantile wish. There almost never is. But there was a way to confirm the view that transformation, rather than disguise, is the more accurate view of this dream's "work." This was accomplished by the simple means of listening to the dreamer's own interpretation of her manifest dream: it was a "wonderful dream," and wasn't it clever the way it gave another picture of having had intercourse with her lover the night before. There had been moments when she was not sure she could keep him in the "corral," and it was now difficult to determine whether the dream more accurately depicted her sexual impatience or her more general impatience concerning the lover's impending divorce.

Another person may have had the identical dream, awakened in fright, and not have had the slightest idea what waking experiences the dream referred to. We might well, then, have spoken of the manifest dream as having a disguised latent meaning. But let us be very clear where the element of disguise enters into the sequence: it is in the dreamer's *waking* reaction to the dream, whether this involves clinical interpretation or not. It does not necessarily enter into the process of dreaming as such. In other words, the process of dreaming does involve the transformation of mental contents, whether recent or infantile, into new forms; but the onus of distortion, whether it be slight or massive, falls upon the waking state, a state in which dreams may be interpreted but not formed. In speaking of dream formation, therefore, we are on more solid ground if we accustom ourselves to thinking of the dream-work as transformative rather than distortive. The resulting transformations may subsequently be understood by the waking psyche in ways that make them classifiable as disguises. But they may also be understood by the waking psyche in ways that make them classifiable as revelations or expressions or inspirations or compensations or creative insights or what have you.

This view of the dream-work is not only consistent with our modification of the role of wish-fulfillment in dream construction but suggests the specific condition of the D-state which the ego may exploit for adaptive as well as defensive and expressive purposes: its exceptional deployment of primary and secondary symbolic processes, which we shall shortly consider in detail. Indeed, were it not for Freud's abiding commitment to unconscious wishes as the instigators of dreaming, it is not unlikely that the following of his lines of thought could have brought him to embrace our present view of the dream-work:

> I consider it expedient and justifiable to continue to make use of the figurative image of the two systems. We can avoid any possible abuse of this method of representation by recollecting that ideas, thoughts, and psychical structures in general must never be regarded as localized in organic elements of the nervous system but rather, as one might say, *between* them, where resistances *and facilitations* [Bahnungen] [my italics] provide the corresponding correlates. Everything that can be an object of our internal perception is *virtual,* like the image produced in the telescope by the passage of the light rays. But we are justified in assuming the existence of the systems (which are not in any way psychical entities themselves and can never be accessible to our psychical perception), like the lenses of the telescope, which cast the image.

And, if we pursue this analogy, we may compare the censorship between the two systems to the refraction which takes place when a ray of light passes into a *new medium* (65, pp. 610-11; my italics).

This wider conception gains us something and costs us nothing, since it is awkward to conceive of a censoring agency as serving facilitative functions, while a transforming agency may be conceived to serve facilitative functions or resistive ones, depending on circumstances.

DAY RESIDUE

The role of the day residue in dream formation now warrants reconsideration, especially in terms of the original positing of the need of unconscious wishes for transference to recent indifferent or incidental memories and perceptions. The original formulation followed consistently from attributing to unconscious wishes the ultimate motive force of dreaming. However, having taken the position that the unconscious is but one of the creditors of the dreaming enterprise, we may now respect Freud's appreciation of the frequent inclusion in dreams of recent perceptual and memorial material, while reinterpreting it. If, for example, we were to entertain the hypothesis that dreaming serves some adaptive purpose, whether because of or in addition to or in spite of its wish-fulfilling abilities, we might think in terms not only of the need of unconscious material for transference to day residue, but also of the *need of day residue for transference to unconscious wishes*.

Consider Freud's classification of the types of day residue:

. . . (1) what has not been carried to a conclusion during the day owing to some chance hindrance; (2) what has not been dealt with owing to the insufficiency of our intellectual power—what is unsolved; (3) what has been rejected and suppressed during the daytime . . .; (4) . . . what has been set in action in our unconscious by the activity of the preconscious in the course of the day; and . . . (5) the group of daytime impressions which are indifferent and have for that reason not been dealt with (65, p. 563).

For some reason (probably his preoccupation with the metaphor of the censor) Freud chose to refer his formulations of the day residue's role in dream formation to the third, fourth, and fifth of these categories. Now, having found it useful to broaden our conception of the dream-work, we may refer our formulations of the role of the day residue in dream formation to all five categories. Thus, as repressed impulses may "prefer" rejected or indifferent preconscious impressions as nexes around which to weave their connections for the purpose of achieving discharge, so may incomplete or insufficiently resolved or interrupted preconscious impressions "prefer" repressed impulses as nexes around which to weave *their* connections for the purpose of achieving completion or resolution or, in the Piagetian sense, adaptation. However noxious these repressed impulses may be, they have the virtue of being familiar. Of course, the more noxious they are the more would the completion or resolution be likely to be defensive rather than adaptive. But, in the immobile, albeit existentially compelling, experience of dreaming, little could usually have been lost in the attempt, and there could always be the possibility of a secondary gain, i.e., of the repressed materials becoming increasingly subject to ego synthesis in the process.

This revision permits us to view dreaming as an adaptive process from two complementary points of view: from the point of view of reintegrating the *mal*adapted past, and from the point of view of integrating the *un*adapted present.

THE SYSTEMS
PCS AND CS

The system Pcs is one of the most problematic constructs in all of psychoanalytic theory. It has come to be used in two quite different ways: (1) as a kind of storage bin for thoughts and memories which are not, but could become, conscious; and (2) as a kind of converter, ceaselessly engaged in transforming old thoughts, memories, and perceptions into new symbolic forms. The first version, used exclusively by Freud in the theory of dreaming, is conceived as being governed in the main by the secondary process. The second version, deriving from the work of Kris, Kubie, and Klein, is conceived as being governed in the main by the primary process. The second version is obviously much more compatible with our present view of the dream-work, and it is tempting merely to adopt it. However, second thoughts have determined a more moderate course. While many studies (e.g., of subliminal and incidental registration, microgenetic perception, serial reproduction, sensory deprivation, as well as of dreaming) can be cited in support of what Kubie calls the "preconscious stream" (156), it is unlikely that this conception of preconsciousness, the conceptual properties of which differ so markedly from the older conception, can simply be interposed for the older one without large scale modifications being made necessary in the use of the theory as a whole. Therefore, I propose that for the purpose at hand we conceive of the system Pcs in the topographical sense in which Freud conceived it in all of his formulations about dreaming, but that we conceive of this system as being governed by the secondary process *or* the primary process, depending on its deployment in relation to the systems Ucs and Cs, as graphically represented in the tri-phasic model of the sleep-dream cycle proposed in Chapter Three. In this way we shall avail ourselves of Freud's many provocative speculations concerning the participation of the system Pcs in dream formation—some of which were prophetic of the D-state—while achieving consistency with our recast views of the wish-fulfillment and of the dream-work.

Let us observe Freud as he struggled with the question of the role of the system Pcs in dreaming:

> As regards the embittered and apparently irreconcilable dispute as to whether the mind sleeps at night or is as much in command of all its faculties as it is by day, we have found that both parties are right but neither is wholly right. We have found evidence in the dream thoughts of a highly complex intellectual function, operating with almost the whole resources of the mental apparatus. Nevertheless, it cannot be disputed that these dream thoughts originated during the day, and *it is imperative to assume that there is such a thing as a sleeping state of the mind.* Thus even the theory of partial sleep has shown its value, though we have found that what characterizes the state of sleep is not a disintegration of mental bonds, but the concentration of the psychical system which is in command during the day upon the wish to sleep. The factor of withdrawal from the external world retains its significance in our scheme; it helps, though not as the sole determinant, to make possible the regressive character of representation in dreams. The

renunciation of voluntary direction of the flow of ideas cannot be disputed, *but this does not deprive mental life of all purpose,* for we have seen how, after voluntary purposive ideas have been abandoned, involuntary ones assume command (65, pp. 590-91; my italics).

It is impressive how neatly Freud anticipates in this passage many of the monitored sleep findings in the above remarks as regards: (1) presence in the nonwaking state of highly complex intellectual functions, (2) connections of these with previous waking concerns, (3) the need to assume some special organization which is not to be characterized as mental disintegration but as a reordering of the priorities characteristic of waking life, and (4) the probable central significance in dreaming of motor inhibition.

The one piece of knowledge that Freud did not anticipate, and which has proved decisive, is that nonwaking life is divisible into two separate states, the sleeping state and the D-state. Lacking this knowledge he was drawn to attribute all relevant conditions to "a sleeping state," and consequently to view preconscious activity during dreaming in terms of the "wish to sleep." Now that we have reason to believe that the fulfillment of this "wish" is in far more reliable hands than any psychological system could provide, it remains for us to meet the theoretical condition which prompted Freud to posit the "wish to sleep" in the first place: that the end product of dreaming must be a result of compromises taking place between the systems Ucs, Pcs, and Cs. In other words, with our present knowledge, we are entitled to ask: If the role of the system Pcs in dreaming is not the wish to sleep—since sleep will return like clockwork in any event and since, in fact, most dreaming seems not to take place in "sleep"—then what is it? Before trying to answer this question we should recall the primary waking function assigned by Freud to the system Pcs: it is that of overseer of the muscle and motor systems. "I am unable," says Freud,

to say what modification in the system Pcs is brought about by the state of sleep; but there can be no doubt that the psychological characteristics of sleep are to be looked for essentially in modifications in the cathexis of this particular system—*a system that is also in control of access to the power of movement* . . . (65, p. 555; my italics).

We are no longer unable to say what modifications in the system Pcs are brought about by the state of sleep. We are able to say that *in sleep* preconscious mentation is largely secondary process mentation and that access to movement is greatly reduced, although not altogether impossible. Whereas *in the D-state* preconscious mentation is largely primary process mentation, and access to movement is altogether precluded by preemptive neurological functions.

Consider the line of thought on which we have embarked: we have a psychic agency that is inherently engaged in transforming thoughts and memories into new forms (both discursive and presentational, i.e., by means of secondary and primary symbolic processes). In the waking state this agency is also in control of the access of these thoughts to movement, in the state of sleep it is partially relieved of its latter duties, and in the D-state it is almost entirely relieved of them.

Let us turn next to the role Freud conceived for the system Cs in his original formulations of dreaming:

> I must assume that the state of sleep makes the sensory surface of consciousness which is directed towards the Pcs far more insusceptible to excitation than the surface directed toward perceptual systems. Moreover, this abandonment of interest in the thought process during the night has a purpose: thinking is to come to a standstill, for the Pcs requires sleep. Once, however, a dream has become a *perception* it is in a position to excite consciousness, by means of the qualities it has now acquired (65, p. 575).

The major portion of this statement would now seem to be disconfirmed by the sleep monitored findings, which indicate that we can hardly ascribe "abandonment of interest" in thought processes to sleep proper. It seems that the perceptual qualities of dreams displace the ongoing thought processes of sleep rather than that they are reverted to after an "abandonment of interest" in thought processes. Nevertheless we remain indebted to Freud for focusing our attention on one of the qualities of dreaming which is often overlooked, namely, its conscious, indeed, *hyper*-conscious qualities.

As to the role of the system Cs in waking life Freud is much less tentative. It is

> that of a sense-organ for the perception of psychical qualities. . . . In its mechanical properties we regard this system as resembling the perceptual systems, as being susceptible to excitation by qualities but incapable of retaining traces or alterations—that is to say, as having no

memory. The psychical apparatus, which is turned towards the external world with its sense-organ of the perceptual system, is itself the external world in relation to the sense-organ of the Cs. . . . Excitatory material flows into the Cs sense-organ from two directions: from the perceptual system . . . and from the interior of the apparatus itself. . . . We know that perception by our sense-organs has the result of directing a cathexis of attention to the paths along which incoming sensory excitation is spreading. . . . We can attribute the same function to the overlying sense-organ of the Cs system. By perceiving new qualities, it makes a new contribution to directing the mobile qualities of cathexis and distributing them in an expedient fashion (65, pp. 615-16).

Without knowledge of the D-state Freud could only base his speculations on the role of the system Cs on the obvious, namely, that in the state of sleep this "sense-organ" was relieved of the need to attend excitatory material emanating from extrapsychic sources, being thus made subject, so his wish-fulfillment leanings drew him to reason, to the regressive pressures of repressed infantile wishes. We now know that the D-state adds to the sleeping condition of diminished susceptibility to external stimulation the distinctive conditions of activated cortical and visual activity. This can suggest that in the D-state the "sense-organ" of the Cs is especially obliged to attend material emanating from intrapsychic sources.

What, then, can we say about the characteristic deployment of the systems Pcs and Cs in the D-state? In respect to the Pcs we have a psychic agency whose inherent function is the symbolic transformation of thoughts, memories, and perceptions into new discursive and presentational forms, and which in waking life, and to some extent in sleep, is also engaged in regulating the access of these transformed thoughts and memories to motoric expression. In the D-state this agency is almost completely relieved of the latter function, and either obliged or freed to perform the former function in the presentational mode—whether due to influences exerted by early memories and wishes, or to its momentary freedom from executive functions in regulating access to movement, or both. In respect to the system Cs we have a psychic agency whose inherent functions are the perception of new qualities and the directing of these qualities along new paths, which must divide its attention in waking life between extrapsychic and intrapsychic sources of stimulation, and which in sleep is for the most part relieved of extrapsychic stimulation. In the

D-state this agency is not only relieved of extrapsychic stimulation but, it would seem, is also especially obliged to attend intensified intrapsychic activity.

It is, I think, plausible to speculate that in the D-state the systems Pcs and Cs, relieved as they are of their waking and sleeping "duties" by supervening inhibitions of sensory and motor activity, while simultaneously subjected to supervening activations of the cortical and visual systems, must enter into a particularly intimate kind of mutual interaction. To what adaptive psychological use this kind of interaction may have been put in human evolution emerges as an open question. Conceivably it could be mutually enriching or enhancing or corrective or refreshing. But that has been our objective all along: to open the question of what psychological purpose human dreaming may serve.

If these speculations are valid, then we are afforded a fresh perspective within which to regard one of the distinctive properties of dreams, namely their fused perceptions of internal and external qualities of experience. We are also in a better position to account for the hyperconscious quality of dreaming and for its peculiar admixture of discursive and presentational symbolic forms. Moreover, we are in a better position to account for what Freud saw as the "completely egotistical" nature of dreams:

> It is my experience, and one to which I have found no exception, that every dream deals with the dreamer himself. Dreams are completely egotistical. Whenever my own ego does not appear in the content of the dream, but only some extraneous person, I may safely assume that my own ego lies concealed, *by identification,* behind this other person. . . . On other occasions, when my own ego does appear in the dream, the situation in which it occurs may teach me that some other person lies concealed, *by identification,* behind my ego. , . . *These identifications should then make it possible for me to bring into contact with my ego certain ideas whose acceptance has been forbidden by the censorship* (65, pp. 322-23; my italics).

What Freud means by the term "identification" in this statement closely resembles what was meant when we surmised a particularly intimate kind of interaction between the systems Pcs and Cs to be characteristic of the D-state. Consider, too, that when Freud speaks of these identifications making it possible for the ego to gain contact with ideas which are otherwise forbidden, he implies a process by means of which dreaming may serve adaptive functions.

The advantage of our initial assumption that dreaming is an augmentative response of the human psyche to the distinctive neurophysiological conditions of the mammalian D-state may now be brought into better relief. More theoretical leverage is afforded on both the psychological and physiological aspects of the D-state— some of its dimensions conceivably making the process of dreaming possible (increased cortical activity, decreased muscle tonus, and differentially deployed perceptual activity), others conceivably being the *result* of dreaming (variable respiration, variable pulse, etc.)— although much more research will be necessary to sort all this out.

THE FUNCTIONS OF DREAMING

Nothing in the foregoing theoretical revisions precludes the safety-valve function which Freud attributed to dreaming. If, however, we assume these revisions to be valid, then we are obliged to determine what *other* psychological functions dreaming may serve—including, certainly, adaptive ones. In this it will be instructive to observe how close Freud came to ascribing adaptive functions to dreaming in the original theory and to note the conceptual lapse which prevented him from doing so.

It was noted in Chapter Two that the process of psychotherapy itself is a conceivable additional source of analogical insight into the nature of dreaming. As it happened Freud did not overlook this source. In the midst of his discourses on dream formation, having made much of the symptom-dream analogy, he refers briefly to his experience in *treating* symptoms:

> As soon as the memory of [a traumatic experience] is touched, it springs into life again and shows itself cathected with excitation which finds a motor discharge in an attack [of hysteria]. This is precisely the point at which psychotherapy has to intervene. Its task is to make it possible for the unconscious processes to be dealt with finally and to be forgotten. . . . What performs this work is the preconscious, and *psychotherapy can pursue no other course than to bring the Ucs under the domination of the Pcs* (65, p. 578).

Returning to the subject of dreaming, he continues:

> Thus, there are two possible outcomes for any particular unconscious excitatory process. Either it may be left to itself, in which case it eventually forces its way through at some point, and on this single occasion finds discharge for its excitation in movement; or, it may come under the influence of the preconscious, and its excitation, instead of being *discharged*, may be *bound* by the preconscious. *This second alternative is the one which occurs in the process of dreaming* (65, p. 578).

But, having created a logical opening for considering dreaming as an adaptive process, by showing the parallel between dreaming and psychotherapy in reference to the preconscious binding of unconscious materials, Freud immediately reverts to the position that we have rejected: the only purpose that could be served in an interaction between the system Pcs and Ucs during sleep is satisfaction of the "preconscious wish to sleep":

> It was indeed to be expected that dreaming, even though it may originally have been a process without a useful purpose, would have procured itself some function in the interplay of mental forces. And we can now see what that function is. Dreaming has taken on the task of bringing back under control of the preconscious the excitation in the Ucs which has been left free; in so doing, it discharges the Ucs excitation, serves it as a safety valve and at the same time preserves the sleep of the preconscious in return for a small expenditure of waking activity (65, p. 579).

Recalling the heuristic power Freud was able to draw from the dream-symptom analogy, one can only imagine how he might have enlightened us further by way of the dreaming-psychotherapy analogy, had he not been diverted from the attempt by the assumptions that (1) dreaming was somehow related to a "wish" to sleep and (2) dreaming was ultimately governed by the second law of thermodynamics. Having since been disabused of these assumptions, we might well begin our efforts to determine *all* of the functions of dreaming by further pondering this original implication that effective dreaming may be likened to effective psychotherapy. In Chapter Nine we shall pursue this line of thought as we attempt to expand our views of the psychological functions of dreaming. It is first necessary, however, to clarify our understanding of the process of repression in relation to the process of dreaming.

Chapter Eight

REPRESSION
AND DREAMING

As long as wish-fulfillment, as Freud defined it, had to account for the *occurrence* of dreaming, only one kind of stimulus could qualify as having the necessary "motive force": repressed *infantile impulses.* Other conceptions of repression were to prove powerful in bringing psychodynamic understanding to other forms of human experience, but these were excluded from the theory of dreaming by Freud's abiding requirement that the initiation of dreaming be traced to repressions of strong motive force. Only repressed infantile impulses could meet this requirement. However, if the fulfillment of repressed experiences is a consequence and not the cause of dreaming, then we may speculate on how the organization of dreams may be affected by these other forms of "repression." Three such can support serious speculation: Schactel's concept of *conventionalization,* Angyal's concept of *system-subordination,* and Piaget's concept of *unaccommodation.*

None of these need be viewed as a substitute for the Freudian concept of repression; on the contrary, each can be viewed as a supplement.

ERNEST SCHACHTEL

Schachtel begins by calling attention to two shortcomings in Freud's explanation of childhood amnesia:

First, it is not sufficiently clear why a repression of sexual experience should lead to a repression of all experience in early childhood. For this reason the assumption seems more likely that there must be something in the general quality of childhood experience which leads to the forgetting of that experience. Second, the phenomenon of childhood amnesia leads to a problem regarding the nature of repression, especially repression of childhood material. The term and concept of repression suggest that material which *per se* could be recalled is excluded from recall because of its traumatic nature. If the traumatic factor can be clarified and dissolved, the material is again accessible to recall. But even the most profound and prolonged psychoanalysis does not lead to a recovery of childhood memories, at best it unearths some incidents and feelings that had been forgotten. Childhood amnesia, then, may be due to a formation of the memory functions which makes them unsuitable to accommodate childhood experience, rather than exclusively to a censor repressing objectionable material which, without such repression, could and would be remembered (197, p. 4).

The formation of memory functions which are refractory to *all* childhood experience, and which tend to remain so in spite of most therapeutic adult experiences, Schachtel terms *conventionalization.*

Conventionalization is the repression not of specifically taboo or anxiety laden childhood contents but of the symbolizing forms characteristic of childhood. Conventionalization is a culturally influenced process of memory organization which results, in modern Western civilizations, in the formation of memory structures that are unreceptive to and incapable of reproducing the qualities and intensities typical of early childhood experience. In other words, whereas repression, as Freud conceived it, seeks to exclude from consciousness particular memories which were made intolerably painful by uncontrollable elaboration by the primary process, conventionalization seeks to exclude from consciousness the primary process itself.

Conventionalization is not to be conceived as an alternative to repression; nor is it to be conceived as the opposite of repression. Rather, these processes are to be conceived as the two ends of a continuum. In a metaphor which suggests why Herbert Marcuse singled him out as one of the few major contributors to the philosophy of psychoanalysis, Schachtel states:

One might say that taboo and repression are the psychological cannons of society against the child and against man, whereas in normal amnesia society uses the methods of blockade and slow starvation against those experiences and memories which do not equip man for his role in the social process. The two methods of warfare supplement each other and, in the siege conducted by society against human potentialities and inclinations which transcend the cultural pattern, the cannon helps to maintain the blockade, and the blockade and ensuing starvation make it less necessary to use the cannon (197, p. 25).

It is at least interesting to carry this metaphor further, in view of the military truism that every stratagem suggests its own counterstratagem: If the central strategy in civilization's siege against its "discontents" is the coordinated mounting of the repressive cannon and the conventionalizing blockade, whereby the effectiveness of each is supplemented by the effectiveness of the other, then the counterstrategy is clear: divide and then conquer. The metaphor may fetch too far but it is apparently the historical case that the "Triumph of the Therapeutic" (Rieff), which followed Freud's invention of a method for overcoming the repressed, has led to the contemporary search (via the consciousness-expanding means of drugs, human encounter techniques, sensitivity training, etc.) for new ways of overcoming the now diminished effectiveness of conventionalization. And it is probably more than coincidental that those who are conducting this search have adopted as their spokesmen Herbert Marcuse and Norman O. Brown, the two most Freudian of contemporary social philosophers, each of whom has concentrated on the limitations of infantile repression and each of whom has championed regression to infantile experiential forms.

As regards the relation of conventionalization to dreaming, Schachtel states:

In the forgetting and distortion of dreams during waking life it is important to distinguish between that which is due to the resistance to and repression of a specific dream thought or dream content and that which is due to the incapacity of the conventional memory schemata to retain the fantastic general quality and the strange language of dreams. The distortion of a dream thought which resistance wants to keep from awareness has to be distinguished from the process of conventionalization, which more or less *all* dream elements undergo because the medium of dream language is incompatible with the medium of the conventional world of waking life. In the degree of this incompatibility there are, of course, considerable variations between different people and, even more so, between different cultures. But modern Western civilization with its streamlined efficiency, uniform mass culture, and emphasis on usefulness in terms of profitable, material production is particularly and strikingly at the opposite pole from the world of dreams. . . . It is the trans-schematic quality of early childhood experience as well as of dreams which makes it difficult or impossible for the memory schemata to preserve and recall voluntarily such experience. Yet it is also this quality in which potentialities of progress, of going beyond the conventional pattern, and of widening the scope of human life are forever present and waiting to be released (197, pp. 17-18).

If there is merit in this wider view of repression, then we are obliged by our revision of the wish-fulfillment theory to view as consequences of dreaming the conscious entertainment of normally excluded mental *forms* as well as normally excluded mental *contents*. The validity of this conclusion is so utterly self-evident that one may well wonder why it can be offered as the conclusion of a theoretical exercise. The answer must lie, once again, in the extreme success with which Freud identified the meaningfulness of dreams with a particular method of dream interpretation. It is, in fact, often useful to subject a manifest dream to interpretation if we wish to raise to meaningful rational consciousness its repressed mental contents, although it is well to bear in mind that most dreams are, despite their unrationality, more than satisfactorily conscious and meaningful to their makers while they are being dreamed. In bringing to waking consciousness a remembered dream's fulfillment of repressed mental *forms*, however, rational interpretation is not only useless but obscurant, since it must, by virtue of its adherence to the constraints of normal social communication, exert a re-conventionalizing influence on the memory of the dream.

Is this kind of dream distortion any different from what Freud described as secondary revision? Probably not. In fact, a review of Freud's discussion of secondary revision will persuade us that the sense of Schachtel's notions about conventionalization was anything but alien to Freud's thinking. After some extemporaneous debating over whether to include secondary revision with the other processes of the dream-work (condensation, displacement, and symbolism) as a factor of dream construction, or whether to view it as a second agency, to the demands of which a dream must subsequently conform after it is dreamed, Freud chose the former. But he was quick to add:

> In any case . . . of the four conditions for the formation of dreams, the one we have come to know last is the one whose demands appear to have the least cogent influence on dreams (65, p. 499).

And then, as though hedging his own theoretical bets, he went on:

> The following consideration makes it highly probable that the psychical function which carries out what we have described as the secondary revision of the content of dreams is to be identified with the activity of our waking thought. Our waking (preconscious) thinking behaves towards any perceptual material with which it meets in just the same way in which the function we are considering behaves towards the contents of the dreams. It is the nature of our waking thought to establish order in material of that kind, to set up relations in it and to make it conform to our expectations of an intelligible whole. In fact, we go too far in that direction. An adept in sleight of hand can trick us by relying upon this intelligible pattern of the sense-impressions that are offered to us. We often fall into the strangest errors or even falsify the truths about the material before us (65, p. 499).

So for Freud, as for Schachtel, conventionalization of dream memories was a matter of concern.

We may state Schachtel's contribution to our revised theory of dreaming in the form of an hypothesis: *A consequence of dreaming is the repeated conscious utilization of those symbolic forms which in the dreamer's society are relatively useless or irrelevant, and therefore not available to his consciousness in ordinary waking life.* We shall have to await the Marcusan millennium to put this hypothesis to its acid test, for that would require study of some post-Orwellian society whose dreams are worked along logical and lingual lines, in contrast to its cultivation in waking life of "Love's Body" and its renunciation of the "performance principle." But perhaps the world will never see such a society. Or, if it does, perhaps that society may be found to have perfected better ways of dreaming than we now know of. Meanwhile, we must be content to support the hypothesis with retrospective thoughts and, since the D-state is obviously an evolved condition, we must turn our thoughts to evolution. From this vantage some support is to be found: If our basic premise—that dreaming is the augmentative *response* of the *human* psyche to the distinctive neurophysiological conditions of the mammalian D-state—is sound, and if we can further assume that only humans dream, then we may enlist the obvious human contribution to evolution in support of our hypothesis: *Homo sapiens* does not suffer the process of natural selection; by virtue of interposing cultures between himself and physical nature, and this by virtue, in turn, of his capacities for generating and transmitting technologies, languages, and social organizations, *Homo sapiens* has emerged as the naturally selective animal. Furthermore, it is an historical fact that cultures which cannot change lead to the extinction of their societies. It is an equally demonstrable fact that conventionalization is the modus vivendi of cultures. It is but a step from these larger observations to the question of whether cultures change because humans regularly dream the unconventional, or whether humans dream the unconventional because their cultures must change—a question which was implicit in Hall's "Out of a Dream Came the Faucet."

ANDRAS ANGYAL

A key concept in Andras Angyal's contribution to personality theory and to the practice of psychotherapy is what he called the "principle of universal ambiguity." It suggests that the organization of personality may be viewed as analogous to the organization of an ambiguous Gestalt. In this well known one, for example, one perceives an urn or two profiles depending on which of two ways one organizes the total perceptual field (Figure 3). One cannot perceive both simultaneously.

"Man," according to Angyal,

> is to be understood not in terms of any specific traits he possesses, or any specific patterns they form but in terms of the overall pattern that organizes these traits and their multiple interconnection. In the course of my work with neurotic patients I have been·searching for a conceptualization of personality adequate for the practical tasks of education and therapy. The most significant general statement I am able to make as a result of this search is that while personality is pluralistic in the details of its functioning, in its broad outline it is a *dualistic* organization" (1, p. 99).

Figure 3

Speaking from a developmental point of view, Angyal continues:

There is no life course in which every developmental experience has been traumatic, no one from which all deleterious influences have been absent. There are both healthy and traumatic features in every child's environment and in his relations with it; early attempts at relating oneself to the world succeed in part, and in part fail. As a result, the personality of the child develops simultaneously around two nuclei, forms two patterns. . . . One pattern is based on isolation and its derivatives: feelings of helplessness, unloveableness, and doubt about one's prospects. The other is based on the confidence that a modicum of one's autonomous and homonomous strivings may be realized more or less directly. . . . The world visualized in the healthy pattern feels like one's home; it is rich in opportunities, lawfully ordered, and meaningfully related to the person. The world of neurosis is foreign and threatening, full of obstacles and dangers, lawless, capricious, a chaos rather than a cosmos (1, pp. 99-101).

The theory of universal ambiguity has far reaching implications for an understanding of neurosis and for the practice of psychotherapy. It precludes, for example, the conception of a neurosis as a limited growth within the person, which can be extirpated without disturbing or changing the rest of the personality. Rather:

The neurotic person is neurotic throughout, in every area of his life, in all the crannies and crevices of his existence. Conversely, one cannot say that there is in anyone only an element or segment of personality that is healthy. One is healthy throughout and this health extends over one's entire existence, down to the most distorted forms of behavior and the most troublesome symptoms. The so called "healthy core," the patient's real self, will not be found stuck away in some distant or hidden region of his personality; it is to be found right there where it is least expected. Health is potentially present in its full power in the most destructive, most baneful, most shameful behavior. For example:

> As a boy, one patient felt compelled to drink his own urine. Later he managed, with the aid of a contraption of his own invention, the difficult feat of performing fellatio on himself. The most agonizing paroxysms of shame accompanied these revelations, which demonstrated his isolation, his morbid preoccupation with himself, and the fantastic indirections he felt were necessary to achieve gratification. Yet the same behavior expressed diverse "completion" and "fulfillment" motives: "I could have belonged in the family circle only if I had given up the right to be alone; still the circle had to be completed, so I made my own." These distortions also expressed the tendency to experience sensuality to its fullest and a determined wish to affirm his uniqueness in the face of tempting conventional compromises (1, pp. 103-4).

In other words a person's day to day behavioral expressions do not belong independently to either the pattern of health or the pattern of neurosis. All parts belong to both patterns and are assigned their meaning and value by the currently dominant system principle.

> There is therefore no motivational force that a person has to discard in therapy. If the pattern of health becomes dominant, the problematic factors will find their places within it in a system-consistent fashion (1, p. 104).

Thus the term "system-subordination," by which I shall refer to Angyal's conception of repression, since he was content in his lectures on the subject to speak metaphorically of repression as a "two way street":

> In the original formulation of *repression* certain impulses were considered to have been made incompatible with the person's sense of self-esteem by parental reflection of socio-cultural sanctions and therefore excluded from consciousness. According to my theory, the repressed is that which is inconsistent with the dominant organization, whichever it be. Repression remains a very useful concept, but it takes

on new properties. It is no longer a one-way affair but a two-way affair. Not only the neurotic feelings and trends but the healthy ones too may be repressed, in this case by the neurotic organization. Both organizations are repressive, in the general sense of the term, because they are incompatible Gestalts, two total patterns struggling for dominance. If one system gains dominance, the other is *eo ipse* subdued or submerged, and this may take the form of excluding it from consciousness, i.e., of repression in the technical sense of the word. This conception is borne out by numerous observations that one can and does repress feelings and wishes that are in no way socially tabooed and are even considered laudable (1, pp. 110-11).

Like Freud, Angyal interpreted dreams much as he interpreted symptoms, except that he recognized symptoms to be products of the neurotic system in an established position of dominance, revealing the subordinate potentialities of the health system only to the knowledgeable eye. Thus dreams often afforded pictures of the two systems as they competed for dominance, each seeking to organize the same symbolic materials.

Angyal's approach to the interpretation of symptoms was briefly illustrated above in the case of the man with the self-fellatio symptom. It happens that I was the therapist in that case (it was one of my earliest and was being conducted under Dr. Angyal's supervision) and I am therefore in a good position to embellish the illustration:

The patient had entered therapy after failing in a serious attempt at suicide. He entertained little hope that therapy could help him and during the first five or six sessions seemed mostly concerned to inform me that it would be enough if *I* learned something as a student of psychotherapy from these sessions, since he was convinced, after even failing to kill himself, that he was beyond helping. The disclosure about the self-fellatio episodes came in the tenth session after some childhood confessions in the intervening sessions had indicated the possibility he might be investing some hope in our work after all. He was telling of his nightly masturbatory practices. Then he paused, blushed, began to speak, paused again and remained painfully silent for ten or fifteen minutes, during which he became increasingly agitated, clenching his teeth and fists, and alternately looking at me with eyes that both begged forgiveness and damned my presence as a witness. Finally, I said, "You know, whatever it is, you don't *have to* tell me." At this he burst into a fury of tears and self-recriminations, and shouted, "Yes I do have to tell you! Yes I do! God damn you, and God damn me, and God damn this rotten sick life. It's just that I can't understand why I don't *want* to tell you, why I should give a shit what you think of me!" Then he told of how in masturbating he would hold himself in a fetus like position with the aid of a kind of harness he had devised, so that he could ejaculate into his mouth through a short rubber tube.

I came away from the session pleased with this demonstration of the patient's involvement in therapy but confused and worried over the prognostic signs that I read in his disclosure: the extreme "narcissism," the "acting out potentials," the "schizoid primitivity," etc.

In my next consultation with Dr. Angyal I reported the episode but did not voice my fears, expecting that he would confirm them himself. I recall his response vividly. He complimented me on having earned the patient's confidence in so short a period and then, as though sensing my unspoken reservations, he said: "Now, that little trick of his, have you ever heard of such a thing before?" "No," I said, "and I have not read of it either." "Neither have I," he said, looking into the inner distances of his longer experience. "You know, the man must have a quite stubborn taste for some kind of privacy, a special capacity, perhaps, for some unusual form of personal integrity. Think of the lengths to which he is going to be self-contained, a complete unit." Then he shook his head and said, "But look how he is frittering all of that away in that silly trick of his, which only tells him how helpless and alone he can be. Perhaps you would point that out to him some day."

In a similar way Angyal employed his patients' dreams to dramatize the basic choice that his theory led him to assume was theirs: Whether to allow the power of conscious decision to continue in the service of the neurotic system, or whether to place conscious influences at the disposal of the health system. For example:

We are in Israel, near the Jordanian border. Soldiers. We decide to cross the border to conduct a commando operation. We want to go to Egypt, only we cross into Jordan (irrationally) on the way. We are dressed in civilian clothes, carrying rifles. We are three: me, my commander, and someone named Howard. We step across the border into Jordan and walk southward not far from the border. We pass farmhouses, green land (rather like Vermont). Nobody much notices us. At one point a car comes near and we duck behind another car.

I drop my coat and rifle. I think I have dropped it, but the other officer (who is rather faceless) returns it; he had been carrying it.

On a rise to our left we see several shacks. We know there are prostitutes in them. They are walking around the shacks. Two are not bad looking. Someone says, "Now I remember the Arabic word for homosexual." It is something like "fil-wen," the meaning of which at the time I do not understand. In a while, scared, we re-cross the border. Oh yes, the commander calls commando operations *piduyim.* Which is reminiscent of *fedayeau* which actually means redemption. *Fil-wen* may mean in what place?

This dream was reported near the end of a successful course of psychotherapy. The patient, a twenty year old college student, had begun therapy because his sexual fantasies had caused him to fear he was homosexual. During the course of treatment he had come to perceive his "homosexuality" as basically motivated by a more general set of characterological aspirations to be a "deep, attractive, odd, and intriguing" person, rather than the empty and insignificant one that certain early experiences had hinted he might be. He had also concluded, in his own words, that he stood on the threshold of "two worlds." In one he was "alone, angry, dry, crotchety, isolated, hurt, self-concerned, useless, and unknown." In the other he was "warm, tender, perceptive, involved, and the possessor of quite distinctive talents in the use of language." I found these to be apt descriptions of his neurotic and health systems, respectively, although I was content, of course, to discuss them as his "two worlds." In the session preceding the dream we had talked a bit of the approaching end of therapy, and I had tried to sum up the main conclusions we had reached, namely, that his basic choice, the one he would have to make every day of his life, was not whether to be homosexual or not, but which of his two worlds he would try to live in. His "homosexuality" was a choice, too, but not the basic one, since conceivably he could be homosexual or heterosexual in either of his two worlds.

The patient's interpretation of his dream can stand without modification as a nice illustration of Angyal's approach to dreams:

All the business about borders—that, of course, refers to my two worlds. The commando operation reminds me of my therapy sessions; they've been like that sometimes, making the very most of small pockets of strength against well entrenched and seemingly superior forces. The faceless commander who had carried my gun, that's you. It reminds me that pretty soon I am not going to have you around to take care of me. Not that you have, really; which accounts for why, in the dream, I thought I had dropped the rifle myself. The good looking prostitutes probably symbolize my recent life as a heterosexual. But where the dream really tied into things was all that play on the Arabic word for homosexual, and knowing that crossing over into Jordan is a hell of a way to get from Israel to Egypt, but doing it anyway. That feels like when I am in that dry isolated world and I know I want out of it, but instead I go further into it. Damn it, I mean to get to that promised land of mine, so I've got to learn how to just start walking straight toward it, one foot after the other. And that's where the word-play comes in: you told me yesterday that homosexuality wasn't the basic issue, and I agreed. But here is my dream—my very own dream— saying (somewhat confusedly to be sure, and that is some consolation): "No, homosexuality *is* the main issue." So what happens? I am in Jordan, further from Egypt than ever, and not even sure I can carry my own gun!

As we have been at some pains to emphasize in previous chapters, the artfulness of a dream interpretation says nothing directly about the process of dreaming. It merely says that the remembered and interpreted products of the dream process sometimes lend themselves to more sensitive perceptions of waking life. However, as emphasized in Chapter Two, useful dream interpretations may be heuristic in the psychology of dreaming. Thus, Angyal's conception of repression, as understood in the context of his holistic theory of personality, and his approach to dream interpretation, combine to suggest the hypothesis that *a consequence of dreaming is the exposure to consciousness of shifts, or potential shifts, in the balances of power which take place from night to night between an individual's two potential systems of organizing his total personality, under the conditions of freedom from the constraints of social expediency that are characteristic of sleep.* Bear in mind that this exposure to consciousness would have taken place whether or not the dream is subsequently remembered. What varying factors may further enter into the engineering of these shifts, vis-à-vis their day to day counterparts, is widely open to conjecture. Perhaps one's more "healthy" days are challenged by one's more "neurotic" nights, or the converse, which would jibe well with Jung's "compensation" approach to dream theory. Perhaps one's more "healthy" days invite and are reinforced by even more healthy nights, or the converse, which would accord well with Hall's "cognitive" theory of dreams. Or, perhaps the shifts are entirely random, or partially influenced by principles of compensation and reinforcement and partially random. If we could settle any of these questions we could certainly make more sense of the phenomenological fact that on some days we do get up "on the right side of the bed," and on other days we get up "on the wrong side of the bed."

JEAN PIAGET

[NOTE: For years many scholars have recognized that Piaget's work probably contained an important key for opening Freud's theory of dreaming to the systematic refinement it deserves, but most of us have steadfastly shrunk from the task of looking for it. One scholar who *has* undertaken the task is Dr. Peter Castle, of the Department of Psychology, Simmons College, Boston. The discussion of Piaget in this chapter is adapted from a longer work by Castle not yet published.]

A dream can be characterized as a form of thought which is experienced as action. It thus occupies a unique place in the spectrum of symbolic functioning since it seems to be what it is not, i.e., action, and is what it does not seem to be, i.e., thought. As a result of this we normally take a dream completely seriously while we are asleep and tend to dismiss it when awake. Thus, dreams seem to exist outside the mainstream of adult experience in the form of either thought or action.

It is at this juncture that Piaget's thinking commends itself. Although he was not centrally concerned with dreams or dreaming, he made two major contributions in this area. The first was an empirical and descriptive study of how children understand dreams, this study being part of his larger effort to analyze children's understanding of thought as a whole which was published as *The Child's Conception of the World* (175). The second was his major theoretical work on play, dreams, and imitation whose general purpose is better suggested by the original French title, *La formation du symbole chez l'enfant* (176). The latter work includes a systematic critique of Freud as well as a comparative analysis of dreaming.

Piaget starts his critique of Freud's theory of symbolic thought by comparing the structure of dreams and play in young children. In both he finds an analogous expression of a variety of wishes, concerns, and interests of the young child, some of which the child is consciously aware of and some of which he is not. Piaget demonstrates that there is a close similarity between play and dreams, both in terms of their contents and in terms of the way these are assimilated by the child. This being so, Piaget feels that for the young child at least it does not make sense to dichotomize unconscious and conscious modes of symbolizing. He agrees with Freud that there are levels of meaning found in any symbolic product which can be categorized in terms of their relationship to the child's awareness of their significance, but does not feel that this fact, in and of itself, means that nonconscious aspects of symbolizing are the product of a special or separate system of thought. Rather they result from the fact that many of the so-called unconscious or hidden aspects of thought remain out of conscious awareness simply because they are taken for granted by the child:

> As to the child's relations to parents, brothers, and sisters, a comparison of all the games in which they are symbolized clearly shows how revealing the detail of the symbolism is of tendencies and feelings many of which the child is not clearly aware of, for the simple reason that he never questions them. . . . While accommodation of thought is generally conscious, because external or internal obstacles call forth consciousness, assimilation, even when rational, is usually unconscious . . . symbols cannot be classified once and for all as either primary or secondary. Every symbol is, or may be both, i.e., it may have, in addition to its immediate meaning which is understood by the subject, more remote meanings, in exactly the same way that an idea, in addition to what is consciously involved in the reasoning of the moment, may contain a set of implications of which the subject is temporarily unaware, or of which he has long or even always been unaware (176, pp. 172-75).

Thus, in order for awareness to be an integral aspect of thought there must be some sort of opposition between the ideas involved. This results in an effort to fit these together in which consciousness is usually involved. This means that the presence or absence of a specific form of awareness regarding a symbolic product is not, in and of itself, indicative of the presence of a defensive or censoring process. In the case of a specifically repressed idea, in which the absence of awareness is often accompanied by some manifestation of anxiety, such a process may indeed be involved. But in other situations a lack of cognitive opposition may be responsible for the lack of self-conscious awareness on the part of the thinker. It is this which' explains the range and continuity of such awareness as exists in a child's understanding of his play or dreams or thoughts. For children, because of their cognitive immaturity, take for granted a whole host of ideas which adults find quite foreign to their way of thinking. Thus a box in the play of a four year old can readily be a truck, a house, or an animal, in much the same way that it might in a dream. At this stage in the child's development, a sphere of thought (dreaming) and a sphere of action (play) can clearly be seen to be structurally equivalent despite their differences. Some of these ideas come, through a variety of pathogenic circumstances, to make up the content and structure of the repressed in adulthood. The majority of them, however, normally continue to exist as schemas which can find their expression in various forms of thought and whose structure, taken as a whole, constitutes the functional basis of certain basic aspects of thought. In particular, the schemas elaborated during the period from birth to about seven years, which Piaget calls preoperational structures, are the ones which contribute largely to the structure of dreams and in adulthood find little opportunity for expression other than in this form of thinking.

In his detailed analysis of Freud's thinking, Piaget starts with this lucid summary:

The two fundamental facts discovered by Freud and his school are: firstly that infantile affectivity passes through well-defined stages, and secondly that there is an underlying continuity, i.e., that at each level the child unconsciously assimilates present affective situations to earlier ones, even to those most remote. . . . Intelligence also passes through well-defined stages which correspond in the main with those of emotional development. . . . Corresponding to the affective level of "object choice" there is construction of substantial objects and the organization of external space, while the beginning of socialization of thought corresponds to the level of transfer of affectivity to others. Moreover, the whole genetic analysis of thought shows continuous assimilation of present data to earlier schemas and to those of the child's present activity, the progress of intelligence consisting in the progressive decentration of this assimilation, while its errors take the form of unconscious fixation on what may be called repressed intelligence "complexes" (176, p. 185).

He then proceeds to examine Freud's concepts of memory and consciousness and suggests that they are based on a position which ascribes too much permanence to the mental processes, particularly those of young children. With regard to the problem of memory he states the following:

> For Freud, the whole of the past is preserved in the unconscious. Consciousness, having no memory, can only throw light on the memory-images which lie immediately below the surface in the unconscious. . . . It is, of course, impossible to know what becomes of a memory in the intervals between its disappearance and recall. . . . We can only experiment with conscious memories, and when a forgotten memory is evoked the process may be either reconstruction or extraction. . . . [But] on being asked what I did at seven o'clock this morning, I am obliged to deduce the answer, and it was unlikely that it was noted [on a record kept up to date] in my unconscious. . . . In accordance with their hypothesis, the Freudians make the beginnings of memory coincide with those of mental life. Why is it that we have no memories of our first years, and more particularly of our first months, which are so rich in affective experiences? The Freudians reply that there has been repression. But the theory of reconstructive memory provides us with a much simpler explanation. There are no memories of early childhood for the excellent reason that at that stage there was no evocative mechanism capable of organizing them (176, p. 187).

Since we are particularly concerned with action schemas and their role in dreams and dreaming, the above critique is of considerable importance. For it is clear that all the schemas elaborated by the young child during roughly the first eighteen months of life cannot exist or be stored in a form that is capable of being directly evoked in images. How then can they contribute to dream formation? Piaget implies that they can only do so by becoming incorporated into a form of representation which can become conscious in image or thought form. Although at first glance this formulation would seem to create complications for our understanding of dreaming, since it means that we have to discard the idea that a child has an image or idea of being held at the breast, being handled and rocked, etc., it does relieve us of the problem which was thereby created relative to consciousness. For on this former basis, consciousness can only play a selecting or censoring role as it picks and chooses among the supposed complete memory storehouse of images and associated feelings existing in the unconscious. This then raises the question of who or what decides which of these image-memories shall enter consciousness (censorship) and in what form, since consciousness itself, in the metaphor of a searchlight, is essentially passive.

> [Freud's] idea of censorship, linked with his conception of a passive consciousness, is obscure. Consciousness censors, we are told, when it wishes to remain unaware of a repression. But how can consciousness be the cause of ignorance, i.e., of unconsciousness? Such a state of affairs is only comprehensible if consciousness is compared to a searchlight lighting up certain points and avoiding others at the will of its manipulator. If consciousness is activity and intelligence, however, it is completely incomprehensible, the more so because a difficult repression usually requires the collaboration of consciousness for its completion (176, p. 191).

If, however, dreaming is in part a form of remembering, then consciousness is the result of an active effort of reconstruction, and we are relieved of the infinite regress inherent in the censorship model.

> For Freud, censorship is a product of consciousness, and symbolism a product of unconscious associations which elude censorship. In our opinion, it is worth considering whether these two terms might not be reversed; censorship merely being the expression of the unconscious, uncomprehended character of the symbol, and the symbol itself being the result of a beginning of conscious assimilation, i.e., an attempt at comprehension (176, p. 191).

On this basis a dream, by dint of achieving conscious representation, is understood as a manifestation of intelligence, i.e., as an effort at adaptation. This idea is also in line with Piaget's demonstration that both play and dreams involve a range of symbolizations which vary from conscious to unconscious for the child himself. This indicates that:

> Symbolism, and more particularly unconscious symbolism, extends far beyond the field of what can be censored or repressed, and rather than being a disguise or camouflage, seems to constitute the elementary form of consciousness of active assimilation (176, p. 191).

And since the active assimilations of the child by no means all lend themselves readily to representation in verbal-rational form, play and dreams serve to represent these more adequately.

The fact that children as well as adults do remain to varying degrees unaware of all the meanings of their symbolizations remains to be explained. This is the central fact which led Freud to make his analysis of symptoms and resulted in his concept of defense. In the case of adult dreams, which more often than not seem essentially incomprehensible to the dreamer, how, we may ask, can they be contributing to adaptation as an aspect of intelligence?

For Piaget the schemas involved in nonrational and autistic thought are predominantly affective in nature. This means that they are structured in terms of the person's internal interests and values in contrast to his external knowledge and ideas. In Piaget's terminology this means that they are assimilative in nature. That is, they operate in a manner which centers on the subject rather than the object pole of the person-world interaction, and thus are creative rather than reactive in nature. The other aspect of cognition for Piaget is accommodation which results from a centering of thought on the object pole of experience, adapting the person to the external circumstances of outer reality. All thought involves a complex balance of these two types of processes, since obviously neither can exist completely divorced from any trace of the other. In addition, the functional properties and consequences of assimilation will vary as a function of the developmental level of the cognizer and the symbolic mode involved. However, this distinction is ". . . a question of degree and not of watertight compartments, since all symbolism implies interest and affective significance, as does all thought" (176, p. 171). There is a much greater likelihood that "symbolic," as distinct from rational, thought will remain obscure to the thinker. There are several reasons for this, among which Piaget would include repression only as a special case:

> The inability of the subject to understand a symbol, and therefore its unconscious character, is accounted for by the fact that egocentric assimilation is carried to the point at which all present accommodation, i.e., all contact with present reality, is suppressed, involving at the same time suppression of consciousness of the ego. A repressed tendency is one which the subject refuses to accept, and to which he therefore denies all accommodation to reality. It is consequently

driven out of his consciousness . . . since repression makes it incapable of awareness by refusing it any possibility of accommodation. . . . If, in spite of this, it seeks support, it can be only by means of egocentric and unconscious assimilation, i.e., by means of a symbolic substitute. In our opinion therefore, to talk of "disguise" even in this case is to give a false picture. There is a symbolic realization of the desire, since it is repressed and this symbolic assimilation remains unconscious just because it is only assimilation without accommodation to reality (176, p. 203).

Thus the primary reason for the uncomprehended character of certain symbolic thoughts in the adult, and to a lesser degree in the child, is their comparative unaccommodation to *present* reality. This disparity may on occasion be the result of repression proper, but it is more likely to be the result of the formal differences between more primitive and more advanced schemas. To put it another way, children as well as adults are constantly in the process of adaptation, of coming to terms with change. The sources of change derive from shifting expectations of others, from maturational changes in body structure and capabilities, and from the process of adaptation itself, which always involves an interaction between the person and the world. A change in the way a person thinks will in turn produce changes in the way he perceives the world and the way he acts in it. This change is neither in the person nor in his world. It is a change in the relationship between the person and his world, which is essentially what cognition and thought consist of. In order for a person to think effectively he must be able to "mutually assimilate" the enormous variety of schemas he has available to him that are relevant to his world. In fact thought can only proceed in this manner, since its very structure is made up of these schemas and their relationships. Since, over the course of his development, a person will have employed various forms of thought, verbal and nonverbal, not all of his ideas on a given subject will exist in the same form. Some will be stored in the form of schemas of action and reaction (enactive), some will be stored in image form (iconic), and some will be stored in verbal form (ratiocinative). It is necessary, then, that there be available ways for these disparate forms of thought to become mutually assimilated. Dreaming is one such way, and the reason it seems puzzling to most adults is that it is not a form of thought readily assimilable by waking consciousness. But this is a consequence of the development of thought itself and not of any process of disguise. For, as the socialization of thought and action proceeds, the symbolic forms which determine the perceived and experienced relationship between a person and his world shift definitively in the direction of consensual validation and linguistic abstraction. In Piaget's terms, waking thought becomes capable of reversibility and generalization and loses its initial dependence on specific perceptual configurations. Before roughly twelve years of age:

> Any change in configuration modifies the predications accordingly. That is why there is not generalized conservation or "awareness of necessity" at this level. There is only consciousness of perceived or factual relationships, but not yet of any system of possible transformations of these relationships. [Subsequently] the change from one configuration to another becomes more important. Such changes are not understood as part of actions, but of reversible actions. Such reversible actions are called *operations*. They can alter one configuration into another one, and vice versa. It can therefore be said that conservation in all its aspects results from a *combination of operations*. At the primitive stages of his development, however, the child does not have the notion of conservation because his reasoning is not yet reversible but remains preoperational (177, pp. 138-39).

A dream, therefore, being preoperational in its structure in the sense described above, is not, by and large, understandable in the waking state since the images, objects, and configurations involved are not experienced as representative of or examples of general categories. Thus, for example, a box in a dream is not simply one among many possible boxes with a variety of shapes, some of which could perhaps be substituted for the one envisaged. Instead it is simply and wholly a particular box with a particular shape, color, etc., and perhaps with a particular affective significance as well: sinister, familiar, pretty. All this is given in the experience of this box in the dream and this experience is such that the box stands only for itself. In Piaget's terms this is a function of the nonreversibility of the schemas involved, of the lack of any way of transforming the configuration involved without changing its total significance. It is for this reason that each dream experience defines and creates its own perceptual world, each different from the others, despite superficial similarities. It is this general character of dream experience which makes it readily approachable from the waking vantage point in terms of aesthetic understanding. It is also this character which leads to the need for some form of interpretation, some method that will define a way of generalizing or extending the dream image so that it can point beyond itself.

To illustrate further the nonreversible structure of dream thought, consider one of the ways in which people commonly appear in dreams. This is when a dream figure, usually familiar to us, who initially appears in a form which is quite recognizable as his own, then becomes another person while remaining also himself and is thus in effect a double figure. The dreamer does not experience this as a contradiction; the person simply *is*, say, both his mother and his teacher. At first glance this appears to be a transformation, of one person into another, thus indicating a similarity or parallel of some sort. But it is not experienced as such. It remains an experience of simultaneous or successive identity in which there is only one person. Thus there is no possibility of real transformation, which would involve two separate people who shared a common quality and in which this quality of one could lead to the other and vice versa because the quality was separable from both or either as particular. And the reason for this is that the dream mode deals almost exclusively in perceptual configurations which preclude the possibility of such reversibility, transformation, and generalization. Waking thought, which from about twelve years on is dominated by operational structures and transformations, is thus at a loss to deal with dream thought on its own terms, and resorts for its understanding to interpretation. On this basis the simultaneous identity described above is assumed to be the result of a process of condensation. From this vantage point dream thought appears to be a diminished form of waking thought. Although the understanding brought to bear by thinking of dream configurations as condensations may be considerable, we must avoid falling into the error of *post hoc ergo propter hoc*. For this is a way of looking at the dream retrospectively and does not do full justice to the quality and structure of the experience. The dream experience indicates that the people are one, not two, and there is little ambiguity on this point.

Psychoanalytic dream interpretation assumes that causal relations exist in the process of dream formation. That is, it assumes that the actual similarity between the two figures led to an effort to combine them to transform each in terms of the other.

> Freud was trained in an atmosphere of classic associationism . . . consciousness is a mere lighting-up, an "internal sense organ," whose only role is to throw light on existing associations resulting from resemblances and contiguities between unconscious memories. This means that he denies to conscious activity what for most contemporary authors is its essential characteristic, i.e., the constitution of thought, which is a real constructive activity (176, p. 189).

For Piaget, consciousness does not have a causal relationship in thought but rather one of implication. By this is meant that, unlike physical relationships,

> . . . consciousness is at the source of connections that depend on systems of meanings. . . . In affectivity, consciousness constitutes a system of values. Interest is perhaps the most primitive affective mechanism in the child. From the physiologic point of view, interest is a causal process that can be described by regulation of energies; interest facilitates action by freeing available energies. From the point of view of consciousness, this means that certain values are being attached to certain objects, persons or actions. None of these values is determined by the law of cause or effect, but by implied relationships. Here is an example: A child may be interested in drawing; therefore he attaches value to pieces of paper that he would otherwise disregard. The value attached to drawing (value of goal) entails or implies value attached to paper (value of means). Here we have a relationship of implication rather than causality. . . . While causal mechanisms, physiologic or social, can explain the unconscious determinants of emotional life, consciousness of values is obviously a reality in the field of affective behavior. It deals with implication of value rather than of knowledge, but is otherwise as irreducible, specific and original as consciousness of cognitive implication. Therefore affective and cognitive consciousness are parallel rather than opposed to each other. These two aspects of consciousness can, of course, never be separated even though they are distinct . . . in perception, as well as in other areas, consciousness always represents a system of *meanings*. However, the most important difference between perception and higher processes is this: in the higher mental processes meanings are always distinct from the signified; they are attached to "signs" (language, etc.) or to "symbols." In perception, however, meanings are attached to the "cues": that is, to signifiers that are relatively undifferentiated from their respective signified (177, pp. 142-44).

In terms of our example, the doubled identity of a dream person is not the product of a condensation from the point of view of consciousness, but represents a relationship of the two figures by implication. To put it another way, the two figures go together because they have become part of a common system of meanings. This system is a new one, created by the dream process, although the basis for the relationship obviously has its foundation in meanings which existed prior to the formation of the dream. But the new relationship is not simply the sum of whatever the figures have in common, nor is it any simple matching or overlapping of congruent properties. Rather, in this particular system of meanings the two people *are* one. It is because of this relative lack of differentiation that dream thought has the character that it does. In any case, as a form of conscious experience its meanings constitute legitimate constructions within this framework of expression and are hardly accurately described as disguised manifestations of waking thought. If, however, one addresses oneself to the relationship *between* dream thought and waking thought, then one may in various instances discover, as Freud did, that the relationship is such that a set of meanings which exist in one mode do not evoke a complementary or parallel set in the other mode. This may be due to a number of factors, the majority of which Freud lumped under the general heading of defense, which includes the specific effects of repression. It was this approach that Freud took in the *interpretation* of dreams, i.e., the relating of dream thought to waking thought. Difficulty arises, however, when the understandings obtained from this approach are extrapolated in an effort to account for dreaming as a process and the mechanisms of dream *formation.* For, as Freud was aware, dreaming is a form of thought and must be understood as such. This requires that it be approached directly in terms of the form it assumes.

The same general problem of the inferential relationship between interpretation and creation is often encountered in the field of art and art criticism. Here it takes the form of the relationship between the public meanings of a poem or a painting and the meanings intended by the artist, wittingly or not. Here too, interpretations of the product (the work of art) are often used to analyze the processes assumed to have been involved in its creation. Whatever the usefulness of such interpretations, the result is often to prevent one from really experiencing the work of art in terms of its own system of meanings.

One might well ask at this point why in adulthood the preoperational systems of meanings found in dreams, and to varying degrees in allied forms of thought (art, poetry), are still operative at all. What may account for the persistence of these early systems of meaning which have, over the course of development, been either displaced or incorporated in various ways by more differentiated forms? In the case of dreams and dreaming this amounts to asking what function they serve in the life of an adult. Perhaps the most important part of the answer to this question can be given in terms of our previous discussion of thought and its relationship to consciousness. Once a system of meanings, which is to say an articulated system of representations, has become elaborated there is created, *eo ipse*, a "need to function," as Piaget describes it. One reason for this is that since meaning is not simply expressed by symbols but is in point of fact created by them, there is no simple equivalence possible between meanings in one symbolic mode and those in another. As a consequence, one system of meanings, however developmentally primitive, can never be wholly substituted for by another. Since we have all been children there is no real substitute for getting out and exercising, moving our bodies in space, however refined a form it may take in adulthood. Thinking about getting exercise just will not do it, although dreaming about it would perhaps come close. So it can be said that a fundamental reason for the persistence of early systems of meanings is that once established these can only find adequate expression in their own fundamental form, albeit a more elaborate or refined version of it. The child runs and yells for the sheer fun of it, while the adult plays tennis or climbs mountains using highly developed skills but also, at root, for the sake of the activity itself. Since dreams are made up of images, it is important to analyze how images make their appearance in development. Piaget's solution to the problem raised by the emergence of the image as a form of thought is to understand it as a consequence of the interiorization of the child's ability to imitate, which is itself a manifestation of the process of accommodation.

The image is as it were the draft potential imitation. . . . When the accommodation of sensori-motor schemas takes the form of visible gestures, it constitutes imitation proper, but when, sufficiently developed to need no external experiment, it remains virtual and interior, would it not lead to interiorized imitation, which would be the image? (176, p. 70).

When a child imitates some aspect of the external world, he is accommodating himself and his own system of schemas to the world. At the sensori-motor level this process need not and does not involve an intermediary image. Rather the copying process is based on a direct and immediate transfer, action to action. Eventually, however, the child becomes able to imitate, and thus reproduce, absent models or behaviors. This capacity, originally founded in action, results in the establishment of the capacity for internal representation which underlies all forms of thought proper. Thus the image and the capacity to form representations of which it is the first example do not emerge *de novo* but have their roots in the history and structure of sensori-motor functioning, a period in which thought is action and vice versa. The image then is a bridge between action without representative thought and representative thought without action. It is important to note in this context that the sensori-motor period is eminently rational in its organization, albeit nonrepresentative, since during it the child progressively becomes able to organize his actions in ways which allow him to construct the Euclidean world. It is during the period following this, namely that of egocentric representative thought, that the mechanisms of thought which are found in dreaming become elaborated. And these are based on the representations of actions, not on action itself. This distinction is important because it underlines the fact that only *representative* thought can be described as nonrational, since it is able to create and express meanings—something actions cannot do by themselves. Thus the mechanisms of dream thought cannot be derived in any simple way from action patterns themselves but only from the representation of such action patterns.

Once the image as a form of interiorized and abstracted accommodation becomes available to the child as a form of representation, thought and experience acquire a new dimension. Now images can be evoked in a way that serves to create for the individual a flexible continuity of meaning over time and a whole new realm of knowledge and expression. Prior to this, despite the great sophistication achieved on the practical level of sensori-motor functioning (which is also achieved to a significant degree by many of the higher mammals), the child has not had available to him the symbolic mechanisms which would permit the development of meanings and thus the differentiation of the self and the world beyond the action level. Now, however, the past and present can become differentiated, thus creating the possibility of the future. And this creates the possibility of envisioning and implementing change. Now new situations can be compared and understood in terms of old ones, and vice versa.

The relationship between signifiers and the signified, which becomes possible only when means of representation become available, is what constitutes symbolic meaning. It is this relationship which is of particular interest to us as regards the adaptive function of dreaming. As Piaget makes clear, the key to the development of representation is the differentiation of the signifier from the signified, this being what is lacking in sensori-motor functioning. As he states:

> But the symbolic function raises a psychological problem . . . the problem of the differentiation between signifier and signified. . . . This differentiation between two kinds of schemas, "signifiers" and "signified," does in fact become possible precisely through the differentiation between assimilation and accommodation. . . . During the sensori-motor period . . . "signifier" and "signified" are undifferentiated, the only "signifiers" consisting of "indices" or "signals" which are merely certain aspects of the object or of the schema of action. As soon, however, as imitation has become sufficiently flexible and reliable to function as a separate unit, it becomes capable of evoking absent models and consequently of supplying "signifiers" for the assimilating activity, providing that the latter is capable of connecting them with present data. Thus by the very fact of their differentiation, assimilation and accommodation acquire the capacity for being integrated in new systems that are more complex than sensori-motor actions, and are formed by extension of these actions to the nonperceptible field. Whereas sensori-motor activity involved accommodation only to present data, and assimilation only in the unconscious practical form of application of earlier schemas to present data, representative activity demands a two-fold interplay of assimilations and accommodations. In addition to accommodation to present data, it requires imitative accommodation to nonperceptible data, and thus involves, besides the meaning of the present object (provided by perceptual assimilation), the assimilating meanings of the signifiers. This complex mechanism is,

of course, both simplified and made socially uniform by the use of collective signs (words), but the use of such signifiers presupposes that the child learns them. This he does precisely through imitation, by means of which he has become capable of representative thought. Moreover, the interior imitative images continue to serve as individual signifiers even when language comes to be used (176, pp. 278-79).

I have quoted this passage at length because it constitutes a description of the framework suitable for an adaptive theory of dreaming. It indicates that for the creation of any symbolic system there must exist a means of signification which is separate or separable from that to which it refers. Such a system will then become capable of processing present data or stimuli in terms of these meanings, and this, in turn, will result in the extension of the system itself, i.e., in the establishment of new meanings within the system. It is important to emphasize that symbolic systems function in this way because, according to Sapir:

> . . . The symbol is always a substitute for some more closely inter-mediating type of behavior, whence it follows that all symbolism implies meanings which cannot be derived directly from the contexts of experience (196, p. 493).

A symbol system is thus by its very nature creative since it is not made as a copy of reality but as a construction of it.

Language, of course, supplies the dominant framework within which most symbolic functioning intersects. This is because of its critical importance in the social organization of a culture. Onto-genetically, however, the first coherent form of symbolic representation would seem to be the image which is derived from perceptual functions and largely from visual ones. And it is this form which we encounter in dreams. As Piaget indicates, however, images continue to serve as individual signifiers or symbols even after language has become well established as the primary vehicle of socialized thought and communication. This is because the meanings which have been generated and stored in this system continue to be of significance for the individual. That is, they do not exist simply as memories, stacked up like so many frozen cod, but as a system of meanings which is capable of extending itself, of being used in the course of assimilating, if and when assimilation in the present is capable of connecting previous meanings with present data. That is, when a situation arises in which individual meanings—those derived from the individual and idiosyncratic course of personal history—are of primary concern, there will be a natural tendency for thought and the meanings generated by it to take the form of imagining. Such a situation can arise under a number of circumstances, running the gamut from waking reverie to psychosis. During sleep, dreaming is a normal accompaniment because under these egocentric circumstances thought is, of necessity, in this mode. The state of withdrawal from the socialized world which characterizes sleep promotes not so much a regression, as Freud saw it, but a shift of form. It is true that this form is one that has primitive developmental origins but so does language. In other words, the image form is quite as capable of expressing and generating meanings which are appropriate for individual adaptation in the present as is language. Such meanings will be of a qualitatively different order than those generated by most waking thoughts and will tend to be experienced as nonrational by adults for this reason. But, as Piaget suggests, the system of meanings found in dream thought has a structural coherence and individual relevance simply because it is one that every individual develops. And once a system of meanings comes into being, it is never simply abandoned or superseded, as Freud and all other developmental psychologists have repeatedly demonstrated.

Having established that images are capable of serving as an adequate means of representation and thus of being organized into a system of thought, we must now examine how this form of thought functions. Since for Piaget all thought is based on assimilation and accommodation this means understanding the relationship between these processes as manifested in dreaming. Piaget sees symbolic functioning, a term which he uses in a restricted sense to contrast with intellectual functioning, as being closely involved with affect and thus as utilizing affective schemas. By this term he means personalized and imaginative representative schemas, which convey relatively idiosyncratic as opposed to socialized meanings. Affect is thus not separate or separable from intellect. He goes on to state:

> Since affective life is adaptation, it also implies continual assimilation of present situations to earlier ones . . . and continual accommodation of these schemas to the present situation. It is in so far as this

equilibrium between affective assimilation and accommodation is achieved that there is the possibility of conscious regulation of feelings, and of the standards of values constituted by moral sentiments, under the direction of the will. But when this equilibrium is not achieved, assimilation of present to past continues to be a vital necessity, and it is this primacy of assimilation over accommodation which is expressed by unconscious symbolism, in complete continuity with conscious symbolism. . . . In dreams . . . affective life goes on, but without the possibility of accommodation to reality. It is for this reason that in dreams there is constant recurrence of symbolic thought analogous to that of the child's play. . . . Symbolic thought is then the only possibility of awareness of the assimilation which takes place in affective schemas. This awareness is incomplete and therefore distorting, since by the very nature of the situation the mechanisms which symbolic thought expresses are incapable of accommodation. It is, however, only awareness and not disguise (176, pp. 205-10).

So from Piaget's point of view dream thought and other forms of imagination all owe their basic characteristics to the great preponderance of assimilation over accommodation, that is, to a state of cognitive disequilibrium. Adaptation in his view results from an even balance or state of equilibrium between assimilation and accommodation, at any given developmental level. This equilibrium is what constitutes intelligence. This explains why dreams are relatively personalized, idiosyncratic, and unique and lack the property of straightforward communicability normally found in more socialized forms of thought. They do represent a form of awareness, that is, an effort at symbolic comprehension, since they involve the creation and expansion of meanings, specifically that which Piaget calls affective meanings. Among these meanings are schemas which are unaccommodated due to repression proper and thus create a continuous state of disequilibrium. In addition, there are schemas which are more temporary in nature, resulting from situational circumstances which Freud described as the day residue. Finally there are those schemas which simply cannot achieve ready expression because they violate the rules of waking possibility as laid down by language and cultural expectations.

At first glance it would appear that there is no room in Piaget's view for considering that dreaming serves adaptive purposes, since by definition it cannot achieve equilibrium. However, closer examination of Piaget's work reveals this limitation to be an artifact of Piaget's intellectualist bias. An illustration will help to clarify this point. The dreams of young children usually have in them a far greater percentage of animal figures than do the dreams of adults. Assuming that dreams serve to express and represent some of the child's important concerns about himself, his fears, wishes, etc., most of which are intimately bound up with people—his parents in particular—why do so many animals appear? Why are the dreams not populated with people, as is the child's life? Usually in the dream there are good animals, menacing animals, friendly animals. Moreover each animal usually plays a particular role relative to the dreamer. Now in their waking relationship to their parents and other people, children are, for a long time, relatively undifferentiated as persons. As physical objects people come fairly early to have distinct and separate existences. But as people, who are protectors and punishers, whom one both loves and hates and who themselves enter actively into the relationship of nondifferentiation to varying degrees, they do not. In dreams, therefore, it is difficult for people and particularly adults to serve as adequate representations of the child's efforts at affective differentiation and specification. In this regard the child's capacity for thought outstrips the limits of his own experience and his ability to organize that experience. In short, people cannot readily take on roles in the child's view, and be understood in those roles, separately from their other functions. Animals, however, can do this; as most children's stories attest there is the bad fox and the silly duck and the wise owl, etc. Animals, then, are more adequate for the task of representing the child's concerns and ideas in a way that will promote their own differentiation and thus understanding of the world, and this is why they appear so frequently in his stories and dreams. As Piaget suggests, this is not simply a process of disguise but a way of achieving awareness ". . . because radical egocentrism makes consciousness of the ego impossible, and the only means by which affective assimilations can have any consciousness of themselves is by incorporating images as a support" (176, pp. 211-12). To put it another way, this is the form in which the child thinks a good deal of the time and which is continued in adulthood on the individual level primarily by dreaming. There are, however, changes within the dream mode, it also having a developmental course, as for example in the decrease in the relative frequency of animals in favor of persons in the dreams of adults. This change is a consequence of a change in the way the person perceives himself and his possible relationships with other people, which is itself one manifestation of the general developmental process of differentiation of the person and his world.

Piaget's work, as a whole, has explored this general process from a particular vantage point, being concerned almost exclusively with the growth of deductive scientific understanding and logic, as is shown in his studies of conservation, causality, time, etc. His approach might be crudely described as one which has focused on the relationship of the person and the world *with both ultimately conceived as objects*. Some of his understandings and theoretical concepts, however, are capable of being applied to the problem of the relationship between the person and the world *with both being conceived as subjects*. Piaget himself has more or less deliberately ignored or avoided this possibility by restricting his focus to directed thought and intelligence. This is ironic since he is one of the few systematic psychologists who has been able to conceptualize the function and structure of imagination as being both legitimate and coherent in nature, by choosing to analyze it in a developmental context. But, having done this, he then chose to view it either as transitional or "exceptional" as regards its role in adaptation as a whole. He has been justly criticized for this, as in the recent critique by Sutton-Smith who states:

> From Piaget's viewpoint as undirected thinking, fantasy, play, etc., are specifically childlike and mainly compensatory, that is, having nothing to do with the development of particular kinds of intellectual operations, they may be confined to the infantile stage and regarded as irrelevant to the nature of adult intellectual operations. . . . But to rest play's positive contribution on such grounds is to lead to a disjunction of cognitive and affective functions. . . . If play has a constitutive affective function of this sort (ensuring ego continuity), Piaget's general position on affective-cognitive relations requires that it should also have a constitutive intellectual function (219, pp. 107-8).

In point of fact, as Sutton-Smith is also aware, Piaget has suggested what is the function of symbolic play and, by implication, other imaginative forms:

> . . . for the child, assimilation of reality to the ego is a vital condition for continuity and development, precisely because of the lack of

equilibrium in his thought, and symbolic play satisfies this condition both as regards signifier and signified. From the point of view of the signified, play enables the child to relive his past experiences and makes for the satisfaction of the ego rather than for its subordination to reality. From the point of view of the signifier, symbolism provides the child with the live, dynamic individual language indispensable for the expression of his subjective feelings, for which collective language alone is inadequate. . . . Symbolic play, then, is only one form of thought, linked to all the others by its mechanism, but has as its sole aim satisfaction of the ego, i.e., individual truth as opposed to collective and impersonal truth . . . (176, pp. 166-67).

He then goes on to *restrict* the relevance of this extremely suggestive and original analysis to the *young* child, and by doing so turns his back on the possibility that dreaming continues to serve this same important function in the adult.

Since we now know that dreaming is a recurrent rather than an exceptional phenomenon, it seems highly probable that in adulthood as well as childhood it is indeed serving the function of giving form to affective schemas and thus generating ideas on the level of "individual truth." The way in which this operates in adulthood will of necessity differ in various ways, since within the mode of dream thinking itself development will presumably have taken place in the general direction of differentiation and hierarchical integration. Empirical investigation of these differences has been practically nonexistent since content rather than structure has remained the almost exclusive focus of developmental dream studies. The likelihood that dream thought at all levels does indeed have a "constitutive intellectual function" is supported by the Clark University studies on microgenesis (246), among others, which demonstrate that even our most abstract waking thought has its roots in a more primitive form out of which it develops. Thus it is by no means a radical or wholly novel step to suggest that dreaming in adulthood can perform the same functional role that symbolic play does in childhood. Symbolic play is, of course, a form of thought which takes place in action, involving the child's own body, its motions and those of imaginatively transformed physical objects. As we develop, action takes on more and more socialized forms and we no longer make the chair in our living room into a boat afloat on the water, even if we are alone. Representative thought remains private, however, simply because it can be kept to oneself. And dreams are in many ways both the most private and at the same time the most active form of internal representation. Thus it is not surprising that dreaming is a form of thought which is experienced as action, since action is the mode in which it originated.

For the child symbolic play serves to extend his understanding and comprehension of the world by means of his acting upon it and making it part of him by transforming it in terms of his own wants and needs. Even under these highly assimilatory circumstances the child's activity neither is nor can be completely devoid of accommodation. For the adult, dreaming seems to serve the same purpose, but it has a much wider range of representations with which to work since it starts with representations themselves and then transforms these in turn by assimilating one to another.

On the basis of Piaget's thinking, then, dreaming both in childhood and adulthood can be understood as a form of thought. It operates in the same general way as all thought does, namely by the assimilation and accommodation of systems of meanings. The image mode constitutes one such symbolic system. A variety of affective meanings are stored in this mode, in part because of its close relationship to action. These meanings have functional significance throughout the life of an individual and thus are capable of extending and transforming themselves as the individual develops. Dreaming is one regular and recurrent manifestation of such transformation in this mode or system of schemas, which occurs from a psychological point of view simply because it is an occasion for thinking in a highly egocentric context.

THE
PSYCHOLOGICAL
FUNCTIONS
OF DREAMING

Chapter Nine

The amplified perspectives on the possible functions of dreaming, which we were able to derive from the theories of Schachtel, Angyal, and Piaget, were only slightly dependent on the new bases for a psychology of dreaming discussed in Chapters Three through Six or on the revised psychoanalytic theory of dreaming as proposed in Chapter Seven. Now, therefore, we shall try to bring all of the views so far presented, including those developed in the last chapter, to focus on the question of why humans dream. The plan of our deliberations is as follows: We shall first review the biological functions which have been ascribed to REM sleep; next we shall review the psychological functions which have been ascribed to dreaming; then we shall take some tentative positions of our own.

In Chapter Three we took note of five different biological functions that have been ascribed, on the basis of incomplete and far from conclusive evidence, to REM sleep: (1) a *neutralizing* function, in counteractive relation to some noxious by-product of mammalian metabolism; (2) a *stimulating* function, in compensatory relation to the periodic sensory deprivations which are characteristic of mammalian sleep; (3) a *reorganizing* function, in response to the disorganizing effects of mammalian sleep on the central nervous system; (4) an *alerting* function, in preparation for mammalian fight and flight patterns; and (5) an *innervating* function, in the specific service of mammalian depth perception. We concluded that each of these hypothetical functions was plausible, and we foresaw no reason why the eventual confirmation of any one of them should necessarily be grounds for rejecting any of the others.

Let us now suggest, as a purely heuristic exercise, that the biological functions of REM sleep and the psychological functions of dreaming may be analogous. Thus as REM sleep may neutralize this or that cerebral toxin, so dreaming may neutralize this or that noxious impulse or memory. Similarly, as REM sleep may stimulate the cortex in this or that state of efferent deprivation, so dreaming may stimulate emotion or memory in this or that state of experiential deprivation. Similarly, as REM sleep may reorganize firing patterns in the central nervous system in response to the disorganizing effects of sleep, so dreaming may serve to reorganize patterns of ego defense or ego synthesis in response to the disorganizing effects of waking life. Similarly, as REM sleep may serve an alerting function in respect to potential threats to physical integrity, dreaming may serve an alerting function in respect to potential threats to psychosocial integrity. Finally, as REM sleep may help to establish and maintain depth perception, dreaming may, if you will, help to establish and maintain "perceptiveness in depth." Although these analogies are more speculative than hypothetical, each will serve as an heuristic point of view from which to clarify further the new perspectives on dreaming.

NEUTRALIZATION

Recall that to conceive unconscious wish-fulfillment as one of the consequences rather than as the cause of dreaming does not require rejection of Freud's formulations concerning the role of unconscious wish-fulfillment in the *process* of dreaming. The importance of maintaining this point of emphasis may now be seen by observing that the psychoanalytic theory of dreaming, *as revised*, remains viable in ascribing to the dreaming process a neutralizing function. In other words, the hypothesis that dreaming serves as a periodic "safety valve" in respect to the periodic psychonoxious effects of repressed infantile wishes stands as a powerful leading hypothesis in the psychology of dreaming, as capable as ever of ordering accumulated observations that dream contents regularly include hypermnesic infantile images and perceptions. Nor does our rejection of the economic point of view and its reductionistic concepts of psychic energy compromise our acceptance of the safety-valve hypothesis, the latter being an authentic theoretical attempt to explain observable phenomena and, as Klein has insisted, in no need itself of being further explained by hypothetical references to unobservable phenomena. The theoretical modifications proposed in Chapter Seven merely suggest the possibility that dreaming serves more than cathartic functions.

STIMULATION

The views of Schachtel (Chapter Eight) and Silberer (Chapter Five) combine to suggest that dreaming may serve a stimulating or restitutive function in response to recurrent psychological impoverishments imposed by certain external and internal conditions which are characteristic of human life. Recall the hypothesis derived from Schachtel's theory of repression that a consequence of dreaming is the repeated utilization of those symbolic forms which in the dreamer's society are relatively useless or irrelevant and therefore not available to consciousness in ordinary waking life. In most literate societies it is of course the primary process which is most often found to be useless or irrelevant. Thus dreaming, which tends to be governed by the primary process, may be seen as a recuperative response to the unavoidable conventionalizing influences of everyday life in literate societies—thus routinely reminding Man of his capacity for the unconventional, possibly creative, response.

Similarly, dreaming may be seen as a recuperative response to the neccessarily recurrent intra-psychic conditions of apperceptive deficiency and apperceptive insufficiency, as defined by Silberer, the one stemming from recurrent situations of reduced psychic power (of which sleep itself is one), the other stemming from unavoidable situations of growth and development. Actually one major category of the day residue, as Freud defined it ("what has not been dealt with owing to the insufficiency of our intellectual power—what is unresolved" 65, p. 554), is but another way of referring to the condition of apperceptive insufficiency.

These views have received recent support from the quite independent and refreshingly literate thinking of Arthur Koestler on the subject of dreaming in his epic work *The Act of Creation:*

> . . . The fact that art and discovery draw on unconscious sources indicates that one aspect of all creative activity is a regression to ontogenetically or phylogenetically earlier levels, an escape from the restraints of the conscious mind, with the subsequent release of creative potentials—a process paralleled on lower levels by the liberation from restraint of genetic potentials or neural equipotentiality in the regeneration of structures and functions. The scientist, traumatized by discordant facts, the artist by the pressures of sensibility, and the rat by surgical intervention, share, on different levels, the same super-flexibility enabling them to perform "adaptations of a second order," rarely found in the ordinary routines of life (150, p. 462).

The levels of mental organization have been compared to the archaeological strata of ancient and prehistoric civilizations, buried, but not irretrievably, under our contemporary towns. The analogy is Freud's but I would like to carry it one step further. Imagine for a moment that all important written records and monuments predating the industrial revolution had been destroyed by some catastrophe like the burning down of the library in Alexandria; and that knowledge of the past could be obtained only by archaeological excavations. Without digging into the underground strata, modern society, ignorant of the culture of the renaissance, of antiquity, pre-history, and the age of the dinosaurs, would be reduced to an unimaginably superficial, two-dimensional existence: a species without a past and probably—for lack of comparative values—without much future. An individual deprived of his dreams, of irrational impulses, of any form of ideation except articulate verbal thought would be in much the same position. Dreaming, in the literal and metaphorical sense, seems to be an essential part of psychic metabolism—as essential as its counterpart, the formation and automatization of habits. Without this daily dip into the ancient sources of mental life we would probably all become desiccated automata (150, p. 181).

The possibility that dreaming may serve as a psychological stimulant has also been proposed by Alan Leveton in a paper provocatively titled "The Night Residue." Leveton defines the night residue as being "a psychological phenomenon which (1) is derived from the return of repressed material under the special conditions of sleep, and (2) persists in some form into the waking state owing to incomplete re-repression during the process of waking" (161, p. 506). The manifest dream is part of the night residue but in Leveton's view the latter is the broader term including all forms of mentation which arise in sleep and persist into waking life with variable effects, from inconsequential ones to highly influential ones.

In their more dramatic instances these effects may take pathological forms, such as onset of psychosis or morning depression, brought about by pressures of incompletely re-repressed materials on the ego's defense capabilities. Or they may take adaptive forms, such as resolutions of identity conflicts or recent anxiety states, made possible by the opportunities for ego synthesis created by these same incompletely re-repressed materials.

These views are congruent with our previous suggestion that the day residue's role in dream formation may be an exploi*tive* one, using, as it were, the psychological resources represented by repressed imagery and affect to further the ego's organizational purposes, as well as an exploi*ted* one, in which it is used as a vehicle for cathartic purposes. Leveton's views are also consistent with Lowy's position that a dream need not be remembered in waking life in order to be presumed to have served its purposes, since the night residue includes "all forms of drive derivatives . . . even those which do not include imagery or affect, whose presence may be known only by the reactions of the ego to intrusions of . . . released repressed material . . ." (161, p. 506).

REORGANIZATION

The idea that dreaming affords special opportunities for reorganization of ego functions has been explicitly advanced by French, Jones, Breger, and Dewan (19, 36, 63, 64, 120, 129).

The main lines of French's focal conflict theory of dreaming were reviewed in our discussion of his approach to dream interpretation. We shall focus here on two specific principles of ego reorganization which are considered by French (and Fromm) to be frequent aspects of the dream-work: "increased cognitive grasp," in which previously unnoticed facets of the focal conflict or its historical background are brought into view, usually by way of analogy, and "prophylactic defense," in which the ego seeks to achieve an optimal degree of commitment to the focal conflict, again usually by way of analogy. The implication in both instances is that increased mastery of the analogous materials may be transferred to subsequent encounters with the focal conflict in reality. Thus in the highway dream we may speculate that the symbol of "the flames in the rear view mirror" served to bring to notice certain potentially destructive aspects of the conflict aroused by the luncheon conversation with my friend, which were not included in my waking ruminations over that conversation. However, so this theory assumes, I have dealt successfully with flames of mysterious origins before, and so I may expect to do so again. Similarly, as regards "prophylactic defense," we have already considered that the shift in the highway dream from the familiar scene of passing a truck to the unfamiliar scene of driving through a fiery hoop may have served to readjust my problem solving efforts from a very defensive posture to a less defensive posture. However, we may now further speculate that a still less defensive posture may have been taken had the dream included my turning around to assess the damage which earlier on I did not think to prevent. That the dream did not include such a sequence may be taken to suggest that this degree of commitment to the resolution of the focal conflict fell outside my ego's margin of defensive safety. But again, so this theory assumes, I have safely held back from ultimate confrontations before and may expect to do so again.

French makes frequent references in his writings on dreams to integrative ego functions. However, as I have noted elsewhere, his descriptions and illustrations reveal an almost exclusive emphasis on ego defenses as traditionally conceived, doubtless reflecting his exclusive dependence on observations drawn from the clinical practice of psychoanalysis (120, 125). Defensive ego functions may of course be viewed as serving adaptive purposes, so in claiming that his dream analyses reveal adaptive processes, French cannot be faulted. However, it can hardly be claimed that defenses are the only adaptive processes available to the ego in its governance of the dream-work. In a previous monograph I proposed the hypothesis that dreaming serves ego synthesis functions as well as ego defense functions (120). It seemed to me that this hypothesis could best be studied by subjecting manifest dreams to an analytic method derived from a theory of adaptive human development. And I chose for that purpose what I believe is our most viable such theory: the epigenetic dimension of psychoanalytic theory, as originally formulated by Erik Erikson. The hypothesis was systematically stated as follows:

> . . . a manifest dream is the product of a confluence of psychodynamic forces: (1) A motivating repressed wish of infantile origin; (2) the defense ego, which so discharges the energy of the repressed wish as to maintain a healthy state of sleep; and (3) the synthesis ego, which so governs the setting, style and rhythm of the dream's formation as to support a subsequently adaptive state of wakefulness (120, p. 43).

I described this third process as involving the preconscious re-differentiation and re-integration of previous epigenetic successes and failures in the context and under the pressure of contemporary developmental crises. I went on to illustrate the epigenetic method of dream analysis, which I hoped would underscore the plausibility of that part of the hypothesis which referred to the "synthesis ego." For example, a manifest dream reported by a female college student, was as follows:

> An image of walking down Eighteenth Street toward Barnes and Noble's. When I got there I kept looking around at all the people who were passing the book store. At first I was puzzled that I did not see anyone that I knew but soon I felt deserted and began to cry. The next thing that I remember was the consciousness of being near a brook; the brook was running past me, and I was standing on a rock nearby. At first I just stood there, but eventually I began to prepare to dive from the rock into the water, but I could not force myself to do so (120, p. 44).

The analysis, which assumes some familiarity with Erikson's developmental concepts, was as follows:

> . . . The locomotor zone (walking) in association with the passive-incorporative mode (kept looking around at all the people who were passing) activates feelings of ambivalent trust (was puzzled that I did not see anyone that I knew) and then feelings of mistrust (felt deserted). A break in the continuity of the dream is followed by a sequence which seems to be a variation of the same rhythm (at first I was puzzled . . . but soon . . .; at first I just stood there, but eventually . . .) on a similar theme: the inhibited locomotor zone

(standing on a rock . . . just stood there), in association with the passive incorporative mode (the brook was running past me), which leads to an inhibition of the intrusive mode (I began to prepare to dive from the rock into the water, but I could not force myself to do so). Throughout the dream there are ambivalent overtones of the identity crisis: she first looks for familiar others, and then finds puzzlement and desertion in aloneness (120, p. 44).

And the theoretical discussion was as follows:

What significance may we derive from his transcription, viewing the dream as a reconstruction of the synthesis ego? First, note that the dream is woven entirely of references to the first and third epigenetic phases. Recall our tentative hypothesis that in female identity-formation a synthesis of the first and third phases is critical, whereas in male identity-formation a synthesis of the second and third phases is critical. The phase specific task of the dreamer is, of course, identity formation. May we take this first observation, then, as evidence of normal female synthesis activity?

Consider also that the note on which the dream concludes is not one of repressed intrusiveness (since the dream figure was not threatened with drowning, or injury or any of the similarly dire consequences that are readily available to the machinations of dream formation) but one of *inhibited* intrusiveness.

Recall that a ratio of inclusiveness over intrusiveness has been postulated as characteristic of normal female development. May we count this second observation too, then, as evidence of identity-syntonic synthesis activity?

Next, what of the regressed note on which the first segment of the dream ends: mistrust? . . . . It is first . . . important to note that the consequence of this regression is neither sleep-disruption nor hallucinatory compensation. Rather, it is a shift in perspective, and progression to a mode (intrusive) that is phase specifically linked with the zone (locomotor) from which the regression had its start. Might it be, then, that we are observing an instance of "regression in the service of the ego"—or more precisely, regression in the service of the *synthesis* ego? In other words, is this a review of a trust-mistrust ratio established in the dreamer's past, testing, as it were, its potentially adaptive support in the resolution of a current developmental crisis? And might we now say the same as regards the inhibition of intrusiveness, which while it is the latest identifiable epigenetic referent in the dream, is still a regressed position for the dreamer?

Finally, what of the rhythmic qualities in the structure of this dream—the 3-1—3-1—3 pattern? Might this reflect a pattern characteristic of the dreamer's synthesis ego, as, for example, a sequence analysis of her Rorschach productions might reveal characteristic patterns of defense ego functioning? (120, pp. 45-46).

Since the publication of *Ego Synthesis in Dreams* I have received a number of justifiable complaints that the examples of epigenetic dream analysis contained in that monograph are neither sufficiently numerous nor clear to enable other investigators to employ the method. Sometimes these complaints have been accompanied by requests for an explicit statement of the definitions and criteria that had been my frame of reference when composing examples of ego synthesis processes in dreams.

In due time I shall respond to such requests with a scoring manual complete with definitions, criteria, examples, and a scheme for summarizing and perhaps quantifying the results of epigenetic dream analysis. All I can offer at this writing is a more lucid and systematic example:

Recall the series of dreams collected by Dement and Wolpert from one normal male EEG monitored subject over the course of a single night of sleep (Chapter Four above).

1. "We were swimming and doing a lot of things. Everybody was in bathing suits at the swimming pool and I seemed to be admiring my body all the time. In one of the sequences there was this race, and then the racing stopped, and I was swimming down towards the end of the pool. I must have swam it awfully fast, although kind of leisurely. I climbed out and there was some guy sitting there who I immediately disliked. He seemed to epitomize all the guys who make asses of themselves parading around in bathing suits who I grudgingly admit do look good in bathing suits, but who are so conscious of it. And he was oiling himself. Anyway, it seemed as though I was afraid that my friend—I can't remember, he is just a blank . . . or even she, is just blank—was going to be attracted to this guy and not to myself. But for some reason I wasn't afraid as I ought to have been. I seemed to have some sort of metamorphosis. I became just like a strong-muscled Greek god. There was a lot of diving, and once my bathing suit almost came off. It seemed like I was in a white bathing suit. Then it seemed like we were all waiting for a TV program that Miss X [a well-known Hollywood actress] was to be on just before the bell went off."

2. "A and B [two prominent Hollywood entertainers] were lying on a bed in this room, and I was apparently with them. The door suddenly opened and B . . . no A . . . fired this gun, started firing his gun and the panels dropped out of the door and the whole door came crashing down. Then a half-visible man started walking in and said, 'I'm Mr. Blank, I want the plans.' He walked over to A and put his hands around his neck and started to squeeze. It was odd because he was intangible but it seemed as though A could feel him squeezing. We all started trying to squeeze him back and all of a sudden he became tangible or something, but anyway I started to hit him and I just knocked the hell out of him, the poor little fellow. And I remember standing there in a kind of a triumph just as the bell rang."

3. "I dreamed I was coming into this room and I didn't have a key. I walked up to the building and Charles R. was standing there. The thing was, I was trying to climb in the window. Anyway, Charles was standing there by the door and he gave me some sandwiches, two sandwiches. They were red—it looked like Canadian bacon and his were boiled ham. I couldn't understand why he gave me the worst sandwiches. Anyway, we went on into the room and it didn't look like the right place at all. It seemed to be some kind of party. I think that it was at that point when I started thinking about how fast I could get out of the place if I had to. And there was something about nitroglycerin, I don't quite remember. The last thing was somebody throwing a baseball."

4. "I was talking to my aunt about how you got in touch with the underground left over from World War II. She told me about a number of other undergrounds and we were just talking and wandering around the house and I played with my dog a little bit and so forth and she asked me about my work. Finally it seemed like it was time to get dinner and I knew that my mother had been cooking when we started talking. We went down to the dining room and I asked my mother about the underground, and just as I was waiting for her to tell us what the World War II underground was, I said, 'Don't you think we can settle the question?' And the bell went off."

5. "Uh, this dream had something to do with a lecture. It was something about Economics but anyway I was sitting watching Professor Z. and he was lecturing in a queer way. All the students were sitting down at the front of the lecture hall behind a long table, and Professor Z. was standing out in the middle of the room on one of the desks. All of a sudden, this big argument broke out while he was talking and

they were both going on at the same time—his lecture and the argument. Claude R. and somebody else were arguing like that and all of a sudden I realized I was awake" (35, pp. 571-72).

Dement and Wolpert, raising the question of whether the dreams in this series are in any way related, comment as follows:

All the dreams in this sequence seem to express a general theme of conflict and violence. In dreams one and two of the series, an identical plot line is seen as the dreamer experiences a physical triumph over a male adversary. The triumph is associated with an abrupt metamorphosis in both cases. In the first dream, the dreamer becomes powerfully built "like a strong-muscled Greek god" and in the second, Mr. Blank suddenly becomes tangible and accessible to the dreamer's blows. Although the theme is constant, the setting is quite different; in one a bedroom, in the other a swimming pool. Only in the second dream does the conflict erupt into actual physical violence.

Dream three finds the dreamer on the receiving end of his friend's hostility as he is given the "worst" sandwich. He also dreams "something about nitroglycerin." This "something" and the ball thrown by "somebody" and the question of how fast he could get out if he had to would seem to signify that the dream was about to disintegrate into a more open expression of violence as the awakening occurred.

In dream four violence is displaced in time to World War II and the underground, but the dreamer's query, "Don't you think we can settle the question," seems to imply a concern over some present conflict.

In dream five the violence is again verbal and is attributed to others whom the dreamer is watching from a distance.

Thus, in this sequence, the theme of violence and conflict builds up into an actual physical outbreak in dream two. It is then seemingly contained verbally in the last two dreams after being allowed abortive expression in dream three (35, p. 572).

The epigenetic method of converting these dreams into research materials runs as follows: All the dreams in this sequence seem related to the normal growth crisis of autonomy versus shame-doubt, as formulated in Erikson's epigenetic theory of ego development. In dreams one and two of the series, the dreamer experiences feelings of shame, embarrassment, or humiliation. In the first dream he swims leisurely, takes a dislike to a show-off whom he nonetheless grudgingly admires, and is surprised to find that he is not afraid of being rejected. In dream two his sense of triumph is mixed with sympathy for the "poor little fellow" whom he is knocking hell out of. In dream three the emphasis shifts to ineptness and doubt—as he finds himself having to climb in the window for lack of a key and unable to understand why he is getting the worst sandwiches. Dream four finds him again in control of a situation in which his position is potentially weak as he takes the initiative in "settling the question" with his mother. In dream five there is some ambiguity as to who is feeling autonomous and who is experiencing doubt, Professor Z. or the argumentative students, and it is also not clear with which side the dreamer identifies himself.

From this analysis we might conclude that some kind of adaptive dream-work has been concerned in this series with reviewing, updating, or in some other way "working over" the nuclear epigenetic crisis which is central to normal development in the second and third years of life, and which enters more or less significantly into the developmental equations of all periods of life.

At this point a common misunderstanding should be anticipated in order to avoid it. We have shown that the dream series can be analyzed within two different frames of reference. This does not mean that we must choose between them. Dement and Wolpert were interested in spotting whatever common strains might have been governing this series of dreams. If any form of continuity could be shown, then there was a basis for the hypothesis that the dreams were related. These investigators hardly deserve criticism for using a standard tool in testing this hypothesis, i.e., the familiar method of generalizing from the content of the dream to the psychodynamics of the dreamer. They do this expertly, and if the dreamer had been a patient in therapy, one can easily imagine increased insight being the result of their interpretations. The analytic approach used in the second instance adopts a reverse strategy. Here we do not use dreams for the purpose of shedding light on personality; rather we use a theory of personality for the purpose of shedding light on the process of dreaming.

The familiar psychodynamic approach is strongest in showing connections between dreams and the psychological processes of waking life. The epigenetic approach is strongest in its potential for suggesting connections between dreams and the psychological processes of dreaming life: What might it mean when all five dreams of a series are attuned to the same nuclear stage of ego development? How might the processes that produce such a series differ from the processes that produce a series involving a *range* of nuclear crises? What might be suggested by a dream series that begins on a note of "trust," say, and ends on a note of "mistrust," or vice versa; or, as in the present series, when it begins on a note of autonomy, pauses on a note of doubt, resumes the autonomy theme, and ends on the fence? Consider the slant of these questions: they are more dreaming oriented than dream oriented. They seek to make amenable to investigation the nature of dreaming, the functions it performs, and the processes by which it performs them—whether the dream is interpreted or not.

But let us sound a note of caution. We have supposed that some kind of overall adaptive intelligence is at work in this series of dreams. This is a very large supposition, supported almost entirely by theory. Any attempt at empirical documentation is bound to be conjectural. Erikson's theory can support the conjecture, but only if we utilize more of it than we have so far. A few words, then, about the theory: The nuclear growth crises—trust/mistrust, autonomy/shame-doubt, initiative/guilt, industry/inferiority, etc.—have enjoyed an enthusiastic reception in psychological circles. Erikson has a way with words, especially English words, and has fortunately not subverted this talent by any misguided dedication to Big Science. (See Chart 2.) Column G is therefore pleasing to the eye, but this should not blind us to the congeries of psychoanalytic observations which Column G is primarily designed to order; namely, the systematic inter-connectedness of (1) man's prolonged and distinctly programmed physical maturation (Column Z), (2) his distinctively elaborate development as a symbolizing creature (Column M), and (3) the distinctive adaptive premium which is placed on his development of social skills (Columns P and Y). Failing to appreciate these complexities one can use the worksheet as a way of avoiding, rather than a way of following, the theory that produced it.

With these reminders, let us turn to the conjectural task: Dream one seems to base its autonomy resolution along the psycho*sexual* dimension on the active incorporative mode (admiring my body all the time), and on the conceptual modes (he seemed to epitomize; I seemed to have some sort of metamorphosis). Along the psycho-*social* dimension, the resolution is based on the eliminative and retentive modalities of "letting go" and "holding on" (immediately

Chart 2. Revised Epigenetic Worksheet

	Z *Psychosexual Zones*	M *Psychosexual Modes*	P *Psychosocial Zones*	Y *Psychosocial Modalities*	G *Normal Growth Crises*
1.	Oral-respiratory-sensory-kinesthetic	a. Passive incorporative b. Active incorporative	Maternal person	a. To get b. To take	Trust/mistrust
2.	Anal-urethral-muscular	a. Retentive b. Eliminative	Parental persons	a. To hold (on) b. To let (go)	Autonomy/shame-doubt
3.	Infantile-genital-locomotor	♂ Intrusive ♀ Inclusive	Basic family	To "make" (= going after) To "make like" (= playing)	Initiative/guilt
4.	Cerebral-cortical*	Conceptual*	"Neighborhood," school, community*	To turn to*; to know how* To make things (= completing) To make things together	Industry/inferiority
5.			Peer groups and outgroups; models of leadership	To be (oneself)—or not to be To share being oneself	Identity and repudiation/identity diffusion
6.			Partners in friendship, sex, competition, cooperation	To lose and find oneself in another ♂ To have and hold* (= protect) ♀ To have and hold* (= give in = produce)	Intimacy and solidarity/isolation
7.			Divided labor and shared household	To let be* ♂ To make be ♀ To take care of	Generativity and authority*/self-absorption
8.			"Mankind" "My kind"	To be through having been; to face not being; to be a has-been*	Integrity/despair

* Modification or extension of Erikson's worksheet.

disliked; waiting for a TV program). In dream two, the psycho-*social* emphasis remains on the retentive and eliminative modalities ("I want the plans"; started trying to squeeze him back; knocked the hell out of him), while on the psycho*sexual* dimension the symbolism of intrusiveness is brought into play (fired his gun)—the autonomy resolution holding firm. In dream three, in which the autonomy resolution devolves into doubt, the emphasis on intrusiveness continues (trying to climb in a window: throwing a baseball) but this time in conjunction with the passive incorporative modality of "getting" (he gave me some sandwiches). In dream four, which reintroduces the autonomy resolution, the active incorporative modality (asked my mother about the underground) is linked with the retentive modality (don't you think we can settle the question). In dream five, the active incorporative modality (listening to a lecture) is brought into conflict with the retentive modality (a big argument . . . going on at the same time), and the resolution is ambiguous.

Two lines of conjecture emerge from this exercise: (1) The passive incorporative modality would seem to be problematic in that it only appears once and when it does in dream three the crisis is resolved on the side of doubt. This line of thought is strengthened by the observation that the intrusive mode, which also figures in dream three, held strong in dream two, where it was associated with a different modality. (2) Retentive social skills seem to be a stable ego resource in that they appear in every dream of the series *except* dream three. They are conjoined with the active incorporative and conceptual modes in dream one and with the intrusive mode in dream two—facilitating autonomy resolutions in both instances. In dream four, they are combined with the modality of active incorporation with encouraging results. And in dream five they are opposed to the modality of active incorporation with ambiguous results.

Could it be that we are observing here a recuperative or growth process in which a component of ego strength and a component of ego weakness are being systematically deployed in various juxtapositions under the singular conditions of dreaming sleep? This is what we are left with: an hypothesis about *how* dreaming may function as a process of personality development, independently of any subsequent efforts to "interpret" the dreams.

In a recent thoughtful paper, "Function of Dreams," Louis Breger makes very good use of three advantages in addressing the subject of this chapter. He is cognizant of the studies reported in Chapter Three and of the developmental and evolutionary perspectives which have been generated by these studies in respect to the possible functions served by REM sleep; he is familiar with French's focal conflict theory; and he has been persuaded that Freud's economic point of view is untenable. He then refers the question of the function of dreaming to an interesting admixture of clinical psychoanalytic theory and information theory:

> . . . Dreams are one output of particular memory systems operating under the guidance of programs that are peculiar to sleep. These programs stem from certain early modes of psychological operation and, hence, dreams may be said to be regressive, though not in exactly the way that Freud used the term. Certain memory systems have been activated during the period prior to sleep and have set into operation emotional reactions that feed back and keep these particular systems active or "ready." Such activation may have been initiated by a specific event—for example, a rejection by an important person—or by a train of thought or fantasy. But the involvement of emotional reactions serves to potentiate these systems as opposed to the many others that are in operation during the pre-sleep period. . . .

> Upon going to sleep certain memory systems are more "ready" than others and, when the normal periods of nightly activation (the REM periods) occur in their cyclic fashion, it is these ready or primed systems that are brought into play. Dreams are one output of these memory systems, an output which includes images, thoughts, and feelings and a variety of psychophysiological reactions. The quality of dreams, that is, their creative and sometimes bizarre nature, is due to the special programs guiding the internal transformations and output of the memory systems during sleep (19, p. 19).

In essence, these views are very similar, if not identical, to those of French. Breger's thesis merits particular attention, however, at two points: (1) It is less equivocal in assigning an actively initiating role in dream formation to the day residue. (2) It demonstrates that information theory may bring to the theory of dreaming just those systematizing influences that psychoanalytic energy theory sought futilely to exert.

A fourth view of dreaming as a reorganizational process has been proposed by Edmond Dewan (36). It is very similar to Breger's view except that Dewan takes the further step of referring the question of dream function to the analogy of information processing devices. Dewan asks us to view the brain as a computer and then to consider the hypothesis that the purpose of sleep is to program or reprogram the brain. The function of dreaming is then hypothetically seen to be that of "sorting" (or "addressing") memories as well as motor and perceptual "sub-routines" with respect to drives and goals by using labels provided by associated feelings or emotional nuances.

It is too early to say whether this cybernetic model will be able to generate testable hypotheses with specific relevance to the psychology of dreaming, as distinct from the psychophysiology of sleep and the D-state. Dewan has made a promising beginning in this direction but at present the primary value of his work is its congruence with Breger's psychological model.

VIGILANCE

We have already touched on Ullman's hypothesis that the function of dreaming is not to preserve sleep but to maintain an optimal state of vigilance. We have also noted that in advancing this hypothesis Ullman anticipated Snyder's evolutionary theory of REM sleep. In this section we want to specify in more purely psychological terms what Ullman means by "an optimal state of vigilance," and we want to gain a clearer view of how Ullman's conception of vigilance may amplify that of Snyder.

The human organism, says Ullman, shares with lower forms of life a need for vigilance:

> Unique in the human, however, are the manner and form of vigilance operations. Behavior, consciously directed in the waking state, is geared toward the maintenance of relatedness to the *social* environment. Potential threats arise out of the context of *social* existence, and the diffuse ramifications of the threats extend to experiences that expose the flaws, gaps, inadequacies and misconceptions of consciousness. Such threats now extend to any experience that challenges value systems, social status or psychologic mechanisms of defense. In the every day experience of the human being, threats of this nature overshadow direct threats to physical existence. While he is awake, vigilance is tempered by adequate conceptualization, communication and behavior. . . .

The problem of vigilance comes into focus more sharply in connection with the sleep-wakefulness cycle: the necessities which confront the human organism in connection with sleep are of a two-fold nature. With the inception of the sleeping state there arises the need to effect a radical transformation in the activity of the individual. Social orientation and relatedness to the external environment give way to a form of activity governed primarily by physiological needs and hence occurring at an involuntary level.

Similarly, the transition from sleep to wakefulness in response to any stimulus of sufficient strength impinging upon the organism is characterized not simply by the process of awakening, but more significantly by the resumption of consciousness of one's social existence. In the human being these significant stimuli now include symbolic as well as direct sensory effects. The state of vigilance during sleep has shifted from one involving danger to the organism at an animal level, viz., in terms of physical attack, to one involving danger to the organism in its relatedness to society (236, pp. 529-30; my italics).

Let us now examine Snyder's evolutionary theory in detail. His first premise is:

. . . that there is survival advantage to a maximal extent of sleep compatible with the satisfaction of nutritional needs, and that this would have been especially true in the primitive mammalian predicament (212, p. 130).

Further:

. . . a built-in physiological mechanism to bring about brief but periodic awakenings for the purpose of sampling or scanning the environment, without significantly disturbing the continuity of sleep, would make extended sleep both feasible and adaptively advantageous (212, p. 130).

He then notes that precisely such periodic arousals do occur between REM periods and resumed sleep in all mammals so far studied. His second premise is that these brief periods of arousal following REM sleep served a "sentinel" or vigilance function in mammalian evolution, which had adaptive value in the largely predatory conditions to which mammals were adapted. But why, Snyder asks, should these periodic arousals have been preceded by such an elaborate process as REM sleep? His answer:

Periodic awakenings during sleep would be of doubtful survival value unless the organism were already sufficiently prepared for fight or flight.

It is my third premise that the REM state provides such preparatory activation prior to each sentinel awakening (212, p. 131).

In summary, Snyder's hypothesis is that REM sleep

. . . not only maintains the constancy of the internal environment during sleep, but at the same time helps to insure the status quo in relation to the external environment as well (212, p. 131).

Snyder's focus, then, is on the vigilance function of *REM sleep* and its adaptive value in *mammalian* evolution, in which readiness to flee, attack, or hide is at a premium. Ullman's focus is on the vigilance function of *dreaming* and its adaptive value in *human* evolution, in which adaptation by way of social organization is at a premium. There emerges from a conjoinment of these views perhaps our first truly psychobiological hypothesis regarding the functions of the D-state—with good support at the levels of both phylogenetic and ontogenetic considerations. Moreover, as we move to considerations of individual human development it is reassuring to note how immediately Ullman's discussions of vigilance to problems of relatedness to social environments, changes in value systems and in psychological patterns of defense, suggest the views of French, Erikson, and Jones.

PERCEPTIVENESS
IN DEPTH

We were obviously engaged in a play on words when we assumed that the cultivation in dreaming of "perceptiveness in depth" might be the counterpart to what Berger has proposed may be the role of REM sleep in the development and maintenance of human depth perception. Surely we cannot expect the analogy between the functions of REM sleep and the functions of dreaming to lead to as nice a fitting at this juncture as we observed to be the case with the respective views of Snyder and Ullman. The lead is worth pursuing, however, because it will allow us to focus the contributions of Jung, Angyal, and Piaget on the question before us.

Let us first remove the quotation marks from "perceptiveness in depth" by defining the term. We mean perceptiveness *of self*, awareness of diversity within self, self-insight—in the senses that modern psychology has come to associate with psychological health and the optimal development of self-actualizing personality patterns.

Now recall that Jung's approach to dream interpretation was based on the assumption that the human psyche is a self-regulative system in which unconscious processes function in compensatory relation to conscious processes, seeking, as it were, to check conscious excesses and to challenge conscious attitudes of false complacency when either of these tendencies threatens to compromise an individual's capacities to develop his particular potentials to their fullest. Recall also that in Jung's view dreams are the spokesmen for these compensatory efforts of the unconscious.

This assumption has earned a good amount of clinical credibility over the years, by virtue of having guided countless therapeutically effective dream interpretations. However, when psychologists have tried to assess the theoretical merit of Jung's assumption, difficulties have arisen. For, with Jung, one is invited either to accept the assumption on faith or to refer judgment of its credibility to further assumptions involving the "collective unconscious," inherited "archetypes," and so on. And, however successfully one seeks to keep an open mind in respect to these provocative intangibles, they are of no help in imagining what potentially observable psychological processes might be involved in the compensatory function of dreaming.

It is here that Angyal, working within an independently conceived theoretical system, based on premises which lend themselves to empirical scrutiny, may be seen to have provided just the credibility base for the compensation assumption that Jung's theoretical system cannot give it. Recall the hypothesis, derived from Angyal's theory of personality, that a consequence of dreaming is the exposure to consciousness of shifts in the balances of power which take place from night to night between an individual's two potential systems for organizing his total personality, under the conditions of freedom from the constraints of social expediency which are characteristic of sleep. Whether or not a person takes advantage in his waking life of these nightly showings of his diverse potentials for self-development, as, in Jung's terms, whether or not a person follows the guidance of his compensating unconscious, is not a matter that need concern us. What merits our attention here is that the hypothesis derived from Angyal's theory is, within the framework of the psychology of dreaming, an almost exact restatement of Jung's compensation assumption. Consider, moreover, that the hypothesis has two distinct advantages: (1) It was generated by an ontogenetic theory of personality development, and (2) it does not imply, as does Jung's assumption, some vaguely inherent affinity between unconscious processes and health on the one hand, and between conscious processes and neurosis on the other.

It might be objected that Angyal's theory, while closer to observable facts than Jung's, is far from being our most articulate theory with respect to the *developmental* aspects of self-perception. In that event we have Piaget's theory from which we have seen the position derived that dreaming is a highly egocentric form of thought, experienced as action, a function of which is that of "giving form to affective schemas and thus generating ideas on the level of individual truth" (176, p. 167).

The combined views of Jung and Angyal, in addition to those of Piaget, may thus be seen to suggest the hypothesis that dreaming serves to exercise man's unique capacity for self-perception in depth. It might be argued that this is less an hypothesis than an obvious and commonly observable fact. The same could be said of dreaming as a wish-fulfilling experience; yet Freud thought it worthwhile to try to invest that obvious and commonly observable fact with the properties of a scientific hypothesis. Our objective has been the same.

SUMMARY

How to take a discriminate position in respect to the diverse hypotheses which have been reviewed in this chapter? As in our review of the various hypotheses regarding the functions of REM sleep, the evidence does not exist which might support an attempt to choose from among them, nor even to weigh one against another. I shall therefore second the sentiments expressed by Snyder who in a similar predicament had this to say:

If my juxtaposition of these several hypotheses appears eclectic or even indiscriminate, that is by design, for none is sufficiently well based at this time to justify the exclusion of the rest. Beyond the fact that the proverbial analogy to the blindman examining the elephant is probably applicable to the early exploration of any complex visage of nature, there is nothing to assure us that the adaptive function of the REM state need be unitary. Within the general requirement of serving survival, the waking state certainly has multiple specific functions, and perhaps that is characteristic of each of the three modes of existence (212, p. 132).

In conclusion, however, I do wish to share a set of convictions about the functions of dreaming which have inevitably and imperceptibly developed in my own purview of dream psychology over the course of the various exercises which went into the writing of this book. I think Snyder's sentinel hypothesis is the most promising of those which seek to understand the purposes served by REM sleep in phylogenesis, the more so in that the sentinel hypothesis is both sufficiently specific to explain the apparently exclusive role of REM sleep in the evolution of mammals, and sufficiently general to take cognizance of its variations in duration and intensity from species to species. Thus, as Snyder notes, the sentinel hypothesis provides ample conceptual space for including the various proposed developmental functions of REM sleep if any or all of these prove to be valid. Among the various analogous hypotheses regarding the psychological function of human dreaming, I think Ullman's vigilance hypothesis is the most promising. It commends itself as our best leading hypothesis, first because it accords so naturally with Snyder's evolutionary theory, and second because it has similar properties: it is sufficiently *psychophysiological* to promise an eventual understanding of how it is that dreaming may be an augmentative human response to the D-state, and it is at the same time sufficiently *psychological* to provide a framework within which to understand the functions of dreaming from the point of view of species adaptation *and* from the point of view of individual adaptation. The point of view of species adaptation requires that we show dreaming to be functionally relevant to man's three distinguishing adaptive achievements: technology, social organization, and language. The point of view of individual adaptation requires that we show dreaming to be functionally relevant to the capacities of individual humans to utilize both the constraints and the liberties, to which these species adaptations have committed all of us, in the service of perpetuating the only kinds of mutations that can help us now, in that they require particular technologies, particular forms of social organization, and particular languages to be adapt*ive*, rather than adapt*ed:* namely, new ideas.

In other words it may be that once Nature committed Man to his point of no return, his capacity to make his own culture—as she committed the tiger to his tooth, the elephant to his trunk, and the baboon to his troop—she then equipped him with the means to make the most of it. This, by making it not merely possible but *necessary* that he dream—every night—about every ninety minutes.

REFERENCES

1. Angyal, A.: *Neurosis and Treatment: A Holistic Theory.* E. Hanfmann and R. M. Jones, Eds. New York, John Wiley & Sons, 1965.
2. Ansbacher, H. and L.: *The Individual Psychology of Alfred Adler.* New York, Basic Books, 1956.
3. Antrobus, J., Antrobus, J., and Singer, J.: Eye movements during daydreaming, visual imagery, and other internally produced cognitive processes. Report to the Symposium on Eye Movements, Eastern Psychological Association, New York, 1963.
4. Antrobus, J., Antrobus, J., and Singer, J.: Eye movements accompanying daydreaming, visual imagery, and thought suppression. *J. Abnorm. Soc. Psychol.,* 69:244-252, 1964.
5. Antrobus, J., Dement, W., and Fisher, C.: Patterns of dreaming and dream recall: an EEG study. *J. Abnorm. Soc. Psychol.,* 69:341-344, 1964.
6. Aserinsky, E.: Periodic respiratory pattern occurring in conjunction with eye movements during sleep. *Science,* 150:763-766, 1965.
7. Aserinsky, E.: Physiological activity associated with segments of the rapid eye movement period. *Res. Publ. Ass. Res. Nerv. Ment. Dis.,* 45: in press.
8. Aserinsky, E., and Kleitman, N.: Regularly occurring periods of eye motility and concomitant phenomena during sleep. *Science,* 118:273-274, 1953.
9. Aserinsky, E., and Kleitman, N.: Two types of ocular motility occurring in sleep. *J. Appl. Physiol.,* 8:1-10, 1955.
10. Aserinsky, E., and Kleitman, N.: A motility cycle in sleeping infants as manifested by ocular and gross bodily activity. *J. Appl. Physiol.,* 8:11-18, 1955.

11. Baldridge, B., Whitman, R., and Kramer, M.: The concurrence of fine muscle activity and rapid eye movements during sleep. *Psychosom. Med.*, 27:19-26, 1965.

12. Berger, R.: Tonus of extrinsic laryngeal muscles during sleep and dreaming. *Science*, 134:840, 1961.

13. Berger, R.: Experimental modification of dream content by meaningful verbal stimuli. *Brit. J. Psychiat.*, 109:722-740, 1963.

14. Berger, R.: Oculomotor control: a possible function of REM sleep. *Psychol. Rev.*, in press.

15. Berger, R., and Oswald, I.: Effects of sleep deprivation on behavior, subsequent sleep, and dreaming. *J. Ment. Sci.*, 108:457-465, 1962.

16. Berger, R., and Oswald, I.: Eye movements during active and passive dreams. *Science*, 137:601, 1962.

17. Bertini, M., Lewis, H. B., and Witkin, H. A.: Some preliminary observations with an experimental procedure for the study of hypnagogic and related phenomena. *Arch. Psicol. Neurol.*, 6:493-534, 1964.

18. Boss, M.: *The Analysis of Dreams*. New York, Philosophical Library, 1958.

19. Breger, L.: The function of dreams. *J. Abnorm. Psychol. Mono.*, 72:1-28, 1967.

20. Brown, N. O.: *Life Against Death*. New York, Vintage Books, 1959.

21. Cartwright, R. D., Monroe, L. J., and Palmer, C.: Individual differences in response to REM deprivation. *Arch. Gen. Psychiat.*, 16:297-303, 1967.

22. Cartwright, R. D., and Monroe, L. J.: Effects of dream deprivation under two experimental conditions. Paper read at meeting of Association for the Psychophysiological Study of Sleep, Santa Monica, Calif., April 1967.

23. Dement, W.: Dream recall and eye movements during sleep in schizophrenics and normals. *J. Nerv. Ment. Dis.*, 122:263-269, 1955.

24. Dement, W.: Effect of dream deprivation. *Science*, 131:1705-1707, 1960.

25. Dement, W.: Experimental dream studies. In: *Science and Psychoanalysis: Scientific Proceedings of the Academy of Psychoanalysis*, J. Masserman, Ed. New York, Grune & Stratton, 1964, Vol. 7, pp. 129-162.

26. Dement, W.: Recent studies on the biological role of rapid eye movement sleep. *Amer. J. Psychiat.*, 122:404-407, 1965.

27. Dement, W., and Fisher, C.: Studies in dream deprivation and satiation. Abstract in: *Psychoanal. Quart.*, 299:671, 1960.

28. Dement W., and Fisher, C.: Studies in dream deprivation and satiation: an experimental demonstration of the necessity for dreaming. Abstract in: *Bull. Phila. Ass. Psychoanal.*, 10:30, 1960.

29. Dement, W., and Fisher, C.: Experimental interference with the sleep cycle. *Canad. Psychiat. Ass. J.*, 8:400-405, 1963.

30. Dement, W., Greenberg, S., and Klein, R.: The persistence of the REM deprivation effect. Report to Association for the Psychophysiological Study of Sleep. Washington, D. C., March 1965.

31. Dement, W., Kahn, E., and Roffwarg, H.: The influence of the laboratory situation on the dreams of the experimental subject. *J. Nerv. Ment. Dis.*, 140:119-131, 1965.

32. Dement, W., and Kleitman, N.: Cyclic variations in EEG during sleep and their relation to eye movements, body motility and dreaming. *Electroenceph. Clin. Neurophysiol.*, 9:673-690, 1957.

33. Dement, W., and Kleitman, N.: The relation of eye movements during sleep to dream activity: an objective method for the study of dreaming. *J. Exp. Psychol.*, 53:339-346, 1957.

34. Dement, W., and Wolpert, E.: Relation of eye movements, body motility, and external stimuli to dream content. *J. Exp. Psychol.*, 55:543-553, 1958.

35. Dement, W., and Wolpert, E.: Relationships in the manifest content of dreams occurring on the same night. *J. Nerv. Ment. Dis.*, 126:568-578, 1958.

36. Dewan, E.: Sleep as a programming process and dreaming ("D-state") as an addressing procedure. Paper read at meeting of Association for the Psychophysiological Study of Sleep, Santa Monica, Calif., April 1967.

37. Domhoff, B.: Night dreams and hypnotic dreams: is there evidence that they are different? *Int. J. Clin. Exp. Hypn.*, 12:159-168, 1964.

38. Domhoff, B., and Kamiya, J.: Problems in dream content study with objective indicators. I. A comparison of home and laboratory dream reports. *Arch. Gen. Psychiat.* (Chicago), 11:519-524, 1964.

39. Domhoff, B., and Kamiya, J.: Problems in dream content study with objective indicators. II. Appearance of experimental situation in laboratory dream narratives. *Arch. Gen. Psychiat.* (Chicago), 11:525-528, 1964.

40. Domhoff, B., and Kamiya, J.: Problems in dream content study with objective indicators. III. Changes in dream content throughout the night. *Arch. Gen. Psychiat.* (Chicago), 11:529-532, 1964.

41. Ephron, H., and Carrington, P.: REM sleep and cortical homeostasis: theoretical considerations. Report to Association for the Psychophysiological Study of Sleep, Washington, D. C., March 1965.

42. Erikson, E.: The dream specimen of psychoanalysis. In: *Psycho-analytic Psychiatry and Psychology*, R. Knight and C. Friedman, Eds. New York, International Universities Press, 1954, pp. 131-170.

43. Feinberg, I., Koresko, R., Heller, N., and Steinberg, H.: Unusually high dream time in an hallucinating patient. *Amer. J. Psychiat.*, 121:1018-1020, 1965.

44. Fisher, C.: Dreams and perception. *J. Amer. Psychoanal. Ass.*, 2: 389-445, 1954.

45. Fisher, C.: Dreams, images and perception: a study of unconscious-preconscious relationships. *J. Amer. Psychoanal. Ass.*, 4:5-48, 1956.

46. Fisher, C.: A study of the preliminary stages of the construction of dreams and images. *J. Amer. Psychoanal. Ass.*, 5:5-60, 1957.

47. Fisher, C.: Psychoanalytic implications of recent research on sleep and dreaming. *J. Amer. Psychoanal. Ass.*, 13:197-303, 1965.

48. Fisher, C., and Dement, W.: Dreaming and psychosis: observation on the dream-sleep cycle during the course of an acute paranoid psychosis. *Bull. Phila. Ass. Psychoanal.*, 11:130, 1961.

49. Fisher, C., and Dement, W.: Experimental manipulation of the dream-sleep cycle in relation to psychopathological states. *World Cong. Psychiat.*, June, 1961.

50. Fisher, C., and Dement, W.: Studies on psychopathology of sleep and dreams. *Amer. J. Psychiat.*, 119:1160-1168, 1963.

51. Fisher, C., and Gross, J.: Relationship between dream content and the REM erection cycle. Report to Association for the Psychophysiological Study of Sleep, Washington, D. C., March 1965.

52. Fisher, C., Gross, J., and Byrne, J.: Dissociation of penile erection from REMP and rebound effect. Report to Association for the Psychophysiological Study of Sleep, Gainesville, Fla., March 1966.

53. Fisher, C., Gross, J., and Zuch, J.: Cycle of penile erection synchronous with dreaming (REM) sleep. *Arch. Gen. Psychiat.* (Chicago), 12:29-45, 1965.

54. Fiss, H., Klein, G. S., and Bokert, E.: Waking fantasies following interruption of two types of sleep. *Arch. Gen. Psychiat.* (Chicago), 14:543-551, 1966.

55. Foulkes, D.: Dream reports from different states of sleep. *J. Abnorm. Soc. Psychol.*, 65:14-25, 1962.

56. Foulkes, D.: Theories of dream formation and recent studies of sleep consciousness. *Psychol. Bull.*, 62:236-247, 1964.

57. Foulkes, D.: *The Psychology of Sleep*. New York, Charles Scribner's Sons, 1966.

58. Foulkes, D.: Dreams of the male child: four case studies. *J. Child Psychiat.*, 8:81-97, 1967.

59. Foulkes, D., Pivik, T., Steadman, H., Spear, P., and Symonds, J.: Dreams of the male child: an EEG study. *J. Abnorm. Psychol.*, 72:6:457-467, 1967.

60. Foulkes, D., and Rechtschaffen, A.: Presleep determinants of dream content: the effect of two films. *Percept. Motor Skills*, 19:983-1005, 1964.

61. Foulkes, D., and Vogel, G.: Mental activity at sleep onset. *J. Abnorm. Psychol.*, 70:231-243, 1965.

62. Freidman, N., and Jones, R. M.: On the mutuality of the oedipus complex. *Amer. Imago*, 20:107-131, 1963.

63. French, T.: *The Integration of Behavior. II. The Integrative Process in Dreams.* Chicago, University of Chicago Press, 1954.

64. French, T. M., and Fromm, E.: *Dream Interpretation.* New York, Basic Books, 1964.

65. Freud, S.: The interpretation of dreams. In: *Standard Edition of the Complete Psychological Works of Sigmund Freud,* J. Strachey, Ed. London, Hogarth Press, 1953, Vol. 4.

66. Freud, S.: *Fragment of an Analysis of a Case of Hysteria* (1905). In: *Collected Papers.* London, Hogarth Press, 1950, Vol. 3, pp. 13-134.

67. Freud, S.: *From the History of an Infantile Neurosis* (1918). In: *Collected Papers.* London, Hogarth Press, 1950, Vol. 3, pp. 473-605.

68. Freud, S.: An evidential dream (1913). In: *Standard Edition of the Complete Psychological Works of Sigmund Freud.* London, Hogarth Press, 1958, Vol. 12, pp. 267-278.

69. Freud, S.: On narcissism: an introduction. In: *Standard Edition of the Complete Psychological Works of Sigmund Freud.* London, Hogarth Press, 1958, Vol. 14, pp. 67-102.

70. Freud, S.: A metapsychological supplement to the theory of dreams. In: *Standard Edition of the Complete Psychological Works of Sigmund Freud.* London, Hogarth Press, 1958, Vol. 14, 217-235.

71. Gerard, R.: The biological roots of psychiatry. *Amer. J. Psychiat.*, 112:81-90, 1955.

72. Goodenough, D., Lewis, H., Shapiro, A., Jaret, L., and Sleser, I.: Dream reporting following abrupt and gradual awakenings from different types of sleep. *J. Personality Soc. Psychol.*, 2:170-179, 1965.

73. Goodenough, D., Lewis, H., Shapiro, A., and Sleser, I.: Some correlates of dream reporting following laboratory awakenings. *J. Nerv. Ment. Dis.*, 140:365-373, 1965.

74. Goodenough, D., Shapiro, A., Holden, M., and Steinschriber, L.: Comparison of dreamers and nondreamers: eye movements, electro-

encephalograms, and recall of dreams. *J. Abnorm. Soc. Psychol.*, 59:295-302, 1959.

75. Green, W.: The effect of LSD on the sleep-dream cycle: an exploratory study. *J. Nerv. Ment. Dis.*, 140:417-426, 1965.
76. Greenberg, R.: Dream interruption insomnia. *J. Nerv. Ment. Dis.*, 144:18-21, 1967.
77. Greenberg, R., Kawliche, S., and Pearlman, C.: Dream deprivation study. Report to Association for the Psychophysiological Study of Sleep, Gainesville, Fla., March 1966.
78. Greenberg, R., and Pearlman, C.: Delirium tremens and dreaming.. *Amer. J. Psychiat.*, 124:133-142, 1967.
79. Greenberg, R., Pearlman, C., Brooks, R., Mayer, R., and Hartmann, E.: Dreaming and Korsakoff's psychosis. *Arch. Gen. Psychiat.*, 18:203-209, 1968.
80. Hall, C.: Diagnosing personality by the analysis of dreams. *J. Abnorm. Soc. Psychol.*, 42:68-79, 1947.
81. Hall, C.: What people dream about. *Sci. Amer.*, 184:60-63, 1951.
82. Hall, C.: A cognitive theory of dream symbols. *J. Gen. Psychol.*, 48:169-186, 1953.
83. Hall, C.: A cognitive theory of dreams. *J. Gen. Psychol.*, 49:273-282, 1953.
84. Hall, C.: The significance of the dream of being attacked. *J. Personality*, 24:168-180, 1955.
85. Hall, C.: Out of a dream came the faucet. *Psychoanal. and Psychoanal. Rev.*, 49:113-116, 1962.
86. Hall, C.: *Dreams of American College Students.* Publication No. 2, Primary Records in Psychology, R. Barker and B. Kaplan, Eds. University of Kansas Publications, Social Science Studies, 1963.
87. Hall, C.: Strangers in dreams: an empirical confirmation of the oedipus complex. *J. Personality*, 31:336-345, 1963.
88. Hall, C.: Slang and dream symbols. *Psychoanal. Rev.*, 51:38-48, 1964.
89. Hall, C.: An empirical investigation of the castration complex in dreams. *J. Personality*, 33:20-29, 1965.
90. Hall, C.: Attitudes toward life and death in poetry. *Psychoanal. Rev.*, 52:67-83, 1965.
91. Hall, C.: *The Meaning of Dreams.* New York, McGraw-Hill, 1966.
92. Hall, C.: A comparison of the dreams of four groups of hospitalized mental patients with each other and with a normal population. *J. Nerv. Ment. Dis.*, 143:135-139, 1966.
93. Hall, C.: Are prenatal and birth experiences represented in dreams? *Psychoanal. Rev.*, 54:157-174, 1967.

94. Hall, C.: Representation of the laboratory setting in dreams. *J. Nerv. Ment. Dis.*, 144:198-206, 1967.
95. Hall, C.: The methodology of content analysis applied to dreams. In: *Dream Psychology and the New Biology of Dreaming*, M. Kramer, Ed. Springfield, Ill., Charles C Thomas, 1969.
96. Hall, C., and Domhoff, B.: A ubiquitous sex difference in dreams. *J. Abnorm. Soc. Psychol.*, 66:278-280, 1963.
97. Hall, C., and Domhoff, B.: Aggression in dreams. *Int. J. Soc. Psychiat.*, 9:259-267, 1963.
98. Hall, C., and Domhoff, B.: Friendliness in dreams. *J. Soc. Psychol.*, 62:309-314, 1964.
99. Hall, C., and Smith, M. E.: An investigation of regression in a long dream series. *J. Geront.*, 19:66-71, 1964.
100. Hall, C., and Van de Castle, R.: *The Content Analysis of Dreams.* New York, Appleton-Century-Crofts, 1966.
101. Hall, C., and Van de Castle, R.: Studies of dreams reported in the laboratory and at home. *Institute of Dream Research Monograph Series*, 1:1-55, 1966.
102. Hall, C., Meier, C., Ruf, H., and Zeigler, A.: The forgetting of dreams in the laboratory. *Percept. Motor Skills*, 26:551-557, 1968.
103. Hall, C., and Lind, R.: *Dreams, Life and Literature: A Study of Franz Kafka.* Chapel Hill, University of North Carolina Press, 1970.
104. Hartmann, E.: The D-state: a review and discussion of studies on the physiologic state concomitant with dreaming. *New Eng. J. Med.*, 273:30-35, 87-92, 1965.
105. Hartmann, E.: The D-state (dreaming sleep) and the menstrual cycle. *Recent Advances Biol. Psychiat.*, 8:34-35, 1966.
106. Hartmann, E.: *The Biology of Dreaming.* Springfield, Ill. Charles C Thomas, 1967.
107. Hartmann, E., Verdone, P., and Snyder, F.: Longitudinal studies of sleep and dream patterns in psychiatric patients. *J. Nerv. Ment. Dis.*, 142:117-126, 1966.
108. Hawkins, D., Knapp, R., Scott, J., and Thresher, G.: Sleep studies in depressed patients. Report to Association for the Psychophysiological Study of Sleep, Washington, D. C., March 1965.
109. Hawkins, D., Puryear, H., Wallace, C., Deal, E., and Thomas, E.: Basal skin resistance during sleep and "dreaming." *Science*, 136:321-322, 1962.
110. Hermann, H., Jouvet, M., and Klein, M.: Etude polygraphique du sommeil chez la tortue. *C. R. Acad. Sci.* (Paris), 258:2175-2178, 1964.

111. Hobson, J., Goldfrank, F., and Snyder, F.: Respiration and mental activity in sleep. *J. Psychiat. Res.*, 3:79-90, 1965.

112. Hollender, M.: Is a wish to sleep a universal motive for dreaming? *J. Amer. Psychoanal. Ass.*, 10:323-328, 1962.

113. Holt, R.: A Critical examination of Freud's concept of bound vs. free cathexis. *J. Amer. Psychoanal. Ass.*, 10:475-525, 1966.

114. Hunter, I., and Breger, L.: The effect of pre-sleep group therapy upon subsequent dream content. *Psychological Issues Monograph Series.* New York, International Universities Press, in press.

115. Jacobson, A., Kales, A., Lehman, D., and Hoedemacher, F.: Muscle tonus in human subjects during sleep and dreaming. *Exp. Neurol.*, 10:418-424, 1964.

116. Jones, E.: *The Life and Work of Sigmund Freud.* New York, Basic Books, 1953, Vol. 1.

117. Jones, R. M.: The return of the un-repressed. *Amer. Imago*, 15: 175-180, 1958.

118. Jones, R. M.: *An Application of Psychoanalysis to Education.* Springfield, Ill., Charles C Thomas, 1960.

119. Jones, R. M.: Epigenetic reconstruction in dreaming. *Percept. Motor Skills*, 13:32, 1961.

120. Jones, R. M.: *Ego Synthesis in Dreams.* Cambridge, Mass., Schenkman, 1962.

121. Jones, R. M.: On the metaphor of the dream censor. *Percept. Motor Skills*, 15:45-46, 1962.

122. Jones, R. M.: Sexual symbols in dreams. *Percept. Motor Skills*, 19:118, 1964.

123. Jones, R. M.: The problem of "depth" in the psychology of dreaming. *J. Nerv. Ment. Dis.*, 139:507-515, 1964.

124. Jones, R. M.: Dream interpretation and the psychology of dreaming. *J. Amer. Psychoanal. Ass.*, 13:304-319, 1965.

125. Jones, R. M.: In and out of a procrustean bed: a review of *Dream Interpretation: A New Approach* by T. French and E. Fromm. *Contemporary Psychology*, 10:402-404, 1965.

126. Jones, R. M.: To "S"—perchance to "D": A review of *The Biology of Dreaming* by E. Hartmann. *Contemporary Psychology*, 13:401-402, 1968.

127. Jones, R. M.: The psychoanalytic theory of dreaming—1968. *J. Ment. Nerv. Dis.*, 147:587-603, 1968.

128. Jones, R. M.: *Fantasy and Feeling in Education.* New York, New York University Press, 1968.

129. Jones, R. M.: An epigenetic approach to the analysis of dreams. In: *Dream Psychology and the New Biology of Dreams*, M.

Kramer, Ed. Springfield, Ill., Charles C Thomas, 1969, pp. 379-398.

130. Jones, R. M.: The manifest dream, the latent content and the dream-work. In: Sleep and dreaming. *International Psychiatry Clinics*, E. Hartmann, Ed. Boston, Little, Brown, in press.

131. Jones, R. M.: The functions of dreaming. In: Sleep and dreaming. *International Psychiatry Clinics*, E. Hartmann, Ed. Boston, Little, Brown, in press.

132. Jouvet, D., Valatx, J., and Jouvet, M.: Etude polygraphique du sommeil du chaton. *C. R. Soc. Biol.* (Paris), 155:1660-1664, 1961.

133. Jouvet, M.: Studies on rhombencephalic sleep. Report to Association for the Psychophysiological Study of Sleep, Palo Alto, Calif., March 1964.

134. Jouvet, M.: Paradoxical sleep: a study of its nature and mechanisms. In: *Sleep Mechanisms (Progress in Brain Research)*, K., Akert, C. Bally, and J. Schade, Eds. Amsterdam, Elsevier, 1965, Vol. 19, pp. 20-62.

135. Jouvet, M., and Klein, M.: Analyse polygraphique du sommeil de la tortue. *C. R. Acad. Sci.* (Paris), 258:2175-2178, 1964.

136. Jouvet, M., and Mounier, D.: Neurophysiological mechanisms of dreaming. *Electroenceph. Clin. Neurophysiol.*, 14:424-430, 1962.

137. Jung, C. G.: *Modern Man in Search of a Soul.* New York, Harcourt, Brace & World, 1933.

138. Jung, C. G.: *Two Essays on Analytical Psychology.* New York, Meridian Books, 1956.

139. Kales, A., Hoedemaker, F., Jacobson, A., and Lichtenstein, E.: Dream-deprivation: an experimental reappraisal. *Nature* (London), 204:1337-1338, 1964.

140. Kardiner, A.: *The Individual and His Society.* New York, Columbia University Press, 1939.

141. Kardiner, A.: *The Psychological Frontiers of Society.* New York, Columbia University Press, 1945.

142. Kardiner, A., Karush, A., and Ovesey, L.: A methodological critique of Freudian theory. I. Basic concepts. *J. Nerv. Ment. Dis.*, 129:11-19, 1959.

143. Kardiner, A., Karush, A., and Ovesey, L.: A methodological study of Freudian theory. II. The libido theory. *J. Nerv. Ment., Dis.*, 129:133-143, 1959.

144. Kardiner, A., Karush, A., and Ovesey, L.: A methodological study of Freudian theory. III. Narcissism, bisexuality, and the dual instinct theory. *J. Nerv. Ment. Dis.*, 129:207-221, 1959.

145. Klein, G. S.: Consciousness in psychoanalytic theory: some implications for current research in perception. In: *Contemporary Educational Psychology*, R. M. Jones, Ed. New York, Harper Torchbooks, 1966, 156-185.

146. Klein, G. S.: Peremptory ideation: structure and force in motivated ideas. In: *Motives and Thought: Psychoanalytic Essays in Memory of David Rapaport*, R. R. Holt, Ed. New York, International Universities Press, 1966, pp. 80-128.

147. Klein, G. S.: Two theories or one? Perspectives to change in psychoanalytic theory. Paper presented at Conference of Psychoanalysts of the Southwest, Galveston, Texas, March 1966.

148. Klein, M., Michel, F., and Jouvet, M.: Etude polygraphique du sommeil chez les oiseaux. *C. R. Soc. Biol.* (Paris), 158:99-103, 1964.

149. Kleitman, N.: *Sleep and Wakefulness*, 2d ed. Chicago, University of Chicago Press, 1963.

150. Koestler, A.: *The Act of Creation*. New York, 1964.

151. Koresko, R., Snyder, F., and Feinberg, I.: "Dream time" in hallucinating and non-hallucinating schizophrenic patients. *Nature* (London), 199:1118-1119, 1963.

152. Kramer, M., Whitman, R., Baldridge, B., and Ornstein, P.: Drugs and dreams. III. The effects of Imipramine on the dreams of depressed patients. *Amer. J. Psychiat.*, 124:1385-1392, 1968.

153. Kremen, I.: Dream reports and rapid eye movements. Unpublished doctoral dissertation, Harvard University, 1961.

154. Kris, E.: On preconscious mental processes. In: *Organization and Pathology of Thought*, D. Rapaport, Ed. New York, Columbia University Press, 1951, pp. 474-493.

155. Kubie, L. S.: *Neurotic Distortion of the Creative Process*. Lawrence, University of Kansas Press, 1958.

156. Kubie, L. S.: Hypnotism: a focus for psychophysiological and psychoanalytic investigations. *Arch. Gen. Psychiat.*, 4:40-54, 1961.

157. Kubie, L. S.: The concept of dream deprivation: a critical analysis. *Psychosom. Med.*, 24:62-65, 1962.

158. Lane, R. W., and Breger, L.: The effect of preoperative stress on dreams. *Psychological Issues Monograph Series*. New York, International Universities Press, in press.

159. Lewis, H., Bertini, M., and Witkin, H.: Hypnagogic reverie and subsequent dreams. Report to Association for the Psychophysiological Study of Sleep, Palo Alto, Calif., March 1964.

160. Lewis, H. B., Goodenough, D. R., Shapiro, A., and Sleser, I.: Individual differences in dream recall. *J. Abnorm. Psychol.,* 72: 225-239, 1965.

161. Leveton, A. F.: The night residue. *Int. J. Psychoanal.* 42:506-516, 1961.

162. Lowy, S.: *Foundations of Dream Interpretation.* London, Kegan Paul, Trench, Trubner, 1942.

163. Luborsky, L., and Shevrin, H.: Dreams and day-residues: a study of the Pötzl observation. *Bull. Menninger Clin.,* 20:135-148, 1956.

164. Marcuse, H.: *Eros and Civilization.* Boston, Beacon Press, 1955.

165. Meier, C. W., and Berger, R. J.: Development of sleep and wakefulness patterns in the infant rhesus monkey. *Exp. Neurol.,* 12: 257-277, 1965.

166. Monroe, L., Rechtschaffen, A., Foulkes, D., and Jensen, J.: Discriminability of REM and non-REM reports. *J. Personality Soc. Psychol.,* 2:456-460, 1965.

167. Muzio, J., Roffwarg, H., and Kaufman, E.: Alterations in young adult human sleep EEG configurations resulting from d-LSD-25. Report to Association for the Psychophysiological Study of Sleep, Palo Alto, Calif., March 1964.

168. Nachmansohn, M.: Concerning experimentally produced dreams. In: *Organization and Pathology of Thought,* D. Rapaport, Ed. New York, Columbia University Press, 1951, pp. 257-287.

169. Offenkrantz, W., and Rechtschaffen, A.: Clinical studies of sequential dreams. *Arch. Gen. Psychiat.* (Chicago), 8:497-508, 1963.

170. Offenkrantz, W., and Wolpert, E.: The detection of dreaming in a congenitally blind subject. *J. Nerv. Ment. Dis.,* 136:88-90, 1963.

171. Ostow, M.: A discussion of and reprinted with Ullman's "Dreams and arousal." *Amer. J. Psychol.,* 12:222-242, 1958.

172. Oswald, I.: *Sleeping and Waking: Physiology and Psychology.* Amsterdam, Elsevier, 1962.

173. Parmelee, A., Akiyama, Y., Monod, N., and Flescher, J.: EEG patterns in sleep of full-term and premature newborn infants. *Electroenceph. Clin. Neurophysiol.,* 17:455-456, 1964.

174. Paul, H., and Fisher, C.: Subliminal visual stimulation: a study of its influence on subsequent images and dreams. *J. Nerv. Ment. Dis.,* 129:315-340, 1959.

175. Piaget, J.: *The Child's Conception of the World.* Totowa, N.J., Littlefield, Adams, 1951.

176. Piaget, J.: *Play, Dreams, and Imitation in Childhood.* London, Routledge and Kegan Paul, 1962.

177. Piaget, J.: Consciousness and awareness. In: *Conference on Problems of Consciousness-Transactions.* New York, Josiah Macy Foundation, 1954, pp. 138-139.

178. Pivik, T., and Foulkes, D.: "Dream deprivation" effects on dream content. *Science,* 153:1282-1284, 1966.

179. Pötzl, O., Allers, R., and Teler, J.: Preconscious stimulation in dreams, association and images. *Psychological Issues Monograph Series.* Vol. 2, No. 3. New York, International Universities Press, 1960.

180. Polanyi, M.: *Personal Knowledge.* Chicago, University of Chicago Press, 1958.

181. Ramsey, G.: Studies of dreaming. *Psychol. Bull.,* 50:432-455, 1953.

182. Rapaport, D.: The structure of psychoanalytic theory. *Psychological Issues Monograph Series,* Vol. 2, No. 2. New York, International Universities Press, 1960.

183. Rechtschaffen, A.: Discussion of experimental dream studies by W. Dement. In: *Science and Psychoanalysis:* Scientific Proceedings of the Academy of Psychoanalysis, J. Masserman, Ed. New York, Grune & Stratton, 1964, Vol. 7, pp. 162-170.

184. Rechtschaffen, A., Goodenough, D., and Shapiro, A.: Patterns of sleep talking. *Arch. Gen. Psychiat.* (Chicago), 7:418-426, 1962.

185. Rechtschaffen, A., and Maron, L.: Effect of amphetamine on the sleep cycle. *Electroenceph. Clin. Neurophysiol.,* 16:438-445, 1964.

186. Rechtschaffen, A., and Verdone, P.: Amount of dreaming: effect of incentive, adaptation to laboratory, and individual differences. *Percept. Motor Skills,* 19:947-958, 1964.

187. Rechtschaffen, A., Verdone, P., and Wheaton, J.: Reports of mental activity during sleep. *Canad. Psychiat. Ass. J.,* 8:409-416, 1963.

188. Rechtschaffen, A., Vogel, G., and Shaikun, G.: The interrelatedness of mental activity during sleep. *Arch. Gen. Psychiat.* (Chicago), 9:536-547, 1963.

189. Reite, M. L., Rhodes, J. M., Karan, E., and Adey, W. R.: Normal sleep patterns in the macaque monkey. *Arch. Neurol.,* 12:133-144, 1965.

190. Rieff, P.: *The Triumph of the Therapeutic.* New York, Harper and Row, 1966.

191. Roffenstein, G.: Experiments on symbolization in dreams. In: *Organization and Pathology of Thought,* D. Rapaport, Ed. New York, Columbia University Press, 1951, pp. 249-256.

192. Roffwarg, H., Dement, W., Muzio, J., and Fisher, C.: Dream imagery: relationship to rapid eye movements of sleep. *Arch Gen. Psychiat.* (Chicago), 7:235-258, 1962.

193. Roffwarg, H., Muzio, J., and Dement, W.: Ontogenetic development of the human sleep-dream cycle. *Science*, 152:604-618, 1966.

194. Sampson, H.: Deprivation of dreaming sleep by two methods. I. Compensatory REM time. *Arch. Gen. Psychiat.* (Chicago), 13: 79-86, 1965.

195. Sampson, H.: Psychological effects of deprivation of dreaming sleep. *J. Nerv. Ment Dis.*, 143:305-317, 1966.

196. Sapir, E.: Symbolism. In: *Encyclopedia of the Social Sciences.* 14:493. New York, Macmillan, 1934.

197. Schachtel, E. G.: On memory and childhood amnesia. *Psychiatry*, 10:1-26, 1947.

198. Schonbar, R.: Some manifest characteristics of recallers and non-recallers of dreams. *J. Consult. Psychol.*, 23:414-418, 1959.

199. Schonbar, R.: Temporal and emotional factors in the selective recall of dreams. *J. Consult. Psychol.*, 25:67-73, 1961.

200. Schonbar, R.: Differential dream recall frequency as a component of life style. *J. Consult. Psychol.*, 29:468-474, 1965.

201. Schrötter, K.: Experimental dreams. In: *Organization and Pathology of Thought*, D. Rapaport, Ed. New York, Columbia University Press, 1951, pp. 234-248.

202. Shapiro, A., Goodenough, D., Biederman, I., and Sleser, I.: Dream recall and the physiology of sleep. *J. Appl. Physiol.*, 19:778-783, 1964.

203. Shapiro, A., Goodenough, D., and Gryler, R.: Dream recall as a function of method of awakening. *Psychosom. Med.*, 25:174-180, 1963.

204. Shevrin, H., and Luborsky, L.: The measurement of preconscious perception in dreams and images: an investigation of the Pötzl phenomenon. *J. Abnorm. Soc. Psychol.*, 56:285-294, 1958.

205. Silberer, H.: Report on a method of eliciting and observing certain symbolic hallucination-phenomena. In: *Organization and Pathology of Thought*, D. Rapaport, Ed. New York, Columbia University Press, 1951, pp. 195-207.

206. Silberer, H.: The dream. *Psychoanal. Rev.*, 42:361-387, 1955.

207. Singer, J., and Antrobus, J.: Eye movements during fantasies. *Arch. Gen. Psychiat.* (Chicago), 12:71-76, 1965.

208. Snyder, F.: The new biology of dreaming. *Arch. Gen. Psychiat.* (Chicago), 8:381-391, 1963.

209. Snyder, F.: Observation concerning REM-state in a living fossil. Report to Association for the Psychophysiological Study of Sleep, Palo Alto, Calif., March 1964.

210. Snyder, F.: The organismic state associated with dreaming. In: *Psychoanalysis and Current Biological Thought*, N. Greenfield and W. Lewis, Eds. Madison, University of Wisconsin Press, 1965, pp. 275-315.

211. Snyder, F.: Progress in the new biology of dreaming. *Amer. J. Psychiat.*, 122:377-391, 1965.

212. Snyder, F.: Toward an evolutionary theory of dreaming. *Amer. J. Psychiat.*, 123:121-136, 1966.

213. Snyder, F.: In quest of dreaming. In: *Experimental Studies of Dreaming*, H. Witkin and H. Lewis, Eds. New York, Random House, 1967, pp. 3-75.

214. Snyder, F.: The physiology of dreaming. In: *Dream Psychology and the New Biology of Dreams*, M. Kramer, Ed. Springfield, Ill., Charles C Thomas, 1969.

215. Snyder, F., Hobson, J., and Goldfrank, F.: Blood pressure changes during human sleep. *Science*, 142:1313-1314, 1963.

216. Snyder, F., Hobson, J., Morrison, D., and Goldfrank F.: Changes in respiration, heart rate and systolic blood pressure in relation to electroencephalographic patterns of human sleep. *J. Appl. Physiol.*, 19:417-422, 1964.

217. Snyder, F., Karcan,, I., Tharp, V., Jr., and Scott, J.: Phenomenology of REM dreaming. Report to Association for the Psychophysiological Study of Sleep, Santa Monica, Calif., April 1967.

218. Stoyva, J.: Posthypnotically suggested dreams and the sleep cycle. *Arch. Gen. Pyschiat.* (Chicago), 12:287-294, 1965.

219. Sutton-Smith, B.: Piaget on play: a critique. *Psych. Rev.*, 73: 104-110, 1966.

220. Swanson, E., and Foulkes, D.: Dream content and the menstrual cycle. *J. Nerv. Ment. Dis.*, 145:358-363, 1968.

221. Tart, C.: Frequency of dream recall and some personality measures. *J. Consult. Psychol.*, 26:467-470, 1962.

222. Tart, C.: A comparison of suggested dreams occurring in hypnosis and sleep. *Int. J. Clin. Exp. Hypn.*, 12:263-289, 1964.

223. Tart, C.: Hypnotic suggestion as a technique for the control of dreaming. Presented in a symposium on "New Frontiers in Dream Research," American Psychological Association, Los Angeles, Calif., 1964.

224. Tart, C.: Toward the experimental control of dreaming: a review of the literature., *Psychol. Bull.*, 64:81-91, 1965.

225. Tart C.: Some effects of posthypnotic suggestion on the process of dreaming. *Int. J. Clin. Exp. Hypn.*, 14:30-46, 1966.

226. Tart, C.: The control of nocturnal dreaming by means of post-hypnotic suggestion. *Parapsychology*, Sept. 1967, pp. 184-189.

227. Tart, C.: On influencing dream content. In: *Dream Psychology and the New Biology of Dreams.* M. Kramer, Ed. Springfield, Ill., Charles C Thomas, in press.

228. Tauber, E.: Eye movements and EEG activity during sleep in the diurnal lizards: Chameleo Jacksoni and C. Melleri. Report to Association for the Psychophysiological Study of Sleep, Gainesville, Fla., March 1966.

229. Trosman, H.: Dream research and the psychoanalytic theory of dreams. *Arch. Gen. Psychiat.*, 9:9-18, 1963.

230. Trosman, H., Rechtschaffen, A., Offenkrantz, W., and Wolpert, E.: Studies in psychophysiology of dreams: relations among dreams in sequence. *Arch Gen. Psychiat.* (Chicago), 3:602-607, 1960.

231. Ullman, M.: Physiological determinants of the dream process. *J. Nerv. Ment. Dis.*, 124:45-48, 1957.

232. Ullman, M.: Dreams and arousal. *Amer. J. Psychother.*, 12:222-242, 1958.

233. Ullman, M.: Hypotheses on the biological roots of the dream. *J. Clin. Exp. Psychopathol.*, 19:128-133, 1958.

234. Ullman, M.: The dream process. *Amer. J. Psychother.*, 12:671-690, 1958.

235. Ullman, M.: The adaptive significance of the dream. *J. Nerv. Ment. Dis.*, 129:144-149, 1959.

236. Ullman, M.: Dreaming, altered stages of consciousness and the problem of vigilance. *J. Nerv. Ment. Dis.*, 133:529-535, 1961.

237. Ullman, M.: Dreaming, life style and physiology: a comment on Adler's view of the dream. *J. Individ. Psychol.*, 18:18-25, 1962.

238. Ullman, M.: An experimental approach to dreams and telepathy: methodology and preliminary findings. *Arch. Gen. Psychiat.*, 14:605-613, 1966.

239. Ullman, M., Krippner, S., and Fieldstein, S.: Experimentally induced telepathic dreams: two studies using EEG-REM monitoring technique. *Int. J. Neuropsychiat.*, 2:420-437, 1966.

240. Van de Castle, R.: The use of dreams to investigate psychological aspects of the menstrual cycle and pregnancy. Paper read to Division 22 of American Psychological Association, Washington, D. C., September 1967.

241. Van de Castle, R.: Some problems in applying the methodology of content analysis to dreams. In: *Dream Psychology and the New*

Biology of Dreaming. M. Kramer, Ed. Springfield, Ill., Charles C Thomas, 1969.

242. Verdone, P.: Variables related to the temporal reference of manifest dream content. Unpublished doctoral dissertation, University of Chicago, 1963.

243. Verdone, P.: Temporal reference of manifest dream content. *Percept. Motor Skills,* 20:1253-1268, 1965..

244. Vogel, G., Foulkes, D., and Trosman, H.: Ego functions and dreaming during sleep onset. *Arch. Gen. Psychiat.* (Chicago), 14:238-248, 1966.

245. Weiss, T.: Discussion of "The D-state" by E. Hartmann. *Int. J. Psychiat.,* 2:32-36, 1966.

246. Werner, H., and Kaplan, B.: *Symbol Formation.* New York, John Wiley & Sons, 1963.

247. White, R. W.: Ego and reality in psychoanalytic theory. *Psychol. Issues Monograph Series,* Vol. 3., No. 3. New York, International Universities Press, 1963.

248. Whitman, R.: Drugs, dreams, and the experimental subject. *Canad. Psychiat. Ass. J.,* 8:395-399, 1963.

249. Whitman, R.: Remembering and forgetting dreams in psychoanalysis. *J. Amer. Psychoanal. Ass.,* 11:752-774, 1963.

250. Whitman, R., Kramer, M., and Baldridge, B.: Which dream does the patient tell? *Arch. Gen. Psychiat.* (Chicago), 8:277-282, 1963.

251. Whitman, R., Pierce, C., and Maas, J.: Drugs and dreams. In: *Drugs and Behavior.* L. Uhr and J. Miller, Eds. New York, John Wiley & Sons, 1960, pp. 591-595.

252. Whitman, R., Pierce, C., Maas, J., and Baldridge, B.: Drugs and dreams. II. Imipramine and Prochlorperazine. *Compr. Psychiat.,* 2:219-226, 1961.

253. Whitman, R., Pierce, C., Maas, J., and Baldridge, B.: The dreams of the experimental subject. *J. Nerv. Ment. Dis.,* 134:431-439, 1962.

254. Witkin, H., and Lewis, H.: The relation of experimentally induced presleep experiences to dreams: a report on method and preliminary findings. *J. Amer. Psychoanal. Ass.,* 13:819-849, 1965.

255. Witkin, H., and Lewis, H., Eds.: *Experimental Studies of Dreaming.* New York, Random House, 1967.

256. Wolff, P.: The developmental psychology of Jean Piaget and psychoanalysis. *Psychol. Issues Monograph Series,* Vol. 2, No. 3. New York, International Universities Press, 1960.

257. Wolpert, E., and Trosman, H.: Studies in psychophysiology of dreams. *Arch. Neurol. Psychiat.,* 79:603-606, 1958.

INDEX